A
Spectrum
Reader

*For William Broadwell Jones,
born January 3, 1991 —*

a future Spectrum Weekly *reader*

Liner Notes

Thanks to: Liz and Ted Parkhurst, for letting us do this book; Karen Hutcheson, for everything else; Cindy Fribourgh, for suggesting it all; our moms and dads; Susan Files; Anne Neville (the Marxist of Love); D'Anna Sharon, who never got proper credit the first time; Dorothy Neville; Michael Keckhaver; Patrick Kelly, Jess Henderson, Tony Moser, Jim Nichols and all the other fine reporters whose work is under-represented in this volume; Charles (for surrendering his hard drive) and the rest of the *Spectrum* staff (for understanding, we think); all the former employees of and contributors to *Spectrum;* Kathleen Harper; Ramona (for the spaghetti we didn't eat); Mary Cameron; Sandy Alan and the Maryland fan club; Carol Sims; everyone who ever gave Phil a ride; Pat Lynch; all the people Steve never called back; Bill Haymes; Rod; T-Bone Burnett; Elvis Costello; Glenn Gould; The Mekons; The Replacements; Frank Sinatra (of the Capitol years); Neil Young; Discount Records (for detente); Markham Liquor; Sweden Creme; Rally's (for staying open late); Vino's (for Guinness and Bass on tap); Mark Abernathy and Juanita's; Community Bakery; Stanley Tiner; Carl T. Hall (for luring Steve to Arkansas); Copes and Di; Stuart and Mick; Dave Black; Gustave Flaubert (for finding so many right words); Henry James (for finding so many extra words); Jonathan Swift (for the savage indignation); Alexander Pope (for *The Dunciad*); Samuel Johnson (for the balanced sentences we attempt but rarely achieve); Paul Fussell; Allan Bloom and the University of Chicago; Kimberly Collins ("Well hast thou fought the better fight" — Milton); Lt. Johnson of the Jacksonville Police Department; and all the drummers we fired before we got famous.

No thanks to: Sundown Slim.

A Spectrum Reader

*Five Years of Iconoclastic
Reporting, Criticism & Essays*

*Edited by
Bill Jones
Philip Martin
& Stephen Buel*

August House Publishers, Inc.
LITTLE ROCK

Published by August House, Inc.
P.O. Box 3223, Little Rock, Arkansas 72203
501-372-5450

Printed in the United States of America
10 9 8 7 6 5 4 3 2 1

LIBRARY OF CONGRESS CATALOGING-IN-PUBLICATION DATA

A Spectrum Reader: five years of iconoclastic reporting, criticism & essays
edited by Bill Jones, Philip Martin & Stephen Buel. — 1st ed.
p.   cm.
Excerpts from the first five years of Spectrum.
ISBN 0-87483-128-8 (pbk.: alk. paper): $9.95.
1. Journalism — Arkansas. 2. Underground press — Arkansas. 3. Arkansas — Civilization.
I. Jones, Bill, 1950-   . II. Martin, Philip, 1958-   .
III. Buel, Stephen, 1958-   . IV. Spectrum (Little Rock, Ark.)
PN4897.A824S64   1991
071'.6773 — dc20   91-570
                                                        CIP

First Edition, 1991

Executive Editor: Liz Parkhurst
Book Design: Stephen Buel
Typography: Spectrum Graphics

This book is printed on archival-quality paper
which meets the guidelines for performance
and durability of the Committee on
Production Guidelines for Book Longevity
of the Council on Library Resources.

AUGUST HOUSE, INC.   PUBLISHERS   LITTLE ROCK

Table Of Contents

Reviews

Postscript

Cartoons

Introduction

Why *Spectrum* Exists

Prototype Issue 0, May 1985.

In 1984, I covered public utilities for the *Arkansas Democrat*, Little Rock's Republican-leaning daily. Utilities were making news at the time, and I wrote volumes about the AT&T break-up, the deregulation of natural gas and how Arkansas Power & Light Company had obligated its customers to pay for an unneeded $4 billion nuclear power plant.

I took my job seriously, and my stories appeared regularly on the front page. Reporters aren't very complimentary by nature, but every so often a colleague would hesitantly say something like: "I can't read much of that utility stuff, Steve, but you seem to be doing good work."

Then I was asked to help cover David Pryor's re-election bid for the U.S. Senate. Since knocking about with politicians in twin-engined airplanes is higher up the reporters' ladder of success, I happily surrendered the utility beat to a very able colleague. He did good work.

I couldn't read any of it.

Here I'd been passionate about utility coverage for 18 months, and yet, mere weeks after changing assignments, I was unable to force myself through even one story on the topic. The problem wasn't that my replacement's stories weren't well-reported or well-written — at least as well-crafted as a reporter can make a story between a 5:00 p.m. trip to the Public Service Commission and a 6:30 p.m. deadline. Instead, I discovered there was something unsatisfying about reading stories prepared under such conditions. Sure, daily utility coverage is important, but it isn't necessarily enjoyable reading. Newspaper reading is an acquired taste that largely follows one's professional or recreational interests, and now that I didn't have to track the daily doings of utilities, I found that wading through the sort of ponderous, jargon-ridden pieces I'd been writing was rather boring.

That's when I concluded that reporting as I'd been practicing it is useful only to the handful of people who possess a job-related need to know about the subject in question. Without taking the time and room necessary to explain the context behind the day's news, daily newspapers do little to make most news seem relevant to their readers. Perhaps this explains why daily newspaper readership is steadily dropping.

By November, I'd about had enough of the *Democrat* and started looking for openings elsewhere. One opportunity stood out; a publisher in Atlanta was seeking an editor for *Southline*, the alternative newsweekly he was preparing to start. I called him up and we talked for about an hour. After convincing myself that I was his man, I wrote him a four-page manifesto on what an alternative newspaper should be.

Todd Evans didn't hire me, or even call me back, and upon rereading my pompous memo to him, I can't blame him. But a seed had been planted, and a colleague of mine at the *Democrat* suggested that we start a similar paper here in Little Rock. It would be called *Spectrum*, and it would cover news, arts and entertainment. She would handle the business side of things and I would handle the editorial product. We would both write lots of long, in-depth stories.

It took Cindy Fribourgh about three months to persuade me to start *Spectrum* with her and a third partner, then unknown to me. Cindy became publisher and I became editor. Neither of us ever got to write too many of those long, in-depth stories.

Although business matters almost immediately crowded writing out of my

Baptism By Fire

The first issue of Spectrum *appeared in Little Rock businesses in June of 1985. Within 48 hours, the paper was sued for $40 million by a Little Rock record store.*

Discount Records owner Jack Garner argued in court that he construed a debut-issue profile of a Klan-sympathizing family as an indication that Spectrum *itself possessed such sympathies. Garner sought $40 million in damages on the basis that he had been defrauded by the paper when he purchased an ad in the first issue. A separate suit named* Spectrum *and eight distribution outlets in an effort to prevent distribution of the issue.*

job description, I did at least manage to edit the paper during its five-and-a-half years of biweekly publication. This book compiles some of the work from that period of which we are proudest. My co-editors and I have selected these pieces with an eye toward universality, omitting many dozens of fine stories which would have no relevance to readers outside our community.

Among the journalistic tenets that characterize *Spectrum* is a lack of faith in the modern concept of "objectivity" in news reporting. Smart Americans know the myth of objectivity is a lie, and they seem increasingly unwilling to see the Sam Donaldsons of the world as anything more than fallible humans with subjective personal biases and points of view. Yet most news outlets persist in the comfortable myth that they are objective purveyors of truths. It's a convenient lie, but one that was necessary for newspapers to adopt as they transformed themselves from their early 20th-century role as subjective partisans for one narrow viewpoint into their current role as newsgathering monopolies seeking to be all things to all readers.

Which came first, this trend toward monopoly or the industry's rush toward a bland, neutral objectivity? The answer to this question, I believe, is hanging on the wall of my office. I collect and display final editions of dead newspapers. Not coincidentally, the two best papers in my collection are also my two oldest — the *Chicago Daily News* and *The Washington Star.* Even in death, both papers possessed some of the uniqueness and identity that once distinguished many American dailies and gave each city a unique identity based on the quality of its daily journalism. There aren't many newspapers with that kind of identity left today. It's no wonder that most American cities have room for only one of the bland "objective" newspapers that typify journalism in the Nineties.

Still, there is no lack of hunger among the reading public for stimulating and provocative news and opinions, and that's where we hope *A Spectrum Reader* fits in. We've divided our book into five sections: reporting, editorials, columns, cultural criticism and reviews. These are significant distinctions, but if the truth be known, such divisions mean less at *Spectrum* than they would at a daily newspaper. At *Spectrum* we're not only happy to confess that our reporting is informed by our opinions, but we're proud of it. Few things, after all, could be more subjective than ranking the relative importance and triviality of divergent points of view and then enshrining some, while ignoring others. Unlike other local news organizations, we simply choose not to adopt the pretense of being dispassionate about such choices. Hence, our reporting occasionally displays some of our opinions about our culture.

To an outsider looking at its media images, America might seem a land of the middle, frightened by extremes. Sometimes Americans forget that our nation's very origins spring from a series of biting, pseudonymous opinion columns which ran in various newspapers in the late 1700s. The 85 essays, which came to be known as *The Federalist Papers,* were aimed at literate and perceptive readers, and their writers — James Madison, Alexander Hamilton, and John Jay — were unafraid of addressing those readers as intellectual peers. *Spectrum* is a token of our faith in the belief that there still exists a healthy audience for journalism directed toward well-educated common readers.

Although the name *Spectrum* does a lamentably poor job of explaining our paper's market niche to potential advertisers, I cannot imagine a name that would better describe our underlying editorial motivations. The word *Spectrum* suggests, by its very connotation, all the editorial schizophrenia we strive for. A certain schizophrenia has always been seen as a virtue at *Spectrum,* and we wear ours on our sleeves — bouncing from topic to topic with a desire to be unpredictable and fresh. We're governed by just two concerns: that our subjects be newsworthy and our writing lively. I've taken to saying that we try to *market* the news at *Spectrum* — that is, we write about serious topics like utility regulation using the same tools an advertising agency might employ if it were trying to sell us a product. We select the content of *Spectrum* with an eye toward making it healthy for its readers, but then we try to make it taste good.

When we started *Spectrum*, friends occasionally asked whether Little Rock was cosmopolitan enough to support our efforts. Then, as now, we rejected the implication behind this question. While *Spectrum* has certainly encountered its share of obstacles through the years, lack of a dedicated reading audience has never been among them. We've always written *Spectrum* with the goal of providing interesting reading for discerning readers, and the demand for the paper has grown steadily.

But just as a large segment of the American reading public is drawn to papers like *Spectrum*, so too is the initial inclination of many advertisers to shy away from any medium which strays too far from the center. Media critic Ben Bagdikian, under whom I studied at the University of California at Berkeley, describes this trend in alarming detail in his book *The Media Monopoly.*

Bagdikian hit upon the great twin tension in American journalism: whether those who possess the inclination to provide unflinching journalism also possess the necessary business stability to support their efforts, or whether those with the wherewithal develop the inclination. Sadly, these two traits seldom seem to exist in opposition. In that, *Spectrum* and I have been quite fortunate to have the support of my partner, Karen Hutcheson. We exist today only through her unflagging commitment to stand by our paper while we've slowly figured out the business side of the equation. For this, I shall be forever grateful.

Karen, the editors of this book and our many fine colleagues all share the belief that it's possible for a paper like *Spectrum* to prosper in a market like Little Rock. The key to success lies not with the urbanity of Little Rock's reading public but with our own efforts. The issue is whether we possess the skill to explain the composition of our audience to potential advertisers as well as we've explained to readers the many topics we cover every week in the paper, and in this book.

Stick around; I think we do. We certainly possess the inclination. We're improving the wherewithal all the time.

Stephen Buel, March 1991

Psst! Hey Buddy!

Got $40 Million?

Spectrum needs subscribers to help finance the $40 million *Spectrum* legal defense fund. We had planned to put our first $40 million back into the business, but now that may have to wait until next month.

We'll graciously accept spare jet planes or Bermuda vacation cottages. But all it really takes to subscribe is $10. That gets you one full year, 26 issues of our lively coverage of news, art and entertainment. And a promise from us that no amount of criticism will deter us from trying to keep you informed about your world.

So cut this out right now and mail it in today with your check or money order. Really.

Name

Address

Zip

Spectrum, 300 E. Markham St., Suite 309, Little Rock, AR 72201

The Rest Of The Story

Spectrum *shortly filed a countersuit against the record store. The paper made light of its fortune in a series of whimsical subscription ads, but chose not to write about the suit for several issues, a decision the staff came to regret once it realized the confusion the affair had sewn in the minds of some readers.*

After it prevailed in the suit for an injunction, Spectrum *and Discount Records began discussions which ultimately resulted in a settlement and an apology being issued by the record store.*

Roughly four years later, Discount and Peaches Records came again to advertise in the pages of Spectrum.

Discount Records tied for the honor of best record store in Spectrum*'s first music awards presentation in 1991.*

We're friends today.

Philip Martin

Robert Leonard Waldrum had

been famous. In 1985, as a staff attorney for the state Public Service Commission, he had looked straight in the face of Arkansas Power & Light Company, the monolithic utility company that always gets what it wants, and told it "No," Arkansans should not pay for any part of the Grand Gulf nuclear power plant. Not even AP&L seemed fearsome to this man who had looked into the eyes of North Vietnamese soldiers and seen his buddies kill and die in Southeast Asian jungles.

Waldrum fought ferociously against a proposed settlement to the rate case. Even after his superiors at the PSC removed him from the case, Waldrum railed against what he believed was a sellout of Arkansas ratepayers, calling for the resignation of Governor Bill Clinton, Attorney General Steve Clark and members of the PSC.

Despite his insubordination, Waldrum was not fired. He left his job of his own accord in February 1986, a few months after the PSC agreed to allow

Worth What It Costs

It was not until the seventh issue that Spectrum *received its first letter to the editor. In September1985, Arkansas Democrat managing editor John Robert Starr, who was unimpressed with the handiwork of his former employees Stephen Buel and Cindy Fribourgh, sent a missive.*

"Where are all the big important stories you were going to run in Spectrum*? All I've seen so far is a lot of garbage like daily newspapers scrounge up to fill Sunday sections.*

"So far, Spectrum *seems to me to be worth exactly what it costs."*

Middle South Utilities, AP&L's parent company, to pass on 80 percent of its Grand Gulf costs to AP&L customers.

Before Grand Gulf, Waldrum had never had trouble finding work. But after Grand Gulf, he never held a permanent job again. He went to dozens of interviews, but for his last 11 months, he was without steady work. There were rumors that he had been blackballed and that no state agency would consider employing him.

Other factors added to Waldrum's depression. His health was not good. He had a stuttering heart valve, high blood pressure and was subject to stress-induced blackouts — a vestige of his service in Vietnam. Friends of Waldrum said he worried about his exposure to Agent Orange, and he told at least one friend that he was afraid to have children for fear of genetic damage. His mother's poor health was another concern. His family told police Waldrum had been taking medication for his sometimes blinding depression; his friends say he was always subject to extreme mood swings, that he sometimes brooded.

Bob Waldrum was 40 years old when he killed himself. On the morning of December 19, 1988 the ex-Marine pushed a .38-caliber revolver up against the right side of his head, squeezed the trigger, and tumbled into nothingness.

Some of his associates weren't surprised.

"It seems morbid to say this, but I had thought about it before," a friend of Waldrum's said. "I knew if Bob was ever going to kill himself, I knew how he'd do it. A head shot. No doubt about it. Get it over with. That was just the way he was."

"My life and my death are not purely my own business. I live by and for others, and my death involves others."

— Thomas Merton,
Conjectures of a Guilty Bystander

JUST THREE YEARS before he shut out the light, Waldrum was so popular with grassroots Arkansans that he had to deny rumors that he was planning to run for attorney general, or even governor. Those who knew him say it is unlikely that he ever seriously considered making a bid for public office, but the support was there — his fan mail and hundreds of favorable phone calls were evidence. Waldrum told reporters, however, that his experience with politicians and the way they did business didn't make him covet their jobs. Besides, he loved his privacy too well.

Waldrum argued that the $3.7 billion nuclear power plant built near Port Gibson, Mississippi, was a mistake by Middle South Utilities management and that Arkansas ratepayers should not be forced to pay a dime for AP&L's share of the troubled nuclear plant. In August 1985, when it seemed that PSC senior management was inclined to settle the rate case, Waldrum walked out of Grand Gulf settlement negotiations. A few weeks later, PSC Director Jerrell Clark removed Waldrum and fellow PSC staff attorney W.W. "Dub" Elrod II from the rate case.

At the time, Clark said the staff attorneys were removed because he felt they would not be "comfortable" with the position adopted by the PSC. Doug Strock, chief counsel to the PSC, took over negotiations.

Within days, the PSC reached a settlement with the state that led to the ratepayers being charged with 80 percent of AP&L's Grand Gulf costs over the life of the plant. AP&L stockholders were to be held accountable for the remaining 20 percent of the obligation. Since the settlement, Arkansas ratepayers have paid close to $300 million in increased rates. More Grand Gulf costs are scheduled to be incorporated in AP&L rates over the next decade.

Waldrum publicly denounced the settlement, calling on Clark, Clinton and members of the PSC to resign. He filed a formal request with the PSC for reconsideration of the settlement. The request was denied.

Clinton defended the settlement, saying that if the state had not settled the case, "federal courts" might have required ratepayers to assume all of AP&L's Grand Gulf costs.

Later, in an interview with Associated Press reporter Bill Simmons, Waldrum explained why he went public with his opposition to the settlement.

"Three reasons," he said. "First. I wanted to generate public interest and debate on what I see as the most significant betrayal of public trust by public officials and agencies in recent Arkansas history. It is so outrageous and so pervasive it's almost insurmountable. I think it discredited the agency I work for and government in general. I think it was constructive to raise that flag.

"I think people like myself and Steve Clark and Bill Clinton and Jerrell Clark have to be accountable for that trust. Now the people who signed the settlement are putting it off on everybody else — the federal courts and so on — but those are just phantoms and shadows. People make things happen. In this case, it was Steve Clark and Bill Clinton and Jerrell Clark and other people who made this happen. You can't blame the courts.

"And I wanted to draw the Legislature's attention to the fact that the process by which rates are supposedly set has been irreversibly corrupted."

Elrod, the attorney who worked with Waldrum at the PSC, said he shared Waldrum's view of the Grand Gulf case. He said the PSC legal staff was at first instructed to "go after" AP&L on the Grand Gulf case.

"They told us to do anything we had to do," Elrod, now in private practice, said. "Any experts we needed, anything at all — they told us they weren't going to settle the case. Then they flip-flopped, and left us in an untenable position."

The Grand Gulf negotiations were a crucible wherein he and Waldrum were subjected to intense heat and pressure. As such forces often do, that heat and pressure bonded Elrod and Waldrum together. They made a good team. Elrod remembers that even under those conditions, he laughed harder with Waldrum than anyone he had ever known.

Their styles were complementary: Dub was the quieter one, the low-profile researcher and brief writer; Bob was the speechifier, the rough-and-tumble rhetorician, the one the press called when they wanted good quote. Bob always gave good quote.

"He just had a way of putting things," Elrod said. "He could come up with these perfect descriptions of things — he once called AP&L a 'corporate outlaw.' He was always coming up with those kind of turns of phrase. And he delivered them in this low booming voice. It was a great trial lawyer's voice. Bob was an advocate ... And once he decided something was right, he was unshakable."

It was good, tough work for two young lawyers — at least until the senior management opted for the settlement and Jerrell Clark removed them from the case.

"After that, after they took us off the case, they kept us on the payroll but they didn't give us anything substantive to do," Elrod said. "They took all our authority away from us. It used to be that the PSC legal staff was like a private law firm: We could do pretty much what we thought needed to be done. And all of a sudden we were relegated to being 'yes men'."

Though neither Elrod or Waldrum were fired — at the time, political consultant Jerry Russell publicly speculated that Waldrum would have been dismissed if his PSC bosses were not afraid of making "a martyr" of him — both left a few months after the emasculation of the legal department.

Elrod said he still believes he and Waldrum were on the right side of the Grand Gulf case — he thinks the episode was "the closest thing to a Watergate in Arkansas history" and the wrong people are still paying for the mistakes of AP&L management.

Issue 90, December 1990.

"The ratepayers took the hit and AP&L has the same corporate structure it did before Grand Gulf." Elrod said. "What should happen when the officers of a company make a mistake is that the board of directors replace the officers, and the stockholders take the hit. If the stockholders decide that the board of directors made a mistake, well, they can elect a new board. None of that happened in this case. Some basic foundations of rate-making law were undermined, but worse, Bob Waldrum's sense of right was offended."

Scott Trotter, a Little Rock lawyer who chaired the consumer advocacy group Ratepayers Fight Back during the Grand Gulf controversy, remembers running into Waldrum at a public hearing on the case a few days after his removal by Clark.

"He was sitting there, all alone but with the crowd all around him," Trotter recalled. "It was kind of like we were in a vacuum together. He had to decide whether or not he wanted to say anything about the settlement. I sat down next to him and he proceeded to explain to me what was going through his mind. I said, 'Bob, have you considered all things? Have you considered what this might do to your career?' He said he had considered everything, and that he felt he had to say something. And he did. I don't know if he should have or not, but he did."

Several friends believe that Waldrum, if not formally put on a "Do Not Hire" list, was at least informally blackballed through an unwritten accord. Trotter says he heard speculation to that effect. Elrod is even stronger in his opinion. Asked if Waldrum was blacklisted, he responded with a one-word answer: "Obviously."

Jerrell Clark, on the other hand, said he was never approached by anyone asking him for information about Waldrum. Had he been, Clark said, state policy would require the PSC personnel department to do no more than verify the dates of employment and grade of the employee.

"Bob Waldrum attracted a lot of attention in the media," Clark said. "That probably contributed to his difficulty in finding a job."

WALDRUM WAS BORN in Pine Bluff in 1948 and, from the age of two, was reared in Little Rock. He grew up in a modest house on South Tyler Street. His father worked for the City of Little Rock. By the time Bob was in high school his parents had retired. Looking back at mid-Sixties Central High School yearbooks, he appears in only a few photos, a serious, thoughtful-looking boy with thick glasses and a tamed shock of colorless hair dipping across his forehead. He is not smiling in any of the photos.

He was in the Beta Club and National Honor Society and apparently had an interest in science. Though he later described himself as something of a high-school hippie, the yearbook gives up no evidence of any of that kind of foolishness.

After graduating in 1966, Waldrum spent a year at Hendrix College, but he apparently wasn't ready. He failed twice in attempts to enlist in the Marines before figuring out that he shouldn't tell them about his his bad back or the crumbly cartilage in his knees. On his third try, they accepted him. Typically, his motive was altruistic — or at least guilt-driven: Years later Waldrum told the AP's Simmons he volunteered because he felt it was unfair that he could avoid service by staying in college while kids who couldn't afford college were "getting blown apart" in Vietnam.

Waldrum was assigned to the 1st Marine Division, I Corps, based south of Da Nang, in a combat artillery brigade that fired 105-millimeter howitzers. Waldrum was wounded in his right calf on March 19,1969, during a six-hour nighttime firefight in which North Vietnamese Army regulars overran his company's outpost at Phu Lac.

Larry Jegley, another lawyer who worked with Waldrum and Elrod on the PSC staff, remembers late nights at the office when Waldrum would sometimes talk about Vietnam.

"He told me they would be running through the jungle, bullets flying around, and all of a sudden, a guy next to you, maybe your best friend in the world who you'd been talking to five minutes before, would hit a mine and then — and these are the exact words he used — 'just be pink foam on the jungle leaves'." Jegley said Waldrum visited the Vietnam Memorial in Washington and spent a whole day looking up names of buddies who had died in the war. It was, he later told Jegley, the first chance he had had to grieve. Only when he saw the names on the wall had he been able to realize what it meant.

Many of Waldrum's later physical problems had their roots in Vietnam, Jegley said.

"He told me that Agent Orange was everywhere, that if you were thirsty you dipped your hand down in a pool that had Agent Orange scum floating on top of it. It was all over everybody and everything."

Waldrum was wounded again just as his 13-month tour of duty was coming to an end. While riding in a Jeep in a convoy on the way to the airfield at Da Nang where he was to board a plane for home, a mortar shell exploded and blew shrapnel into his right wrist and arm.

Waldrum told Simmons he did not report the wound because the Marine Corps had a policy against sending "wounded" men home. So a corpsman pulled out the fragments and gave him some penicillin. A doctor in Okinawa supplied him with some more penicillin, and Waldrum finally sought treatment for his infected arm when he returned to Little Rock. Some who knew Waldrum said the arm continued to bother him occasionally.

Waldrum's first job after law school was as a prosecutor in North Little Rock's municipal courts. The cases he handled were usually sad and messy affairs; the people he prosecuted were usually little criminals — drunks, brawlers and petty thieves.

In the relatively informal municipal court atmosphere, Waldrum stood out. One associate described him as a "gunslinger," fearless and undaunted, always working from the moral high ground. He was a man who saw bright lines everywhere — this was right and this, by God, was wrong and every human being knew in his heart it was wrong. He was a policeman's prosecutor, a zealot who protected his own witnesses while savaging the "bad guys."

"Bob never saw any gray," Jegley said "Things were always black and white with him. I look out the window and I see gray skies, gray trees, gray cars and gray grass. Bob would say, 'No, that's black, that's white, and here's where you divide them'."

Chancery Judge Lee Munson was the Pulaski County prosecutor Waldrum worked for in North Little Rock. Waldrum, Munson said, "had an opinion about everything. And he had a lot of integrity. And if he had a difference of opinion with you, he wasn't afraid of expressing his opinion. He wasn't afraid to fly in the face of his boss."

Eventually, that's what happened to Bob Waldrum the prosecutor. Munson said he got "crossways" with Waldrum over a case, and that Waldrum refused to follow a direct order. Munson did the only thing he could. He fired Waldrum.

"Just because I fired him didn't mean we weren't friends," Munson said. "He understood why I had to do what I did. I wrote him letters of recommendation and helped get him jobs. I kept up with him."

Waldrum soon found a job in the attorney general's office, where he gained some notoriety as he represented the state Board of Nursing and the Department of Human Services Office of Long-term Care during investigations of nursing-home practices when investigations were turning up widespread neglect and abuse of nursing home residents.

By the time Waldrum joined the PSC staff, he had a reputation as a competent, hard-nosed attorney. If he had one flaw, it was that he was not a pragmatist. He never had been fond of compromise. Some lawyers believe that is what the practice of law essentially is — the art of compromise.

After his refusal to compromise led to his departure from the PSC in February 1986, Waldrum floundered. He couldn't find a job, and private practice didn't agree with him. He hadn't liked it during a brief stint before joining the PSC and he felt he hadn't been especially good at it. Waldrum, Elrod said, was not an "attorney" who could sit in an office, count beans and be satisfied with a fat check — he was a "lawyer," an infighter, a man who needed a banner to carry.

And his health was getting worse. Waldrum couldn't meet the physical demands of high-pressure private work. His heart was weak. The physical manifestations of his Vietnam experience — blackouts and headaches — were intensified by those conditions. What Bob Waldrum needed was an administrative job, a job where his communication skills and his tenacity could more than compensate for his lowered tolerance for physical stress.

For a time — from August 1986 to January 1988 — he found a job that met his requirements. Waldrum found temporary employment with the McMath Law Firm, researching state and environmental regulations in connection with a pending case. Former governor Sid McMath and two of his brothers had served in the Marine Corps. "Of course, he was an ex-Marine," Bruce McMath, one of the partners of that family firm said of Waldrum, "and around here, that always matters." At the height of Waldrum's involvement in the Grand Gulf controversy, he received a supportive letter from Sid McMath that closed with the motto of the Marines: "*Semper Fi.*"

But the job was only temporary, and Bruce McMath said Waldrum's deteriorating health unfortunately expedited his departure. "He was an inspiring guy to have around, a real idealistic guy. We just kept pushing back the deadline for Bob's 'retirement date,' first by days, then by weeks, finally by months," he said. "Then we got to a point where it was just a natural break in the case and it became obvious that whoever took it over at that point would need to see it through. Bob couldn't do that — to be frank, his health just wouldn't allow it."

"It's a real shame he couldn't continue as an attorney," said Nathan M. "Mac" Norton, a former PSC chairman and fellow lawyer whom Waldrum occasionally found himself squared up against in court. "He was a good attorney, a real gentleman — he was a pleasure to work with, and even against."

Apart from a few teaching assignments at UALR, there was nothing else for Waldrum to do. The doors to state government were closed to him — perhaps understandably. He had a reputation for being a wave-maker, a loose cannon who wasn't afraid of being fired, a man who might go public with what his superiors saw as internal matters. Bob Waldrum did not have a reputation as a team player.

"He wasn't afraid of anything or anybody," Larry Jegley said. "He told me that. He said once you'd looked in the faces of pissed-off NVA, there wasn't anything that would scare you. He had seen the worst, had walked through Hell, and there wasn't anything they could do to him."

"He intimidated people because they could tell he wouldn't back down," Elrod said. "He wasn't a physically imposing presence, he wasn't a big man, but people always seemed to get the idea he was much bigger than he actually was."

While his body conspired against him, Waldrum would sit for days in his apartment, caring for his sick mother. He would tell friends that he felt great empathy for the "minimum-wage workers" who took care of the infirm. He mentioned to some that he would like to go back to school and become a social worker.

During the last few months, Waldrum continued to go to interviews. Half a dozen people were regularly calling him with job leads. Some suspect he may have stopped following up on the job leads they gave him, that after a while he gave up. He would sit in the apartment, reading Thomas Merton or religious history or maybe not even reading. Occasionally he would call his friends.

Jegley heard from Waldrum about a week before he killed himself.

"He sounded about the same as he always did; we laughed. I think maybe he sounded a little depressed, but that was just Bob. It was just sort of his nature.

"I don't know if anything could have been done. You can think back and find all sorts of things that maybe you might have said or done, but that doesn't do any good. I think there must have been something in his make-up that set him on this track long before any of us even knew him — whether it was Vietnam, I don't know, maybe it was before that. I don't know.

"I just know I'm pissed off at him for killing himself."

(January 1989)

Ruben Gonzalez and his daughter, Brenda.   *Sheri Walker*

JoBeth Briton

Young Americans

In the green heart of agriculture and timber country in South Arkansas, the land stretches out in long, flat configurations — here forested, full of deer and squirrel, and there arable, marked out in fields that bear the last of the season's harvest or which already lie fallow and brown.

The geography also sequesters communities of largely anonymous Hispanics, both seasonal migrant laborers and permanent residents upon whose backs the region's economy rests. At the height of harvest season in late summer, their numbers swell into the thousands.

Hundreds live out of the public eye around Moro Bay on the Ouachita River. Beneath a silver-sprinkled sky the late-night ferry chugs over the county line dividing Union and Bradley counties. It is hushed and deceptively timeless, for the history of this region in reality is rapidly changing. And it is those descendents of 16th-century Spanish explorer Hernando de Soto, who once traipsed the untamed territory in search of adventure and gold, who are more than anyone else rewriting the story of South Arkansas.

In increasing numbers, Hispanics are opting to leave grueling, dirty jobs in poultry houses all over South Arkansas, creating a labor shortage that could significantly affect the state's number-one industry. And the shortage could extend to crop harvesting before long as more and more Hispanics express the desire for jobs with better pay, better working conditions and more benefits.

Without unions, workers and employers are loosely organized, if at all, in a system of independent farms that discourages a unified response to the problems on both sides of the equation. Coupled with an apparent lack of awareness on the part of organizations like the Arkansas Poultry Federation, the farm economy in South Arkansas may be headed for a new crisis.

Ironically, the passage of the Immigration Control and Reform Act in 1986, which was designed to alleviate labor shortage problems in agriculture by extending legalization to a predominantly illegal alien workforce, has contributed to the new shortage. Initially, it both helped farmers to obtain legal workers and reduced labor abuses. But once Hispanic tomato pickers became American tomato pickers, they started looking beyond the tomato fields to the possibilities of getting ahead American-style.

RUBEN GONZALEZ left the farm for a sawmill job. He started coming north with his brothers from Mexico City in 1981 when he was 19 years old.

"We used to work on vegetables and tomatoes," he recalls, "then we saw we were able to make a little more in timber, so we learned to cut. At first, we were very afraid to even touch the power saw."

Gonzalez has been able to get what many Americans dream of — a house of his own, steady work and a family. The small brick home in Warren, which Gonzalez bought with a Farmers Home Administration loan, is a far cry from the days when Gonzalez lived with eight to 15 men in one building.

Two American-made pickups are parked in the driveway and inside, Gonzalez, just off from work, is out of the shower. He joins his wife, Adelina, 21, and their two children in the den, whose only decoration is a painting of a tiger on black velvet.

"It was very rough at the beginning, very rough," he says through an interpreter. "I don't know if that's because I've learned quick about what to do or it is because God is treating me well and leading me to good places."

Near Moro Bay at the Centro Bautista Bartoleme, a mission center for seasonal and migrant laborers, the Rev. Ariel Hernandez tries to explain the trend among Hispanic workers.

"Having a car and being able to go where they want to — they want that," he says. "Many people are leaving the agricultural for better paying jobs. I feel very, very bad because the pay in poultry is very low."

"Hollywood," a 25-year-old father of three who lives with his wife and children in a rented house in Hermitage, visits the Southern Baptist Convention mission center regularly. He has left crop harvesting for more lucrative work in the timber industry. On a Sunday in August, he's dressed in stiff blue jeans and heeled gray boots, with a hand-tooled, silver-buckled belt encircling his boyish waist. He likes "the style of living" in the U.S. and believes there are more opportunities to earn money here than in Mexico. "There are more facilities [opportunities] to have a house or a vehicle some day," he says, allowing Hernandez to interpret for him.

Although Hollywood has legal status — his application for legalization was one of about 900 Hernandez has helped process since 1987 at the mission center — he doesn't want to reveal his name because he has seven brothers in Mexico who may come north to work as illegals. In repeated interviews with people in South Arkansas, almost everyone asked to not be identified by name.

After five years in the United States, Hollywood has settled into a job he likes. He picked tomatoes for a while, he says, shaking his head. When asked if he ever worked on a poultry farm, he grimaces and says no.

"It doesn't smell good and they don't make much money," he explains with an embarrassed laugh.

THE SMELL. It's the first thing you notice. Coming up on one of those long, tin laying or breeding houses in the middle of a hot, dry field in summer, the stink almost knocks the air out of your lungs. The air is stagnant and hot and saturated with dust. The stink and the heat and the dust seem to seep into every exposed pore of skin. Poultry workers live in this environment seven days a week every day of the year. Because the work never stops, poultry workers tend to live on the farm in housing supplied by the farmer. Though one poultry farmer insists that most now treat their workers "better than they treat their families" because they can't afford to lose good workers, the situation still smacks of indentured servitude.

The influx of alien workers into South Arkansas began in the early 1960s — around the time of regional civil rights turmoil, when blacks began getting out of cotton fields and into courtrooms. Before that, the region's farm economy had depended on black labor, stretching back to the slave era.

On the shelves of El Dorado's public library, a book printed in 1936 describes those days through myopic white eyes: "The slaves were happy and sang negro spirituals while working in the fields in the blistering sun. Some were used as house servants and had duties as cooks, maids, seamstresses, butlers, weavers and nurses. They loved their masters for most of them were well treated." It could be a white farmer in 1989 talking about the Hispanic workers he treats as family.

Blacks and poor whites want no part of chicken-farm work. White farmers claim blacks in South Arkansas are too used to welfare to take menial chicken and crop picking jobs, but a Union County housekeeper named Pat, who is black, says the situation is more complex than that and weighted with psychological baggage.

"They don't want to go back. You can't turn the clock back. These aren't slavery days," she explains. She says some white farmers actually do treat black workers like slaves even now. For instance, they may negotiate to hire workers to pick field peas, then require them on-site to do a greater variety of tasks, even to clean the farm house, before paying them. Farmers may not provide cool water to drink or decent bathroom facilities, she adds, even though the law requires them to do so.

BEFORE 1986, when most seasonal workers were illegal, "the view at the time was that Mexicans were taking jobs away from the locals," a white farmer says. The Immigration Act turned illegal aliens into a pool of available legal labor, supposedly making all things equal and creating equal opportunities for blacks, whites and Hispanics.

The pay is undeniably better than what most Hispanics could earn back home. Jobs are harder to come by in Mexico, and wages are lower. Menial labor earns $1.50 per day in Mexico, whereas an able body can earn $150 a week on a South Arkansas poultry farm, plus room and board, medical care and other benefits, according to the inclination of his employer. He can earn $90 a day picking tomatoes but usually must provide his own housing and sometimes his own transportation to the field. In some timber industry jobs, he can earn $100 a day, or $400 a week planting seedlings or logging. Timber workers fend for themselves, too, in lodging, transportation and food.

According to Hernandez, who acts as a pipeline of information for Hispanic seasonal and migrant workers across the United States, most workers send at least half their American earnings out of the country on a weekly basis.

The exchange rate makes that money go a long way in Mexico, where 20 American dollars brings 48,000 pesos. A whole family can buy a basic three-course dinner in Mexico for 10,000 pesos, for instance. The money goes even further in very rural areas of Mexico, which, Hernandez says, is where most of the seasonal workers in South Arkansas come from.

Cecilia and Ruth, of Salvadoran heritage, display their favorite toys.

With a carrot like that dangling in front of them, a number of Hispanics will continue to emigrate north, although the amnesty laws and the 1986 Immigration Act have finally curtailed those numbers.

Agents with the Immigration and Naturalization Service during all of 1960 picked up 3,648 illegal aliens crossing the Rio Grande River from Mexico along the U.S. Border Patrol's 341-mile El Paso sector. During the first week of May 1986, El Paso agents apprehended nearly twice that number. But since 1986, the number of illegal aliens caught has dropped drastically.

In Arkansas, since 1986, the number of illegals caught by Border Patrol agents has dropped by half. Agents arrested 685 deportable aliens between October 1987 and October 1988, compared to 1,382 between those same months in 1985 and 1986.

At the Border Patrol's headquarters in North Little Rock, special agent-in-charge James Hipple says he believes "the vast majority" of Hispanics in South Arkansas are now legal.

But a white poultry farmer confides that a number of farmers still rely on illegal help when they need it, and he speculates that they will do so even more as legal Hispanics continue to abandon poultry jobs. The risk to the farmer is criminal prosecution and fines of up to $10,000 per violation. You can do time for hiring illegals. For the illegal immigrant, the cost has also risen in terms of fees paid to "coyotes," recruiters who get aliens across the border. What used to be a standard $600 fee has risen to $900 in the past few months.

"There are always people on the border trying to take advantage of people coming across," says Rosa, who does not want to reveal her last name. In a two-room house near Warren, she and her husband are raising five children and trying to improve their lives. They work for a poultry farmer at $130 a week. The farmer has provided the house and utilities.

A recent cold snap forced the family to close one bedroom and move into one room, where the open flame of oven burners heats the bare floor and walls. Rosa hopes to buy some furniture soon to extend the two beds and the rolled-up mattress on which the family now relies.

Despite the spartan surroundings, Rosa says the family is better off in Arkansas than in their native land of El Salvador.

"It is a lot better here," she says, balancing a wide-eyed baby on her lap as four other children sit in a row on the mattress. Unlike the other children, Rosa's baby was born in El Dorado, not El Salvador. "Mostly for the education of the kids. They go free every day and they eat lunch free every day."

"The political unrest in the Salvadoran government made it impossible to have jobs," Rosa says through an interpreter.

She and her family, like Hollywood and his, are representative of the 10 percent of Hispanic workers who live as a family in South Arkansas, according to Hernandez. Most workers are single men, who have left families behind in Central or South America. Coming from the family-oriented cultures of those homelands, Hispanics who have left parents and wives and children in order to work in the U.S. face particular emotional and psychological constraints, but those problems pale in comparison to the worker abuses to which they were routinely subjected before 1986.

The abuses and problems of that period are still vivid for Larry Norton, a lawyer now with Pennsylvania Legal Services who once handled farm worker advocacy cases in Arkansas.

"A number of farmers used coercive means to keep [Hispanic workers] there until they had paid off the money they owed the coyote," Norton remembers. Those intimidation tactics included farmers "carrying weapons, saying they were not allowed to leave until they had paid off the money, threatening to have them deported if they left the farm."

Locals tell of one farmer who kept his workers in a cage. Others lived in old chicken coops or abandoned school buses, sandwiched into filthy spaces without regard for hygiene or privacy.

Norton, who worked for a Texas legal aid group until 1984, handled Arkansas cases, including one which he filed in 1983 on behalf of migrant farm workers who were picking tomatoes in Bradley County for Randy Clanton.

Norton recalls talking to Clanton at his house during the advocacy case: "I remember talking with him and he didn't strike me as someone who would shape up easily. He called to one of the workers, whistled to him to come over, calling him 'boy,' and showed his anger by saying to him, 'Go ahead, if you have any problems, tell this lawyer.'"

Clanton is the only farmer in Arkansas who has taken advantage of an alien worker program called H-2A, which is part of that 1986 Immigration Act. The program enables a farmer to hire temporary alien residents for labor, but he must go through piles of paperwork to prove he cannot get local help. He has to conform to strict regulations that govern the provision of housing and transportation and the way in which he keeps records and handles wages. The farmer must also pay $110 per certified job position, up to a maximum of $1,000.

The program, which Clanton used this past summer, worked well for him. "In my opinion, that's the only way to go," he said. He plans to incorporate next year with other farmers to apply for the program again. "That will help defray some of the expense [of applying]," he said.

Clanton doubled his tomato acreage to a 200-acre spread and applied for 200 workers. A third of his workers were U.S. citizens, whom he was forced to hire because of program rules on hiring available help. That group, he said, "went home early" in the harvest because he was not satisfied with their work.

Clanton hired a "contractor on the border" to bring in a group of temporary residents for the rest of his work force, he said. The contractor charged $50. The tomato grower said he did not know if the contractor charged the Mexicans a fee to be included in the group, but such fees are the norm, and so-called contractors, even under government approval through programs like H-2A, exploit Hispanics heading north by charging big fees. It cost $125 a head, excluding wages, to transport workers to his farm and back to the border, as well as to house them.

Clanton's records have been reviewed, as required under the H-2A program, by the Labor Department.

Dean Speer, district director in Little Rock for the department's Wage and Hour Division, which investigates labor conditions in Arkansas, would not say whether Clanton had fully complied with program regulations. When Norton was told of Clanton's apparent success in the regulated H-2A program, he responded dubiously. "Maybe," he said. "Maybe he has become more of a straight businessman now."

While widespread worker abuses have diminished, they still exist on some farms, Speer says. Housing, for instance, "on some of the farms is still atrocious. Those conditions have not changed much," Speer says. "I can understand it's an expensive proposition."

A law called the Migrant and Seasonal Agricultural Workers Protection Act requires farmers to provide specified, adequate housing and working conditions. According to the Labor Department's regional office in Dallas, violations have continued at a fairly constant rate since 1986.

In a five-state region that encompasses Texas, Arkansas, Louisiana, Oklahoma and New Mexico, penalties assessed for violations amounted to $277,000 in fiscal year 1986 (*i.e.*, October 1985 to September 1986), the following year to $142,000, then $140,000 and $134,000 most recently. A single six-figure assessment against one farmer in 1986 accounted for the disparity that year.

Worker abuses at one point led outside organizers and lawyers to infiltrate South Arkansas to force improvements. Farmers still tell bitter stories of efforts in the early part of this decade by the Catholic Diocese of Little Rock to organize farm workers.

Under the auspices of the Campaign for Human Development, the church's war on poverty program, a special three-year program called Arkansas Farmworkers Organizing Project folded in 1985. Today, little visible evidence remains of the groups that banded together to negotiate for better working and living conditions.

Hernandez, a Baptist, who is frequently called in by farmers and officials as an interpreter, mediator and general source of knowledge, says the Catholics' work was perceived in South Arkansas as being too aggressive, or "hard." Hernandez often conducts what he calls "friendly negotiations." He says it is unlikely farm workers will ever unionize because they are too isolated from each other at independent farms.

The labor shortage that forced Randy Clanton to use a government program to find harvesters illustrates how the growing lack of workers already is spreading to perishable crops. Farmers in those crops may get help from a replenishment program called ROWS that is expected to go into effect next year. According to Hipple at the Border Patrol office, ROWS would replenish the pool of legal aliens by extending legalization opportunities offered under the 1986 Immigration Act.

The reason behind instigating ROWS, says Hipple, is that "a lot of legals have gone out of agriculture to other industries."

But there's a catch. When the 1986 law passed, only foreigners who had worked a required period of time in eligible jobs were allowed to apply for legalization. Those jobs were all in perishable crops. Poultry, cotton and timber were not eligible fields in 1986, nor are they expected to be next year when ROWS starts up. Hipple says lawsuits have been filed in efforts to get cotton and some timber products included on the perishable crops list.

"We spent a lot of time [in 1986] helping our workers fill out their papers. It was a mountain of paperwork," a poultry farmer's wife explains. "For us to go through all that just so they can leave and work for somebody else, it's not worth it."

And legalized Hispanics are leaving poultry farms more often these days.

Independent poultry farmers, all of whom are under contract to one of the industry giants — ConAgra or Tyson Foods — say their supply contracts have them locked into tight margin profits and they cannot afford to negotiate away much more.

Senator Joe Yates of Bentonville, a spokesman for the northwestern division of the Arkansas Poultry Federation, predicts South Arkansas poultry houses may convert to automation, as is the norm in Northwest Arkansas's thriving poultry industry. But poultry farmers in South Arkansas, where houses are generally older than in the northwest, point out that building a new automated house costs $140,000. Converting an old house costs $25,000. To date, only one farmer in Union County uses automated houses. Farmers are reluctant to spend that kind of money, when they exist at the whim of the big poultry companies.

One farmer says the poultry companies might decide it would be better for them to convert his houses to breeders after he'd sunk money into automating laying houses.

One solution to cutting production costs and labor shortage problems that could spell real problems for Arkansas's economy would be for poultry companies to go "off-shore" — south of the border. Don Tyson already has entered a joint venture agreement in Mexico, and ConAgra officials plan to convert all their independent farmers under contract to plain old company operators within 20 years, making it easier to move the company, if need be. But Yates says such a move is unlikely even though he sees Tyson's foray into Mexico as one that "spells benefits" rather than threats for Arkansas.

Meanwhile, Hispanic workers in South Arkansas continue to talk about leaving poultry and crop picking jobs for greener pastures, and judging from random conversations and interviews, a lot of them seem to be moving into timber jobs.

In Union County, angry poultry farmers tell stories of recruiters from the timber industry raiding their poultry farms by night to recruit Mexicans and transport them away. Timber officials deny those stories. Still, with more Hispanics working in timber jobs, the industry is struggling to comply with labor laws and other changes that affect the bottom line.

Michael Economopoulos, president of Superior Forestry Service in Tillar, is also president of the Southeastern Contractors Association, a group of 12 to 15 member companies that joined in 1986 "to combat abuses in contracting."

"We're all for worker rights," Economopoulos states, "but basically these people who abused workers were putting us out of business with their competitive edge" by using cheap Hispanic labor.

Economopoulos says the state's timber industry has seen "a drastic reduction in worker abuses over the last 18 months." That's due in part, he notes, to a ruling in February 1988 by the Ninth Circuit Court in Oregon that mandated the Labor Department to enforce MISPA regulations in the timber industry, even though timber was not included in the 1986 Immigration Act as an eligible field for worker legalization.

"MISPA also provides to potentially make timber companies liable for violations," Economopoulos says. "That put a real scare into them.

"Traditionally," he adds, "there has been all kinds of abuse of Mexicans in the forest industry ... Most of the horror stories you hear are probably true. It was rampant, but now it's reduced. You won't find the headline abuses you did two or three years ago. There still is a lot more to do. A lot of it will depend on how the timber companies are regulating themselves."

Clay Hathorn contributed to this article.

(November 1989)

Ramsay Ball

The Other Convention

What Really Went Down in Atlanta

Issue 80, August 1988.

I have it on good authority that George Bush was genetically engineered to rule the world.

My authority is Bob, a self-appointed "intergalactic hero and street person" I met on the second day of the Democratic National Convention. Bob, one of many strange characters I was to meet during my trip to Atlanta, accosted me outside a Chinese restaurant and asked for spare food change. As I usually do in such situations, I offered to buy him a meal rather than give him cash. Whereas most winos just curse you and head for their next mark, Bob readily accepted my offer. As we dined on assorted Far Eastern delights, he told me his story.

Bob said he was working as a CIA custodian several years ago, when he ran across some files describing a project that involved a renegade group of Naval intelligence men who worked for the predecessor to the OSS, which subsequently became the CIA. The project was a primitive method of artificial insemination that was to breed a super spy who would rise to rule the planet. Dick Nixon and Ed Meese were apparently early failed experiments, and Bob said Bush is the last one left. Bush was recently overhauled by the CIA, through the installation of a big Motorola microchip in the back of his head, very similar to the one the CIA put in Bob's head. Bob's duty was to warn the world.

That's why Bob was hanging around the convention. My reason was slightly different. Although my original plan had been to march onto the floor as a delegate for Illinois Senator Paul Simon, this option turned out to be no more likely than Bob's story. So, I took the only offer I could get: to cover the convention behind the convention as a reporter.

It was a good thing that characters like Bob were wandering about, because there was very little else of consequence to observe in Atlanta. The events on the convention floor were little more than a rubber stamping of preordained realities. Mike Dukakis was already the nominee, Lloyd Bentsen was to be his running mate and Jesse Jackson, the prodigal son, would inevitably return to claim his fatted calf.

The real story from Atlanta is that there was *no* real story. What little spontaneous deliberation the delegates participated in occurred either over a drink at one of the many liquor-soaked hospitality suites and late-night parties open to the well-connected, or through interaction with life outside the convention center. Which explains, of course, the relevance of Bob.

Sunday, July 17 — Foreplay to the Convention

11:30 a.m.: The Democratic Party of Arkansas is hosting brunch at the Embassy Suites Hotel in Marietta, distant headquarters of the Arkansas Delegation. The luncheon is to be a gathering of the Arkansas delegates and their friends, roughly a hundred people. The governor's office volunteered to co-host, sending invitations to anyone local who had ever lived in Arkansas. The crowd numbers around 700, ranging in status from U.S. senators to Georgia Tech freshmen. Glasses of champagne, screwdrivers, mimosas and Bloody Marys are passed around to get the crowd in the proper mood. The governor stands at the entrance to the atrium and shakes hands for at least two hours. Clinton is said to

"THE BUS WILL NOT LEAVE
UNTIL EVERYONE IS LOADED."

Jeff Loucks

have 37 events scheduled for the day. Clearly, he is in his element.

2:30 p.m.: The Young Democrats of America are setting up a nerve center in Tower Room 18 of the Peachtree Plaza Hotel. The advance crew is setting up telephones, typewriters and a bar. A quick trip through the service corridor rounds up tables, tablecloths, glasses, ashtrays, buckets of ice and anything else that could be "appropriate." I quickly stake out a corner and turn on CNN. A CNN/*Los Angeles Times* poll reports that 70 percent of "The Party Of The People's" delegates have college degrees, 40 percent graduate degrees, and that more than 55 percent have a household income of more than $55,000 per year.

6:30 p.m.: Back at the Embassy Suites. The Arkansas and Mississippi delegations are going to Marietta to attend a cocktail party and barbecue, courtesy of the mayor and city of Marietta. The convention has commandeered the MARTA Bus System to shuttle the conventioneers from place to place. The transportation volunteers attempt to herd the groups onto the buses, but because of the free happy hour going on in the hotel, it's not too easy. One bus stays to pick up the stragglers. When half of the group gets on the bus and demands to leave in a rather surly fashion, the attendant on the bus announces that "The bus will not leave until everyone is loaded." At this point Dale Evans, a delegate from northwest Arkansas announces, "Well, let's get loaded." He proceeds to lead a group off the bus and back to the bar for a round of drinks.

The delegations finally depart, and the bus winds through Marietta to the mayor's house, where cocktails are being served. It's an odd scene: the stragglers' bus pulls up in the middle of a quiet neighborhood and spits out a crowd of drunken revelers who then proceed to get even drunker and scarf down mounds of cheesestraws and chicken fingers.

At an appointed time, the buses come back to the house, and take the delegations to Marietta Square, where there is an old-fashioned barbecue. Locals dressed up as Southern belles and beaus greet each group.

Delegates are learning to sniff out free meals from half a mile away, and this crowd of drunken Democratic Party animals stampedes to the rapidly forming lines in front of the food tents. Enormous quantities of roasted meats are piled on each plate, along with the necessary side dishes of cole slaw, beans and white bread. After disposing of this snack, bands of roving delegates flock to the taverns and honky-tonks that encircle the square.

At a preappointed hour, everyone returns to the buses, which are parked at a large staging point outside the square. Evans and his friends have appropriated a life-sized cutout of old Jack Daniels himself, and set him up in the back of the bus, plastered with buttons and lipstick. The group returns to the Embassy

Suites, where the drinking continues until the wee hours. The mood of the convention has been established.

Monday, July 18 — The Rubes Arrive

9:45 a.m.: Lib Carlisle, Arkansas State Party Chairman, is giving the Arkansas delegation its marching orders at the morning caucus. Second District Congressman Tommy Robinson approaches and I ask him for a quote. His "quote" consists of a choice expletive comparing me to a specific region of the posterior. From frequent association with the congressman, I realize this is his way of saying "Good morning."

11 a.m.: The *Atlanta Journal-Constitution* has a large convention section, which notes that protests at "authorized sites" in front of the Omni will include demonstrations against left-wing Democrats; a group of former Black Panthers who now support the South African government; and The Committee to Free Darrell Alexander, which is protesting the case of a jailed man who relatives say has been held by the Ghanian government since June 6 on charges of trying to illegally export 2,000 parrots.

12:30 p.m.: Michael Dukakis, Jesse Jackson and Lloyd Bentsen hold a joint press conference and announce that they will still respect each other on the morning after. The immediate speculation in the hotel is about "The Deal" — what Jackson will get for his act of affection — because the convention is his show at this point. It was critical for the Duke to bust up any potential long-term threat of implied racism. Dukakis handles himself well. He's a man with the look of a fighter who knows his opponent is doomed.

3:30 p.m.: Fourth District Congressman Beryl Anthony is hosting a party at Pittypat's Porch, an over-rated eatery in downtown Atlanta. Anthony, a relatively passive figure in Arkansas politics, is *the man* in Atlanta this week. As chairman of the Democratic Congressional Campaign Committee (DCCC) — the organization that doles out money to congressional candidates across the country — he stands over this city like a colossus. He also is the man who controls passes to Flamingo Joe's, the after-hours nightclub that has been appropriated this week for the exclusive use of the DCCC, as well as the passes for the DCCC hospitality suite in the World Congress Center next door to the Omni. Food and drink of every sort flow freely in both places, and no money is needed. Beryl's favor is all that is required.

The Congressman is standing in the doorway greeting everyone coming in, a fine sheen of sweat on his forehead, drinking vast quantities of diet soda. We don't have passes for this event but are waved on in regardless. I hear later that others from Arkansas without passes are required to give the correct pronunciation of El Dorado to prove that they are really from the state.

5:15 p.m.: Back up at the Young Democrat Suite, Ed Fry, president of the Young Democrats of America and a top aide to Congressman Robinson, strides in with what looks like about 10 of every pass available for the convention.

Fry, the ultimate insider, realized early that the real currency of the convention was neither money nor delegate votes, but passes. The passes are different colors and have different legends, representing different areas the bearer is allowed to enter. The lowest form of currency is the World Congress Center orange Convention Guest Pass. This pass allows the bearer to get into the confines of the WCC, where he can watch the convention on closed-circuit television, wander around and buy overpriced souvenirs or possibly get into a hospitality suite — if that suite does not require a separate pass of its own. A green Omni Honored Guest Pass allows one to do all of the above and provides access to the Omni hallways. Unfortunately, the Omni Honored Guest Pass will not let you get onto the floor of the convention — and so you must roam the perimeters or go up into the upper tiers of the hall, where you can barely hear the

He Does

In June 1986, Spectrum *reported that 1st District congressman Bill Alexander was observed in a Jonesboro hair salon, having his "fluffy, but graying, locks touched up." There is no evidence that the revelation damaged the entrenched congressman politically. He continues to represent northeast Arkansas in Congress.*

Issue 86, October 1988

speakers. A green Omni Alternate Delegate Pass will get you all of the above, plus the right to go to the lower alternate seating areas. The green Omni Press Pass will go wherever the Alternate pass is allowed and gives you the right to obtain a temporary red Omni Press Floor Pass, which allows you to mingle with the exalted on the floor for 20 minutes at a time.

Certain red Omni Hall Security Passes will get you anywhere. High in demand is the blue Podium Pass. And, of course, the red Omni Delegate Pass allows you on the floor anytime. But even delegates don't reach the peak of passdom, as they cannot get in the most elite hospitality suites, unless they have additional passes or the right connections, such as those Fry has cultivated.

Ed hands out passes to the group, explaining that the key to the whole deal is getting in the World Congress Center. If you can make it there, he says he can get you anywhere. Everyone wants to be Ed's pal this week.

6:15 p.m.: Fry is as good as his word. Although I already had Omni Press Passes, I'm now sitting in a place only Ed could get me into — inside the Democratic Congressional Campaign Committee Hospitality Suite, just inside the entrance to the World Congress Center. The DCCC suite is probably the finest around, Fry had announced outside, giving us the plan. As he only had about four extra passes on him, we would have to pull the old switcheroo. Four people would go in wearing the passes around their necks on strings. They would immediately proceed to the far corner, where three people would remove their DCCC passes and give them to the fourth person, the relay man. He would go back outside, give the passes to three other people, and the whole process would repeat itself, until all of our people got in. Using this method, we managed to get about 15 people in with no trouble at all.

The DCCC is Beryl Anthony's bailiwick, and he's become a master fundraiser. Although any donation is gladly accepted, the big money commands more respect, and this suite was set up to evidence that respect. There's no cheap whiskey to be found here. The most inexpensive booze is Jim Beam; and Crown Royal, Glenlivet, Meyer's Rum and Beefeaters are par for the course. The wine is good and the food is a cut above the average also, with shrimp, paté and crab cakes on the bill of fare. The sign at the door said this little gathering was being sponsored by Phillips 66. The crowd consists of congressmen and spouses, lobbyists, big-time contributors and us.

7 p.m.: My first trip to the convention floor while the convention is in progress. The floor is jam-packed with reporters, who outnumber the delegates at many times. As I pass Congressman Robinson and other members of the Arkansas delegation, they pay their respects by giving me the single-digit salute.

8 p.m.: A trip to the R.J. Reynolds Hospitality Suite located in the second level of the WCC. Big baskets of cigarettes lie around, all for the taking. Once again, there are table-loads of food and barrels of whiskey. The crowd in here is a little mean and pig-eyed, so I only stay briefly. Before I leave, I read R.J. Reynolds' annual report, which brags that they sold more than "99 Billion Units of Cigarettes last year" and boasts of their overseas markets, where smokers don't have to be bothered with pesky Surgeon General's warnings.

11:45 p.m.: The gavel is down. We are now watching Congressman Robinson on CNN's *Crossfire*, where he says, of all things, that the Democratic party can't win without the support of Jackson. TR speculates on The Deal: "If he (Jackson) got nothing, he made a mistake." Afterwards, I catch a ride back to the hotel with Robinson and ask him for another quote. He just grins and mouths the choicest of expletives.

Tuesday, July 19 — They Take the Early Bus

2:30 p.m.: We arrive at the press desk just as they are closing. I snatch up the daily credentials and head for the upstairs bar, the first opportunity of the week actually to buy food and drink with *real* money. The place is packed with celebrities. Ed Asner sits at a table next to us, ignored by teenage fans who are flocking to get autographs from one of his companions, apparently a soap star. Ed Begley Jr. of *St. Elsewhere* fame is snacking two tables over. Dan Rather hurries by.

3 p.m.: The streets are alive with the truly weird. The most prominent are the idiotic Lyndon LaRouche supporters, who harangue people from almost every street corner, sitting or standing behind card tables with signs in front — HOLD AN OPEN CONVENTION, and DON'T LICK DUKAKIS' ASS, KICK IT. The LaRouchites are really worked up, with scrawny sweating bodies, bulging eyes and rapid chipmunk speech.

5 p.m.: The 10th floor of the Marriott is the scene of a reception for Little Rock Mayor Lottie Shackelford, one of four co-chairpersons of the convention. Three or four hundred people show up to honor Her Honor. The purpose of the reception, according to Bill Paschall of Little Rock, who helped organize the affair, is to "show Little Rock off and to introduce the Mayor to Atlanta and the convention."

7:55 p.m.: Shackelford is on TV. She comes across smooth, poised and well-paced. A supporter says she was uncommitted coming to the convention, but now is committed to Dukakis. She took a lot of heat from the Jackson Delegation, but she stayed above the fray. Still, it made for an interesting sight: Robinson, the white Boll Weevil, making noises about Jesse Jackson, and Shackelford, the black progressive, backing Dukakis.

9:45 p.m.: The Omni Hall is locked up tight — no one not already inside is allowed. Tonight's the night — the Reverend Jesse Jackson is to speak, and everyone wants to hear Jesse. The security guys at the front door tell us that the fire marshals have shut down the hall and that there is no way we can get in. Several delegates are shouting, crying, screaming to be let in, but nothing is going to sway the keepers of the gates. It turns out later that a lot of the hired help had flocked to the galleries to see Jesse, and that his speech may have been the only convention event played out in front of an audience even remotely representative of the Democratic electorate.

Because of the lockdown, the DCCC suite next door is jamming tonight. Many of the delegates denied entry are there, but most of the crowd is there just to watch the Jackson "freak show," knowing they are at a safe enough distance that Jesse can't jump out and bite them on the butt. It's yet another manifestation of the strange and condescending "What Does Jesse Want?" phenomenon. Many people, even many liberal Democrats, seem to view Jackson not as a candidate, but as an aberration. I half-expect 3-D glasses to be passed out.

The crowd is moving around uneasily. From the trace of fear in many faces, it's apparent that some must expect Jesse to denounce the party and announce an alliance with the Arab-Muslim League. Copies of Jesse's speech are being passed around already, and the sober ones in the room are reading it grimly.

Jackson looks a little uneasy at the beginning of his speech but soon gets right into the swing of things. The DCCC Suite begins to erupt in spontaneous outbursts of applause. For one of the few times during the convention there's actually something happening on the floor worth paying attention to.

Jesse talks about the party being a huge quilt. Like the quilt his momma made when the family couldn't afford a blanket to keep them warm on those cold South Carolina winter nights. All the special interest groups in the party, Jackson explained, are patches on the quilt, held together by a single unifying thread. He praises the working poor, those who "take the early bus" to their menial jobs. A few "amens!" are shouted in response.

Of course, Democratic Party Chairman Paul Kirk and much of the DCCC crowd probably hate these references to special interests — they don't want to dwell on the fact that the party is supposed to be the refuge of the poor, blacks, women's groups, unions and gays. Kirk's idea of a special interest group is the Finance Council.

The speech is over now, and the room is animated. I wander over to a table, where I agree to go off the record as to the identity of the speakers. The talk is about "The Deal." Supposedly, Jackson gave that barn-burning speech in exchange for the unlimited use of a big Democratic National Committee jet airplane, an almost infinite expense account and the right to put several of his people on the DNC. Most of those present were sincerely touched by Jackson, but there's still a good deal of cynicism left. One Arkansas politician who speaks warmly of Jackson on the record denounces him as self-important and arrogant once we go off the record. Despite the power of his preaching, it seems Jesse will never convert the entire congregation.

Wednesday, July 20 — Eye of the Storm

4 p.m.: The Friends of Paul Simon are hosting a party for the senator at the Botanical Gardens in midtown Atlanta. Simon represents the progressive wing of the party, and, as such, his presidential campaign was doomed from the beginning. The progressives have been gunned down by the Kirk-led middle-of-the-roaders and technocrats, *i.e.*, the Dukakis people.

I meet Simon at the reception. I approach him and introduce myself as someone who worked on his Arkansas campaign. I'm sweating like a pig, soaking down my shorts, shirt and flak jacket. The Secret Service keeps a wary eye on me as I put my arm around the senator and pose for a picture.

9:45 p.m.: Governor Bill Clinton is about to give his nominating speech for the Duke. The Arkansas delegation goes wild when he is introduced, but the Jackson crew is still wound up from the nominating speeches for their candidate. It might have been wiser for Clinton to have gone first. A Jackson delegate and a man wearing a huge donkey head are dancing some kind of square dance in front of the podium, and the crowd is not paying attention to the governor. Clinton's speech leaves the crowd cold. The beat, or something, is wrong. My floor pass expires, so I leave in mid-speech.

10:15 p.m.: Back in the DCCC suite, the crowd is getting roaring drunk and not paying much attention to the speech. An extravagant spread is laid out on the buffet table, and good Russian vodka is being served up ice-cold at the bar. Those who try to watch Clinton on TV, however, are out of luck. It's hard to keep your mind on the game with the antics that are going down in every direction. In one section of the room, a certain Congressman from New York is dead-dog drunk, singing some kind of Moonlight Melody, and trying to feel up a pretty young congressional staffer.

1:05 a.m.: Congressman Robinson and Ed Fry come into the DCCC suite, chuckling to themselves, like a couple of school kids who've just popped the teacher on the back of the head with a big spitball. Which they have, in a way, since these two uncommitted delegates cast their votes for Jesse Jackson, not Mike Dukakis. Robinson and Fry don't really like Dukakis, who is, in their opinion, something of a "tight ass." They like Jesse, who, if nothing else, has a personality. The head honchos of the Arkansas Democratic Party and the Dukakis people were not amused at their votes, which made it even better as far as Robinson and Fry are concerned.

Robinson walks up and says, "Lemme give you a scoop. I voted for Jesse Jackson. I've admired Jesse for a long time. He and I both come from the wrong side of the tracks. He fights for his people, trying to rid the ghetto of drugs. I fight against drugs. He and I have a lot in common. We both appeal to young people. And another thing — Dukakis didn't ever ask me for my vote — Jesse Jackson did." With that off his chest, Robinson, his wife, Carolyn, and Fry head for Flamingo Joe's for a little honky-tonking.

Thursday, July 21 — The Party's Over

11:30 a.m.: Delegates wander into the hotel restaurant after a hard night on the town. The convention is drawing to a close and the discussion around the table is about Governor Clinton's speech. By this time, it has become a national sensation. Supposedly, according to some of Clinton's staff, the governor was given some general guidelines, then wrote the speech himself. Dukakis's people read it, whooped, and said, "By God, this is the best. Read every word." Now, a day later, the Duke's campaign is putting a little distance between itself and Clinton. The governor's people are even having a hard time rounding up passes for the convention, which is the ultimate sign of estrangement.

The "Ambush Theory" is making the rounds. In this scenario, the Duke set up the governor by having him give a long TV speech rather than a fiery convention speech, then had the floor whips drive the crowd into a "We Want Mike" chant, madly ordering Clinton off the stage. The ambush theory holds that Clinton is being punished for his failure to endorse Dukakis in the campaign's early going, back when it would have mattered. The very existence of this theory demonstrates just how little of substance most delegates had to concern themselves with.

The same was true for the media, because what really hurt Clinton was what happened after the speech. The national media, with no suspense left in the air and nothing else to do, made Clinton's speech an event. In a convention free of real debate or controversy — a convention that made the Supreme Soviet look like a serious deliberative body by comparison — Bill Clinton's flubbed speech was the only surprise of the evening.

Clinton's speech was just one of the letdowns for the Arkansas delegation, however. The previous night, the Arkies had to pass on the first tally because State Representative Bill Walker, a Jackson delegate, was raising hell over the vote count. Walker objected after some uncommitted Arkansas "super delegates" — high party officials who get to attend purely because of their rank — assigned their votes to alternate delegates, which was not allowed. Also, Walker was challenging the credentials of some of the delegates, asking for identification from people he obviously knew.

3 p.m.: In a cab going downtown, Larry Cochran of Fort Smith comments on the fireworks display the previous night, when the conventioneers were walking back to the hotels and buses. "They didn't tell us about them," he said. "When they went off, it scared me to death." There was palpable fear around the convention that some kind of terrorist group was going to touch off a bomb, especially after the U.S. nailed the Iran Air jet over the Persian Gulf.

8:30 p.m.: In the DCCC suite, Craig Smith, a member of Clinton's staff, comes in looking for passes: "Look, I've got the French, Canadian, and Tanzanian ambassadors to the U.S. outside, and they've been locked out of the

Clinton Redeemed

An August 1988 editorial, analyzing the media overreaction to Bill Clinton's disappointing nominating speech for presidential candidate Michael Dukakis at the Democratic National Convention, pointed out that the Arkansas governor had been handed a tough task: "Listening to a verbal rendition of 'The Mike Dukakis Story' — no matter who writes and delivers it — is, by definition, about as exciting as listening to paint dry."

The editorial opined that, with the nomination sewn up, the national news media had "little of real interest" to report or write about and "suddenly smelled blood in the water. It was Bill Clinton's blood, and the sharks went for it." Still, the editorial commented, the governor redeemed himself the following week with an appearance on The Tonight Show With Johnny Carson, *where Clinton played the saxophone with the studio orchestra: "[I]f he's a windbag, that's okay with us. The wind sounds pretty good when applied to Gershwin's 'Summertime.'"*

Omni." Each state is given a couple of ambassadors to shepherd around, and since the DNC didn't anticipate the lockout, the ambassadors don't have the coveted DCCC Hospitality Suite pass that will allow them to while away the hours in civilized comfort.

9 p.m.: Smith and Beryl Anthony have supposedly figured out a way to get the ambassadors into the hall. A plot is hatched.

9:30 p.m.: Smith returns. He found a secret path into the Omni and led the dignitaries into the hall. To hear him tell it, it was a matter of squeezing through a cut fence, crossing over planks spanning a ditch, knocking three times on a bolted door and asking for Joe. No other way in.

10 p.m.: The "Duke and Kitty Show" is going full blast in the Omni. Since it's not very hard to figure out who wins, we head for the real action: the after-hours DCCC party at Flamingo Joe's. It is, as the Reverend Jackson says, time to "catch the early bus."

11:07 p.m.: Flamingo Joe's is a hole in the wall that plays Fifties and Sixties music. The convention is over, and the crowd is letting down its hair as never before. Several party girls and a congressman's daughter are at the front table, a group of lecherous hangers-on is trying to hustle them. The power elite begins to file into the bar.

Midnight: A horrible howl rolls out of the women's bathroom. The moon is rising. Liquor flows like a long, hard rain. On a back table, the congressman's daughter is dancing the Pee Wee. The crowd *likes* it.

Epilogue

I crawl out of bed early the next afternoon. Maybe I should have stayed at the Omni and watched the celebration. Maybe I should have heard the Duke speak. But the Flamingo was too decadent, depraved and rude to have not been experienced. And it was Flamingo Joe's, finally, that was the site of the *real* Democratic Convention.

(August 1988)

Letha Mills

Jingle Master

Issue 85, October 1988.

Jerry Russell turns the key in the ignition and propels the automobile's long nose out into the interstate traffic, leaving the straps of the seatbelt lost in the creases of his driver's seat.

"If I want to wear a seatbelt," Russell says, "I'll wear a seatbelt because I want to wear a seatbelt, not because the government says I have to." His voice is defiant, his attitude challenging. He is a reactionary with a crew cut, a bearded anachronism stuck in a world he did not make and whose shortcomings he does not hesitate to decry.

Jerry Russell — successful political consultant, local imagemaker, respected history buff — is brash, opinionated and often abrasive. His words spew forth in a voice that exudes utter confidence in the absolute integrity of his convictions. Modesty is not his middle name.

Though he is politically astute, shrewd and possesses great campaign cunning, Russell is not particularly diplomatic in expressing himself; he employs tact sparingly. State Senator Charlie Cole Chaffin of Benton, who engaged Russell's services in her successful 1984 campaign, calls him the "Don Rickles of political consultants."

"I really like Jerry's personality," Chaffin says, laughing. "He might come on to some people as sarcastic or insulting, but I kind of like it. That kind of thing makes money for Don Rickles, and I figure it can make money for Jerry Russell."

Russell makes his money turning office seekers into winners. "People hire me to tell them what to do to get elected," Russell proclaims. He tends to speak in proclamations and totes an arsenal of aphorisms like: "Until I'm paid, the deal ain't made," and (the one Chancery Judge Judith Rogers cites as Russell's best advice) "Oughta be ain't is."

For two hours, Russell cruises the streets of the city where he was born (in St. Vincent Infirmary some 55 years ago) and talks — about himself, about his work, about his philosophy.

Sitting at a downtown drive-in waiting for a Diet Pepsi, Russell peers intently through glasses that constantly need to be pushed back up to the bridge of his nose. His customary turtleneck is replaced today by an open-neck shirt. The grizzly whiskers that seem to hide three-quarters of his face are incongruous with the outmoded bristle atop his head. "Some people operate on the premise that 'Life is just a bowl of cherries.' To people at the other extreme, it's 'Life's a bitch and then you die.' In between those two, everybody has a basic premise that their life is founded on. Mine is 'People are such fools.'"

It is upon that cynical foundation that Russell's career is built.

"People are thoughtless, selfish, inconsiderate, egocentric, petty, small-minded and closed-minded," he says. "That's why I'm such a successful political consultant: Because I tell all my candidates how to appeal to all those things or to get past all those things in order to get elected to office."

U.S. Representative Tommy Robinson: *Jerry knows how to do a profile on your opponent and come up with a strategy that will work. He knows how to "get to" your opponent.*

Except for daughter Leigh Anne Russell, who runs Russell's in-home office, his firm is a one-man operation. "I don't have any helpers and I don't want any," Russell says. "People ask how I handle all these campaigns. Well, I'm like the guy in the circus that puts a wand up and starts a plate spinning, and another stick and another plate, and another stick and another plate. I run back and forth, spinning plates."

When the spinning stops, his clients find themselves in office more often than not. Of the nearly 200 races he's consulted on, he boasts, "maybe two or three candidates lost who did everything I told them to do." In March, four clients ran uncontested races. Five others hired him, and Russell claims to have "scared off" the opposition. "Nine other clients would have hired me, but they didn't have an opponent. So 18 of my clients were elected in March. I did not lose a single client."

In 1984, though, the sticks and plates fell right on Russell's head. Most of his clients in that year lost their races. One was W.D. (Bill) Younts, who campaigned against Terry Hartwick for mayor of North Little Rock. Younts is less than agreeable with Russell's insistence that candidates who lose are those who ignore his advice. "I did exactly what he said," Younts said. "I don't think I got anything for my $7,500. I'd go sometimes a week or 10 days without seeing him unless I called him. I feel like I got gypped. And it's not because I lost; I was dissatisfied before I lost."

Russell's self-confidence is not easily shaken. People hire him, he boasts, "because I'm the best around."

Senator Chaffin: *In 1982, several friends told me I should hire Jerry Russell. I said to him, "I don't have enough money to hire a political consultant." He said, "You don't have enough money to run for office if you don't have enough money to hire me." It made me mad, and I didn't hire him. And I lost the race. In 1984, when this seat came open, the very first thing I did was to call Jerry Russell.*

Robinson: *I asked around [in 1980, when he first ran for sheriff], and his name always came out on top. He's not cheap, but he's good. Whatever you pay him, you get your money's worth.*

Russell turns a corner and eases up Seventh Street. "People pay me good money and, in relative terms, big money. I charge anywhere from $6,000 to $10,000 for a race, and I get half my fee in advance."

He upped the ante on his front money (from $500 down followed by monthly payments) for a reason beyond the obvious one of economic self-protection. "I've found that if you pay me $3,000, you listen to me about six times better than if you pay me $500. It's kind of like the guy with the mule and the two-by-four: Thwock! You get their attention."

Russell grabs plenty of attention with his trademark radio jingles. The notoriously corny ditties, conceived by Russell and produced by an associate in Las Vegas, offend listeners with their pandering tone, and often embarrass candidates. But no one argues with their success.

County Judge Don Venhaus: *I think the jingle, "Venhaus in the Courthouse," did a great deal in terms of name recognition. The [1982] county judge's race was by no means a race that was capturing everyone's attention. Terrible Tommy was running, and there were other races.*

Robinson: *I had [a jingle] that was an old country and western song, "Do You Want A Crimefighter For Your Sheriff?" He played it on KEZQ ... not a country-western market. People were saying, "If you don't take that off the air, I'm going to vote against you." I thought he was nuts. But he was right.*

Russell enjoys indulging in the game of "what if," especially as it concerns candidates who chose not to hire him. "Several years ago, Dale Cowling called, running for county judge, wanted to hire me." Cowling procrastinated in bringing Russell his advance fee, so Russell represented Don Venhaus. "I'm convinced in my egotism that if Dale Cowling had hired me, Dale Cowling would probably be county judge today."

Venhaus: *Well, I'm surprised he didn't say that if he had handled a cauliflower, that the cauliflower would be county judge. Jerry is not without ego, and he's certainly not without self-confidence. So I'm sure his perception is that he took this nobody — which I certainly was — and by virtue of his skills and manipulation, made me the county judge. And he's entitled to that point of view. But what the outcome might have been if someone else had been my campaign consultant, I don't know.*

Only a few clients such as Younts openly dispute Russell's record for being right when it comes to calling campaign shots. Coupled with an uncanny talent for political prognostication, his strategizing makes him a potent adjunct to politicos with serious aspirations.

But is he always right? "I won't go that far," Robinson says, laughing. "His ego would blow out the top of his head."

On his way to becoming "the only year-round political consultant in the state," Russell earned a journalism degree from the University of Arkansas in 1958, after a stint in the Army. He passed through a number of professional incarnations in advertising and public relations before starting his present business in 1972.

Wheeling lazily across the Arkansas Arts Center parking lot, Russell elaborates on one of his unbending rules. "I was called a few months ago by [Municipal Judge] Allan Dishongh, who is an old high school acquaintance of mine, and he said, 'This may be my last campaign, and I want you to handle it'." Russell had advised Dishongh in his first two campaigns for the legislature 20 years ago.

Russell recalled that after some quibbling about the high price of consulting and the hefty advance fee, the judge said he'd get back to Russell. Two months later Russell was contacted by backers of Dishongh opponent Jim Neal.

It is here that Russell's house rule, "Until I'm paid, the deal ain't made," comes into play.

"I hadn't talked to Dishongh since. I ... talked to Jim Neal, told him the deal. He gave me the money, I'm working for him."

Dishongh says he discussed some ideas for the campaign with Russell, noting that he is concerned with the complexity of modern campaigns. "Of course, my first obligation is to be [in court] and I felt like with four opponents, it might be well to have somebody running the campaign while I was in court every day," the judge recalls. "But I never did get around to hiring him."

"Dishongh has a good chance of losing because he didn't hire me," Russell drawls. "I've got a good track record of running against incumbents.

"How do you run against Allan Dishongh without being ugly, without being tacky?" His rhetorical question hangs in the air just a beat. "Sometimes I advise my clients to be ugly and tacky, but most of the time I don't."

Russell's strategy is couched in Neal's campaign slogan: "If You Care About Integrity." The message is clear, says Russell. "To people who know what I'm talking about, that's all I need to say."

Dishongh: *He's had a lot of winners. Campaigns now are mostly an advertising gimmick. The days of going out campaigning and speaking are about gone. I suppose you could probably take a dead person and, with the right advertising agency and the right money, you could get him elected.*

The man who claims to have "elected more women to office than any individual I know of" volunteers his thoughts on the differences between the genders. "I'm a male chauvinist. I think women ought to stay home and take care of the kids. I would never — and my wife agrees with me — hire a woman if I could hire a man. Women are probably smarter than men, but men are more stable ... not as volatile. Men don't have as many physical problems, many of which are caused by emotional bases, as women. Women are not sensible and logical."

Leigh Anne Russell: *I assumed he felt that way. I don't consider Dad a male chauvinist. Most men would rather relate to a man, especially [when he's] telling them what to do. And that's what Dad does. When they hire him, he tells them what to do, when to do it, how fast or how slow to do it to get elected to office.*

Senator Chaffin: *Anybody who still wears a flat top and a turtleneck shirt in the Eighties has got to have ideas from the Forties and Fifties, and that's exactly where Jerry Russell is in his ideas about women. I treat Jerry Russell just like I treat any other chauvinistic person that I have to deal with.*

Judge Rogers: *The issue of women's rights is where we really disagree. Probably if he hired some women, he'd be more careful in some of the things he does, maybe not make some of these statements. I think he'd be more sensitive.*

Russell and his second wife, Alice Anne, have four children between them, ranging in age from 23 to 30. Grandson Christopher, 10, and Russell are "best friends," says the child's mother, Leigh Anne. Russell especially enjoys taking the boy to visit the nation's Civil War battlegrounds.

Russell is a noted authority on Civil War and Indian history and is a vocal advocate of battlefield preservation. He is national chairman of several historical organizations. "I get to be national chairman because I am also the founder," he says. The long list of associations which count him as a member include such oddities as the Wizard of Oz Club and the Good Bears of the World [for Teddy Bear aficionados]. So, he's a joiner? "No, I'm a runner. I don't belong to anything that I can't run." He corrects himself: "I belong to groups I don't run, but I don't get active in any organization that I can't run because most people are so inept, incompetent and unable to run anything."

"And after I'm president of an organization," he adds, "I'm seldom very active anymore, because it offends me to see the incompetence and ineptness of my successor." Russell was on the Sesquicentennial Commission and is a former director of the Arkansas Historical Association. He is past president of Arkansas Advertising Federation, the Arkansas chapter of Public Relations Society of America, and Friends of the Library. He was the founding charter president of the Civil War Roundtable of Arkansas and is a director on the board of the Custer Battlefield Historical Museum Association. Russell is a conservative Democrat — some might say nominal Democrat — who says he "won't work for anybody I wouldn't vote for." Like many Southern Democrats, he votes for Republican presidential candidates and would like to see a strong conservative wing of his own party. He admits, though, that "the Democratic Party has no use for conservatives."

Is an intermingling of issues possible? Could a candidate get elected if he or she openly opposed, say, abortion on demand and prayer in the schools? The answer is quick and incontrovertible. "No. Because you're asking people to think. I tell all my clients: If people have to think for you to run, don't run."

Judge Rogers: *But I think the voters do think. I think voters are more discerning than that. Every time I've had an opportunity to speak, I've found that people listen. If you look for the best in people, you'll find it. If you look for the worst, you can find it too.*

Russell pulls no punches, either in conversation or his bimonthly newsletter, in voicing his opinions and voicing them as fact. But he doesn't hesitate to emphasize that facts and truth are irrelevant in the political sphere. Perception, he says, is more important than truth. "Truth and logic have no place in politics," Russell says. "It doesn't matter what the truth is. What matters is what people believe the truth is. The truth is that Bill Clinton could no more have kept Jimmy Carter from putting those Cubans in Fort Chaffee [in 1980] than he could fly, but people believe he should have tried. If Clinton had done that, Frank White wouldn't have beat him.

"Emotion takes the place of logic in a political campaign. You're selling aroma, not recipes. [Some candidates] want to give [voters] the recipe for a plate of rolls and I want to say, 'Hmmm, smell them rolls.' People don't care how the rolls were made if they smell good. You talk to people about what they are willing to listen to ... about what they want to know."

That doesn't, however, give one license to lie, he says. One of his basic tenets is to never lie. "Not because of morality; because if you get caught you're in trouble." Probably the best known of Russell's clients in recent years is Robinson. Russell claims to have built the flamboyant cop-turned-statesman into a "folk culture hero" during Robinson's two terms as sheriff. But their alliance ended when the sheriff wanted to run for Congress.

"I told him to take his job and shove it," Russell remembers. "He got to where he knew more about my job than I do. And a man's a fool to work for somebody who knows more about his job than he does."

Robinson: *He did make some points. [He said,] "Hey, I know that you could win the U.S. Senate race. Why fool around with Congress and have to come back if you ever want to run for the Senate?" And I told him I thought I knew as much about it as he did. That didn't go over well with him. You don't argue with Jerry.*

A disobedient — or even a questioning — candidate is intolerable to Russell. "I can't emphasize strongly enough to clients: You hire me to tell you what to do ... not as a debating partner. I don't want to argue with you. That would presuppose that your judgment was better than mine or at least equal to mine. And I'm here to tell you, your judgment ain't equal to mine." When he was preparing his 1984 campaign for prosecuting attorney, Mark Stodola hired Russell, paying him an advance of $5,000. A month later, Russell returned $4,000, and the two went their separate ways, Stodola to suffer a very narrow defeat by Chris Piazza. Russell recalls telling Stodola, "'If you're not gonna do what I tell you to do, I'm not gonna work for you.' And Mark Stodola will say now, 'If I'd done what [Russell] said, I'd have won'."

City Attorney Mark Stodola: *I would expect him to say that, [but] I honestly feel that there would have been a bigger percentage difference between Chris and myself if Jerry had stayed on. I think I probably don't quite fit the mold that Jerry likes. He likes [candidates who] will follow his directions completely. I did ask a lot of questions relative to the intensity of the direction of the campaign. The more experienced you become by being in the public eye, inevitably the more wisdom you pick up, and therefore you ask a few questions of people like campaign consultants. Ending our relationship was a mutual decision.*

Some of Russell's clients pay him a year-round retainer. "But I work for them in terms of the next election," he emphasizes. "From a political standpoint, Charlie Cole Chaffin will tell you, she wouldn't go to the bathroom without asking me if it's all right."

Chaffin: *That is, in fact, not a far-off statement. Let me give you some examples. I had a person call me and say there was a newspaper reporter asking about this, this and this and trying to tie it to me. And I called Jerry and said, "OK, how am I going to respond to something like this?" And he gave me his advice. I don't hesitate to ask [his advice] over things that have nothing to do with a campaign, but have to do with politics.*

Russell and Venhaus parted company over the issue of his keeping Russell on retainer.

Venhaus: *I did not see any need for continuing involvement by a political consultant. Although I knew nothing about campaigns, I felt like I knew a good deal about managing a public agency. I don't care a whole lot about the political aspects of a given issue. I try to identify what's good public policy and act on that basis.*

Russell is quick to note that he is not a lobbyist. "I don't lobby. Only time my clients ever hear from me is if it's something personal like seat belts. I don't care what they do in the legislature, how they vote, except as it relates to their electability.

"Now, sometimes they'll say, 'If I vote for this, is it gonna get me in trouble?' And I'll say no or I'll say yes or I'll say why don't we work it this way. But I don't try to influence votes in the legislature any more than I try to influence decisions by a judge in court."

Then Russell equivocates: "Now, I have discussed some judicial decisions with some of my clients before they rendered [them], but I'm probably, in that context, [of] more use as a sounding board. I'm not saying I've ever influenced a decision. A lot of times, particularly in chancery, you don't rule on hard and fast facts, you rule on interpretations of things."

Rogers: *There are many times that I call him between campaigns because, even though you may not be running a campaign, there are certain things you do that may affect your ability to run the next campaign. But I make some decisions myself. I have intelligence and experience. I very often just check my decisions against his.*

The 1986 movie *Power* focused on Pete St. John, a fictional political consultant kingmaker. Senator Chaffin recommends the movie as showing "what a political consultant does." What St. John does is to circle the globe in his private jet issuing dicta like, "If you wanta win the uncommitted, you gotta stay uncommitted" and "People don't vote for issues, they vote for people." In the end, St. John sees the light and helps a nobody from nowhere beat a slick, "digested, prepackaged" candidate he himself helped package.

Jerry Russell's pronouncement on that Hollywood ending might go something like this: "That's all well and good, and it oughta be that way, but oughta be ain't is."

Point of Clarification

In the next issue, Spectrum *printed the following clarification:*
"In our story ... about campaign consultant Jerry Russell, Chancellor Judith Rogers was quoted as saying she frequently consults with Russell between campaigns for advice. While Judge Rogers was quoted accurately, our use of her comments may have left an erroneous impression that she was speaking about judicial matters. Judge Rogers's comments were clearly made with regard to politics and not to courtroom matters."

Judith Rogers was elected in November 1988 to the Arkansas Court of Appeals.

(October 1988)

Dixie Knight

Philip Martin

Waiting to Play

Life in the Minor Leagues is Not a Sure Thing

After the game, in the dank clubhouse beneath the stands of Shreveport's otherwise-shadowless Fair Grounds Field, the Arkansas Travelers are stripping off their soggy double-knit uniforms. Imbedded in the unstirred air is the pungent, post-coital aroma of the locker room.

Some players lounge in the afterglow, arranging themselves on the industrial-beige folding metal chairs. Though they have just defeated the Shreveport Captains 6-4, there are no unsubtle demonstrations, no high fives or war whoops; just a few satisfied smiles. Minor-league baseball's long seasons and bus rides beat temperance into the most manic player.

Manager Gaylen Pitts, his sparse hair slicked back with perspiration and heavy undershirt melted to his torso, lifts a 1,000-pound arm to point a Shreveport sportswriter in the direction of tonight's star, second baseman Craig Wilson. Tonight Wilson added four more hits to his team-leading total, including a two-out, three-run double that turned a 2-1 game into a 5-1 game.

In his fifth year of professional ball, Wilson, 24, probably shouldn't even be with the Travelers this year. Last year, he played an entire season a step up the ladder as the third baseman for the Louisville Redbirds, the St. Louis Cardinals' Triple-A farm team. He led American Association third basemen in total chances and hit a respectable .256. Normally, a player doesn't get demoted after that type of year.

"The Cardinals have told me I'm only going to be at Arkansas for a couple of more weeks," Wilson said. "I'm just here until this guy comes off the disabled list. Then, they say I'll move up."

MOVING UP is what they all want to do. Some will, some won't. Double-A baseball, perhaps especially the Texas League of which the Travs are part, is where professional baseball careers are made or broken.

Triple-A teams serve as sort of a taxi squad for their major-league affiliates: proven players are kept on reserve there, and hot prospects receive their final seasoning. When big leaguers fall from grace they land in Triple-A, where they are given time to rehabilitate their skills and to heal injured parts and pride.

Class A leagues — the "bush leagues"— are where players prove themselves worthy of the attention by a major-league club. Except maybe for a highly touted first-round draft choice, players have to play well at that level to even be noticed by the parent club. These leagues serve as sort of an orientation into professional baseball — a boot camp of sorts. Many clubs enforce dress codes. Fundamentals are taught, talents assessed, players are graded and sorted like eggs.

In between Triple-A and the bush leagues, the Texas League and other Double-A systems serve as sort of a DMZ between the near-glory of Triple-A and the near-oblivion of the low minors.

The Texas League is a confluence of younger and older players — "older" in this context being 25 and up. It is possible to make it to the major leagues after seven or eight years in the minors — occasionally, maybe once every couple of seasons, a 30-year-old rookie might make his major league debut. But it doesn't happen often, and, every year beyond 25, the dream fades a little.

ROY SILVER IS 26 YEARS OLD and hitting better than he ever has in his life. "I know I can hit major-league pitching," he says flatly. "I've been able to make adjustments, to concentrate harder, to do what I needed to do to get the job done. All I'm waiting on now is the chance to prove it."

Silver is in his third season with the Travelers. Last year, he played a handful of games at Louisville, but he wasn't surprised when he was reassigned to Little Rock. Off-season surgery to correct chronic shoulder problems has limited his ability to throw. With a healthy arm Silver would likely be stroking line drives in Triple-A ball.

"It's hard to bring me up when I can't play in the field," Silver says. "But the Cardinals could have put me on the disabled list, too. I'm lucky to be here."

While a healthy Roy Silver is versatile enough to play four or five positions — including catcher — this season he is strictly a hitter. When the Travelers play teams affiliated with an American League organization, he gets four or five at-bats a night as the designated hitter. On other nights he sits and waits for his chance to pinch-hit, since pitchers bat against National League-affiliated teams. More often than not, his chance comes — Silver has made an appearance in all but nine of the Travelers' games thus far this season. It is not a bad record for a one-armed man.

And, as Silver lunches on liver and rice off a Ramada Inn buffet line, he is a mere five plate appearances shy of the minimum needed to officially qualify as the second-ranked hitter in the Texas League. Only El Paso outfielder Ramon Sambo has a better batting average than Silver's .344 — and Sambo plays half his games in the Dudley "Dome," a notorious hitter's park which has been the home field of 14 of the past 17 Texas League batting champions.

Out of uniform, Silver looks like a blacksmith in repose, with jackhammer arms and a pit bull chest. But he doesn't hit home runs, and he doesn't lift weights.

"I've always been stocky," he says. "Never touched a weight. I guess I'm just fortunate that way. When I was a kid I had a pull-up bar on my bedroom door. Sometimes I used to do push-ups because my dad did push-ups. But I've never done any training religiously."

Silver grew up in suburban Long Island while his father served for 20 years as a New York City policeman.

"When I was a kid I played all sports, not just baseball. All my friends did. Football, basketball, roller hockey, ice hockey, golf, tennis, stickball. And I ran everywhere. I remember coming home in the evenings and jumping over hedges like they were hurdles. That sort of thing is real good for your motor skills, your coordination.

"Kids don't do that sort of stuff anymore."

Unlike most other switch-hitters, Silver is a natural lefty. His father started him switching when he was about "8 or 9 years old." He believes it may be easier for him to hit right-handed against left-handed pitching than it would be for a switch-hitting right-hander to turn around and hit against a right-handed thrower from the left side of the plate.

"There aren't as many lefties," Silver says of pitchers. "Because of that, they usually make it to the big leagues. You see a lot of lefties up there throwing 75, 80 miles an hour — like Tommy John. The righties who throw like that always seem to get hit."

While it might be simplistic to call Silver a Pete Rose type, the analogy seems to hold. He can play anywhere the team needs him, with the same sort of enervating hustle. He hits singles and doubles despite his powerful physique. He is a student of hitting — and he wants to play forever, or at least "until they take the uniform from me."

"I know I'm never going to play the outfield on a regular basis in St. Louis. It's so big and they have Astroturf — they need someone who can really fly and who has a cannon for an arm. I figure I'm the kind of guy you can stick in and who won't hurt you for a couple of days. Maybe catch a game here and there — play some third, some first, a little in the outfield."

Silver plays baseball for about $1,500 a month during the season, supplemented by $11 a day in meal money when the team is on the road. It doesn't go very far, but it's enough to live on. Last year, because of his shoulder surgery, he wasn't able to play winter ball, so he worked as a substitute schoolteacher in West Palm Beach, Florida. He made $77 a day and worked a lot. But teaching is a fallback, not necessarily an ambition.

"The longer I stay in the game, the further my foot gets in the door as far as a coaching or managing job is concerned," Silver says. "No question, I'd like to stay in baseball. If I get a managerial shot, or something like a roving hitting instructor, I'll take it.... It would be great to coach a junior-college team, say in Florida. It'd be a good life; you could raise a family."

Silver isn't working today. Tonight the San Francisco Giants are in Shreveport to play an exhibition with their farm club. Days off on the road are a drag. The Travelers have a day to rest, to stare at the ceilings in their hotel rooms, whatever. A couple of teammates stop by Silver's table to ask if he wants to go in with them. They want to rent a van and go someplace, any place, to fight the ennui.

"Let's go to the mall or something," utility infielder Opie Moran suggests.

"Sure, I'll go in on it," Silver says. "But I want to go over to the park around four and watch the Giants take batting practice."

Silver says he likes to watch big leaguers — even Triple-A players — take batting practice. "I watch them to see what mistakes they're making," he says

A Farewell to Bums

Reviewing The Dodgers Move West *by Neil J. Sullivan in August 1987, Bill Jones observed that, whether they were winners or losers, "Bums" or "Boys of Summer," the Brooklyn Dodgers "were the raw material of modern urban myth." Set against the backdrop of Brooklyn's decline, Sullivan's account of Walter O'Malley's decision to move his ball club to Los Angeles managed to be sympathetic to both the old fans and the much-maligned owner.*

In the author's view, the relocation was warranted from a business perspective, given the subsequent success of the Dodgers in the warm California sun. Yet, Sullivan acknowledged, the loss of the Bums could never be justified to the Brooklyn faithful. "Three decades may not be too long a time to mourn the passing of household gods," remarked the reviewer, who found The Dodgers Move West *a sad but satisfactory study of "the way reality has of overtaking dreams."*

Issue 48, April 1987.

with a shrug. "Then I tell myself not to do it — over and over, until finally it just becomes part of my game. It's just a mental thing I do."

Shreveport pitcher Scott Gay stops by to chat. Silver has known Gay since they played together on a college summer-league team in Cape Cod, Massachusetts, six years ago. Gay was hurt last year and released from a Triple-A club. He caught on with the Captains and is struggling this year. He compares injuries with Silver, contorting his arm to simulate his pitching motion.

"Does it still hurt?" Silver asks.

"Every time I throw the ball," Gay answers. "But I'm just going to keep throwing until I can't throw anymore."

MINOR-LEAGUE BASEBALL has changed through the years — perhaps not always for the better. The facilities are better, the pay is better. But a good deal of the continuity, the local color, has been drained from the game.

Gone are the days when Homer Peel could spend 23 years bouncing around the minors, racking up a lifetime batting average of .323, without breathing a whiff of major-league air. These days, few players who haven't made the majors by the time they're 25 or 26 will survive in the system. Up until the early 1960s or so, major-league teams belonged to the big cities and the minors to everybody else. But when television became a force, minor-league teams became true "farm teams," with developing prospects for the major leagues their sole *raison d' être.*

Since the big clubs had no interest in older players past their prime — a 19-year-old shortstop who someday might hit major league pitching was a better investment than a 32-year-old outfielder who could do the same thing — the older players disappeared.

At 30, ex-major leaguer Andy Rincon is the oldest Traveler. Reliever Craig Weissmann is 28. Centerfielder Ray Lankford — considered by most observers to be the best prospect on the team — is 21. So is shortstop Julian Martinez. Everyone else on the team is in between. And time is running out for all of them.

MIKE PEREZ has his confidence back. He sits in front of his cubicle bent slightly forward at the waist, drenched with the weary dignity of a split-decision. His brown eyes are soft and calm, and his thick arms look like pythons stuffed with rocks.

Perez used to be a prospect. Two years ago, the Cardinals invited him and his 95-mile-per-hour fastball to spring training. He didn't stick with the big club, but he went out and saved a record 41 games in Class A ball.

Last year, he struggled after being called up to Arkansas and, until about a month ago, he had floundered this year. But after recording three victories, no losses and six saves in six opportunities in May, the 24-year-old Perez looks like he still has a future.

"I think I put too much pressure on myself at the beginning of the season," he says in measured, lightly accented tones. "I got hit and I was a little wild and I just started pressing ... it was the worst thing.

"Baseball is supposed to be fun. I've always had fun playing baseball. I just decided to go out and have fun again."

He nods in the direction of his manager.

"Gaylen knows that I can pitch. He never lost confidence in me. He was my manager when I saved 41 games."

CAUGHT NAKED in the locker room by *Shreveport Journal* sportswriter John James Marshall, a smiling Craig Wilson stands politely and answers questions about his game-winning three-run double. The double came off a high, outside fastball from Shreveport starter Mike Remlinger — "very much out of the strike zone."

Wilson couldn't believe he actually got another chance to face Mike Remlinger after smacking him around all night long. Of Shreveport Manager Bill Evans's decision to stick with his starter, Wilson tells Marshall: "I was surprised, because I thought he would bring in the reliever."

To say Wilson is having a good year may be a mild understatement: He is leading the team in runs batted in, an unlikely achievement for a singles hitter — just one home run so far this year — who hits second in the batting order.

"The guys at the bottom of the batting order have been doing a good job getting on base," Wilson says. "I've felt good at the plate and have been making good contact. Plus with Bernard [Gilkey] hitting in front of me, I know I'm going to see a lot of fastballs."

What Wilson leaves unsaid — what he assumes is understood — is that lead-off hitter Gilkey is perhaps the fastest man in the St. Louis Cardinals minor league system and always is a threat to steal a base. Opposing pitchers know this: when Gilkey reaches base they tend to throw fastballs rather than slower breaking pitches so the ball will get to the catcher an extra split-second faster, giving the catcher a slightly better chance to throw the runner out. Baseball is a game of such close tolerances that split seconds and millimeters mean a lot. And Wilson — like virtually every other hitter in Double-A baseball — hits fastballs rather well.

With the victory at Shreveport, the Arkansas Travelers closed to within three-and-a-half games of first-place Tulsa in the east division of the Texas League.

"I'm a real optimistic kind of guy when it comes to baseball," Roy Silver says. "I like to think I can make things happen — I think we're going to win the first-half championship. I think we're a better team than they are. Don't get me wrong, I think they've got a good team, I just think we're better."

Silver says winning is important for "average" players such as himself.

"If you're a prospect, it doesn't really matter. All you have to do is play pretty good and you'll move up," he says. "But guys like me, if you win a league championship, that's a big deal. We won one in A ball a couple of years ago and a lot of guys off that team moved up. Otherwise you might not get noticed."

Silver forks up some salad. He eats it after his dinner — as dessert. He smiles like a man who enjoys what he's doing.

"Even if I never make the major leagues, so what? I've met some great guys and I've had a lot of fun. I don't want to be sitting in a chair some day thinking about what could have happened if I'd stuck with it; I want to give it my best shot."

The 1989 Arkansas Travelers went on to capture the first half pennant — and the second half pennant as well. By the end of the 1990 season, Craig Wilson, Bernard Gilkey and Ray Lankford were St. Louis Cardinals.

(June 1989)

Issue 65, December 1987.

Elizabeth Shores

New Age Land Rapers

Jan James is a self-proclaimed "fossil nut." Her father first took her to dig for quartz crystals 20 years go, and she remembers the rather small hole near Paron, Arkansas, where she unearthed her first crystals. James recently revisited that spot and found that it had grown about one thousand-fold. It is now an unattractive pit the size of a Volkswagon micro-bus.

Similar pits are turning up throughout the Ouachita National Forest as out-of-state crystal aficionados deluge the forest in search of the country's newest gem stone. "There's more people camping and digging at these places than you can imagine," James added.

"It resembles Gold Rush days," said Montgomery County Sheriff James Carmack, who recently arrested an 18-year-old from nearby Mountain Pine for stealing crystals valued at $4,000 from a Mt. Ida mining operation.

Carmack is not alone in likening the current crystal craze to a gold rush. Once popular as flashy but low-cost souvenirs for tourists who visited the Ouachita Mountains, Arkansas crystals today have a growing nationwide reputation. The industry that flourished in a small, quiet way in Western Arkansas more than a century ago is now booming.

But along with prosperity, the boom has brought with it theft, vandalism and problems with illegal mining, as well as larger concerns of environmental damage. Overshadowing these issues is the question: what is sufficient compensation for the minerals these miners take from federal lands?

Like the crystals themselves, this situation is many-sided and elicits strange reactions from some people. Sheriff Carmack, for instance, seems more concerned than most environmentalists about the lasting damage to the forests from crystal mining. Jan James, on the other hand, digs for crystals almost weekly, yet unabashedly calls the mining "land rape" and mournfully confesses that even she has left one unfilled hole in her wake. Large-scale commercial miner Don Burrows, whose mine was burglarized by the Mountain Pine youth, declined to answer most questions over the telephone, fearing that a reporter might actually be a crystal pirate intent on stealing from him.

The facts behind this fad are as strange as the mineral itself. Hard-core believers say quartz crystals can heal physical ailments, clarify a person's thoughts, "amplify" energy at "sacred power spots" and — if enough individuals would hold the rocks daily — even create peace on earth. Faith in these and other purported powers of the mineral silica have led many people to buy them as jewelry and decorations, for personal use as healing tools and even as energy-saving devices. Put one in your refrigerator and your electric bill will go down, some say. The demand for "specimen crystal," the most attractive pieces, has pushed the sale value up astronomically within the last five years.

But this same faith is causing headaches for the geologists and forest rangers who are stewards of federal lands in Arkansas. None of these mining operations cause damage on the scale of clear-cutting. Still, illegal mines, some of them just a few feet in width and depth, present threats to hunters and hikers who might take a wrong step into one, in addition to potentially damaging the aesthetic quality and watershed of the forest. And thieves are creeping into legal mines at night and on weekends, putting pressure on law enforcement agencies such as Sheriff Carmack's department, which was recently cut from four deputies to two because of budget reductions.

"It's Forest Service land," Carmack complained. "The Bureau of Land

Management gets the money for it and expects me to enforce the laws with no additional resources."

The sheriff said he has encountered a "considerable amount of crystal theft from mines."

"People go in at night and dig around," he said. "They sometimes sabotage or steal equipment, too."

On Forest Service or timber company land, clandestine miners sometimes work under cover of darkness, bringing along an automobile battery to serve as the power source for floodlights. If a large amount of minerals are encountered, the battery may be left behind so as to lighten the load on the trip out. When a good vein is located, the diggers will often cover up their tracks when they leave so that none of the competition will get in on their vein.

"It's like a gold rush, and in that atmosphere a lot of people want to get in on it," Burrows said. "And a few people just want to grab some and run."

Arkansas environmentalists, already fighting hard to prevent timber clear-cuts in nearly half of the state's forests, are waking up to the possible environmental problems from mines that may eventually be "reclaimed" but can never be restored in the way that a new timber stand will eventually grow up.

"There's all this public interest against clear-cutting, but there's less damage and more economic return from that than from crystal mining," Carmack said. "I believe the Forest Service is going to be forced to control its clear-cutting, and the same should go for crystals."

Jim Stanley, a North Little Rock lawyer who represents the Arkansas Conservation Coalition, agrees with Carmack that there is potential for significant environmental impact from crystal mining. The Forest Service's reclamation requirements do not go far enough to repair the damage from large-scale mining, he said.

The coalition has appealed a plan for use of the Ouachita National Forest, largely because it objects to plans to clear-cut large areas. But Stanley said the group is also asking that mining not be permitted adjacent to wilderness areas, streams, trail corridors, recreation areas or habitat of endangered species, or scenic or research areas. The service has suspended the plan until it completes its review of it.

Michael Crawford of Hot Springs, another lawyer and environmentalist, points to reclamation of large mines as the greatest concern among environmental groups. But he also wonders whether the revenues from crystal mining merit the expense to the Forest Service.

"One of their big complaints is they don't have enough money to manage for recreation," he said, suggesting that it is ironic that the service does "manage" crystal-mining.

This conflict illustrates a heated issue, whether the original mandate of the Forest Service — to maintain land for "mixed use" by individuals and industry — still makes sense. The focus of the issue is usually timber "harvests." Should vast tracts of national forests be clear-cut by private lumber companies? Are the loggers really paying a fair price for these trees? And what about the loss to wildlife, hunters, backpackers and those who seek some kind of tranquility in the Ouachita National Forest, only to round a bend and see a hideous clear-cut area, rather like a moonscape or bombed battleground?

Under the Forest Service's mandate, the federal Mining Law of 1872, miners are also able to operate legally in the Ouachita National Forest. And the service does its best to accommodate those miners, according to John Nichols, a geologist in the Hot Springs office of the Forest Service.

"We have never denied a permit" to mine for quartz crystal, he said. After all environmental evaluations are made, he added, "usually, there's a way to get them in there."

About 64 separate legal mining operations are underway in the Ouachita

Issue 16, January 1986.

Forest right now, with more applications for permits under review, Nichols noted.

"There are more people mining for quartz than ever in history," Mike Howard, a geologist with the Arkansas Geological Commission, said recently. "People who used to cut pulpwood for a living are now mining crystal full-time."

After all, mining crystals is "a lot less risky than growing pot," observed a jeweler who buys crystals from several miners and characterizes them as "the type of people you run into at Grateful Dead concerts." This jeweler, new himself to the industry, has nonetheless seen it grow "from nothing to incredible volume in a few months," while prices for the most sought-after types of specimen crystal have increased "six-fold."

Quartz is found throughout the world, but the quality of specimen crystal found in Arkansas is particularly fine, according to Don Owens, a geologist with the Earth Science Department at the University of Arkansas at Little Rock. Because Brazil provides the only other known source for this quality of crystal, Arkansas crystal is renowned nationwide and advertised in the pages of alternative newspapers from New York to Los Angeles.

Although some crystal mining is done on private lands, much quartz crystal comes from the Ouachita National Forest and land held by the U.S. Army Corps of Engineers. All mining is illegal on Corps land, but on Forest Service lands, officials are struggling to regulate the legal mines and stop unauthorized mining.

Within the Forest Service, an agency beleaguered by environmentalists trying to stop its plan to permit clear-cutting within the National Forest, most officials refer noncommittally to the service's mandate to provide for "mixed use" of the forests it manages. Simply put, this doctrine permits timber companies and miners to do their thing alongside the campers and birdwatchers. But one staff officer for the Ouachita says bluntly that crystal miners don't pay enough for the crystals they remove.

"I don't think many of these people understand the significance of what's happening," Nichols said of small-scale miners.

The wildcat miners who dig in the Ouachita without official permits or reclamation plans sometimes leave pits that are five feet deep and six feet across. Rangers say the environmental damage from these small mines may not be great, but the potential danger to hikers and hunters who could step into the open holes is.

"It's getting to be more and more of a problem," according to Norman Alley, the Winona District ranger.

Nichols is also concerned. "You can do a lot of damage with a shovel, especially if you get excited and have a couple of friends," he said dryly.

Some illegal digs involve more than just a couple of would-be crystal profiteers. Howard and Brian Westfall, a geologist with the Corps, tell of groups of as many as 100 people that come from as far away as California, Oregon and Washington. They pitch camps and scratch for crystals, which they can sell for as much as $200 per pound.

"They were out there, bare-handed, ripping the heck out of the hillside," Howard said of one group that was discovered near the north shore of Lake Ouachita.

Glenda Cade, who sells crystal jewelry through Little Rock's Quapaw Gallery, said she and her business partner are frequently visited by out-of-towners they do not know who come to their workshop seeking directions to good crystal digs.

"There are people who will pay you $100 just to take them to a mine and dig," added James, who occasionally shares her crystal finds with Cade and partner Wendy Hannah.

"When I go to Dead shows — like in Wisconsin to sell my crystals, almost everybody I talk to has been to Arkansas to mine," Hannah said.

Corps geologist Westfall, who is responsible for maintenance of 82,000 acres of Corps land in the Ouachitas, expresses no affection for these miners. "They may believe in the healing," he said. "But they're also getting a lot of money for them."

Corps officials conducted a months-long "stake out" of one illegal mine before they apprehended five miners this summer.

Although those miners received only suspended sentences for violating the law against mining on Corps land, Westfall is hopeful that the court action has discouraged some crystal-diggers.

Miners who dig without permission on private or federal property are clearly trespassers subject to criminal prosecution in the unlikely event that they are caught. One wrinkle in the job of catching and convicting these thieves is that crystals, once removed from the ground, cannot usually be identified.

But even authorized mining poses its own array of problems. Thanks to the 1872 mining law, crystal miners who obtain permission from the Forest Service can mine indefinitely on "public domain" lands without paying anything for the rocks themselves. They do have to post reclamation bonds, which Burrows said can vary in size from $2,000 to tens of thousands of dollars, depending on the size of the mining operation. If a miner chooses instead to mine on "acquired" lands, those which the Forest Service acquired after its inception, he must pay the Forest Service a royalty of five percent of the gross selling price he receives in royalties and one dollar per acre in annual rent. The five-percent severance rate is typical for minerals in national forests. Lead, zinc and copper mined in Missouri, for example, also go for five percent of their gross sales price. The Department of Interior charges as much as $16\,^2/_3$ percent for off-shore oil and gas, however.

Herb Wincentsen, senior geologist with the Denver-based Minerals Management Service, an agency of the Department of Interior which collects royalties from miners, said that royalty rates are not specified in regulations but that the five-percent figure is the policy of the department.

Nichols said crystal mining is done in approximately equal portions on public domain and acquired lands. Miners may stake claims on as many contiguous plots of 600 by 1500 feet as they wish. Theoretically, vast tracts of the national forest can come under the control of private mining interests in this manner.

Logging companies, in contrast, must submit formal bids to cut trees in the forest. The highest bidder gets the timber, and then only if that bid reflects the true market value of the timber to be cut, according to Bill Walker, a timber, soil and water staff officer with the service.

Walker said he believes the law that permits free exploitation of crystal veins in the national forests should be updated. He would like to see miners required to make bids in the same way that loggers are now.

Asked if the service's income from mineral leases covers the costs of regulating mines, Nichols just chuckled. In fact, mining requires considerable oversight. Rangers must inspect areas in which miners ask to dig; consider the activity's impact on erosion, groundwater, visual aesthetics and safety; provide miners with specific instructions about mining and reclamation; and coordinate regulation as well as collection of royalties and rental fees with two other agencies of the Interior Department. In some districts of the Ouachita Forest, Nichols said, rangers and their assistants spend 50 to 75 percent of their time dealing with crystal miners.

Ultimately, the Forest Service requires miners to reclaim their mining areas, usually by refilling pits with the blown-apart rock and gravel and then planting grasses. But because miners can use pieces of land indefinitely, these mines can be left idle but unreclaimed for long periods. As an example, James and Hannah cite an abandoned World War II-era manganese mine near Mt. Ida

Issue 111, October 1989.

where they are fond of hunting for crystals. The mine was abandoned long ago and, although subsequently mined commercially for the crystal residue the first miners left behind, has not been actively mined since 1975. Yet no effort has been made to reclaim it in those 12 years.

Crystal mining is a delicate undertaking because fragile specimens can shatter unless they are handled carefully. Miners use low-impact explosives to uncover veins of crystal and then dig with hand tools like screwdrivers to expose and remove the crystal. A typical mine is a trench that is 15 feet wide, 15 feet deep and 100 feet long. Workers use backhoes and bulldozers as well as explosives to dig these pits. Some crystal mines are much bigger, however. Nichols said two in the Oden District of the Ouachita cover five acres.

AT ONE SITE in a clear-cut area of the Winona District, a miner has left a deep, steep-sided pit which is full of rainwater.

"I've got to get a fence here," said Jimmy Reynolds, an assistant ranger responsible for supervising miners in that district, when he showed a reporter and photographer the mine recently.

Reynolds' responsibility is massive. As an assistant ranger, he is in charge of mining, recreation, protection of the watershed and maintenance of lands and facilities in the 108,000 acre Winona District. A recent tour of just four crystal mines under his supervision took four hours of driving.

Reynolds does not complain about the mines.

"This land belongs to the people of the United States of America and my job is to manage it the way they want it managed, as passed on through Congress and the laws of this country," he said. If Congress wants to give away crystals worth hundreds of dollars per pound, so be it, he implied.

Nichols is also careful not to complain about the drain on the Forest Service from legal crystal mining. Asked if he thinks the five-percent royalty is sufficient compensation to the U.S. Government, he said, "Well, that's a question you'll have to ask your congressman."

The service requires miners to begin reclamation as mining continues on such big sites. Nonetheless, "it's not ever going to be possible to make it look like Mother Nature intended" at that five-acre mountainside mine, Nichols said. At best, the area will eventually be "benched" or terraced and will look like a mountain-pass road-cut.

"Once you open up this big hole, that's all you're left — and it's hard to stabilize it and cover it with topsoil," said Gaylen Burnside of Little Rock, who likes to dig for crystals when he gets the chance.

"You're supposed to return the land to its natural state," Jan James added. "Well, that's impossible."

(December 1987)

Barbara Middleton   DeAnn Shields-Marley

Issue 99, May 1989.

JoBeth Briton

Delivering Roe

What Motivates The New Pro-Choice Activists?

Bloody Mary used to be a big name in certain quarters in North Little Rock. That was before 1973, before *Roe v. Wade* and safe, legal abortions. Bloody Mary kept secrets for middle class and poor girls who could not afford to be pregnant and could not afford the professional, albeit illegal, physicians used by their wealthier sisters.

"She did it on her kitchen table," recalled Kaye Clark. "Everybody knew Bloody Mary. I think she was a nurse, or she said she was. If you needed an abortion, that's who you went to see."

A counselor at a Little Rock abortion clinic, Clark was twisted in her bus seat, talking with other women at the start of a chartered trip from Arkansas to Washington, D.C., where more than 300,000 people swarmed like angry bees on the capital to join the April 9, 1989, march for equal rights and the preservation of legal abortion. Touted as the largest social issue march in American history — bigger even than the 1963 march for civil rights — the demonstration was sponsored by the National Organization for Women to show popular support for an issue that the Supreme Court could soon throw back to states' choice.

The high court began hearing arguments April 26 in the case of *Missouri v. Webster*, in which pro-life forces argue that life begins at conception. In Arkansas, last year's passage of a similar law, Amendment 65, signaled a victory for this state's pro-life movement. So it was ironic that the pro-choice men and women who packed their suitcases and hopes into two chartered buses on April 8 and pulled out of Little Rock at 8:15 a.m. numbered 65.

The group included five men, a baby and a toddler, a spoiled pet poodle and three working journalists. A diverse cross-section of people — single parents, married couples, lesbian couples, retired women, law students and lawyers, photographers, house cleaners, carpenters, abortion-clinic counselors — they drove out of Little Rock on Interstate 40, heading into the sun, riding at eye level with the straight-backed drivers of tractor-trailer rigs that pulled alongside and stared at the bus windows plastered with yellow "on-board" signs reading: PRO-CHOICE. PRO-CHILD.

Maybe it was the way the road stretched out for miles ahead — 22 hours' worth of road — and maybe it was the shared sense of mission, but it did not take long for people who were strangers at the start of the trip to become buddies and confidants. People stood swaying in the aisle. They hung over the armrests of their chairs. They stood upright or draped themselves over the backs of neighbors' seats. Intermingled with the sound of incessant talk were occasional songs from the back of the bus — "Amazing Grace" and spur-of-the-moment compositions — and laughter. Before the bus reached Little Rock again, there would be tears, too, because for almost everyone participating — many becoming activist for the first time in their lives — this was a very personal public statement, formed often by intimate feelings and private experiences.

Carolyn Izard, 46, a small, round-shouldered woman with curly, ash-brown short hair, sat with her 30-year-old daughter, Terri Bridges, a Little Rock school teacher with the face and body of a high-school cheerleader. They sat across the bus aisle from Izard's twin sister, Shirley Perry, of Searcy. Her 21-year-old daughter, Jana Perry, of Little Rock, wore her blonde hair down her back like a Botticelli portrait.

"We have discussed abortion a lot, being around Carolyn," Shirley Perry said. "She talks about it a lot. I personally believe it's only right to make my own decisions about anything."

On Sunday in Washington, the twin sisters and their daughters stood with the Arkansas delegation in a throng of bodies that assembled at the Washington Monument to begin the historic march. Pro-choice demonstrators — many of them dressed in white, gold and purple, the traditional colors of the suffragettes — stood for three hours at the base of the monument in a stiff, cold wind before they could move ranks onto Constitution Avenue to start the march toward the Capitol.

Feminist singer Holly Near boomed out over the public address system singing a refrain over and over: "You can't just take my dreams away." All around people's faces swirled by in constant changing patterns as groups and individuals searched to link up with other known groups or persons. Picture high-decibel talking, yelling, chanting. People bearing signs and banners reading: CATHOLICS FOR CHOICE; MORMONS FOR CHOICE; JEWS FOR CHOICE; ANOTHER PHYSICIAN FOR CHOICE; MY BODY, MY CHOICE; KEEP YOUR LAWS OFF MY BODY; WHO MAKES THE DECISION? And, everywhere, the symbolic coat hanger, an icon of the pro-choice movement's refusal to return to back-alley abortions and self-induced tragedies. On placards, buttons and caps, the coat hanger rode along with the slogan, "NEVER AGAIN."

Issue 130, August, 1990.

Izard took it all in. "One of the main reasons I came was because [Amendment 65] passed in Arkansas and because my husband voted for it. It also told me that I had to get active in a women's oganization because I couldn't depend on other women to take care of the problem themselves. And I had never been active and I thought, well, I've got to get out and do my part.

"It also told me, when my husband voted for Amendment 65, that people were ignorant of what they actually were voting for. I mean, you know, here's my husband, who's college-educated, and the first thing I said was 'You are not a stupid man. You are college-educated and you can read and you got up there and voted the very way that you were not supposed to vote.' Well, let me tell you, I have a choice, too, and I am not going to live with a man who does not have my best interest in mind." Izard's daughter, when she heard this, giggled. But Izard continued in a stern, angry voice.

"Since then, he has learned a lesson because I will not live with a man and I certainly will never have sex with a man who doesn't have my best interest at heart." After she became active, Izard started going to NOW meetings, attended a women's rights conference in Louisiana and began to read extensively on the issues that have galvanized her to activism.

"If a woman is not mad, she is not informed," Izard said. In the context in which it was made, that seemed an especially appropriate comment. Many of the lengthy conversations held on this trip among the members of the Arkansas delegation were not just laced with anger, they were volcanic, vituprous, mad. Rape. Job discrimination. Women describing abortion butchery. Women telling of the scars they bore because they had not had abortions — bitterness and resentment towards parents who never allowed the abortion, towards society for not caring when they bore their babies alone and in poverty and were forced to forego dreams and aspirations, to drastically change their lives in order to support their children. Women who gave birth to children whom they were conned into putting up for adoption.

"This is so great, to be able to talk like this," said one successful, 27-year-old career woman who did not want her name published. She and her seat-mate on the bus, a 50-ish woman with a quiet, regal demeanor, discovered not long into the trip that they had both participated in the anti-nuclear march in Washington in 1979.

"I was 14 when I got pregnant," the younger woman related to a close circle of women. That was in 1976 and she lived with her parents on a military base in Hawaii. "I was the only girl in school to get pregnant. No one knew what to do, how to handle it. The kids would throw paper wads at my back." Her father never acknowledged her pregnancy until after the baby was born, but he moved the family to the East Coast during the final trimester of her pregnancy. She was constantly besieged by adoption counselors.

"This one woman acted so nice. She acted, you know, like she was really interested in me and said I seemed really intelligent so she was going to have me take all of these IQ tests, just to help me out. Well, you know what she was doing! She was testing me to see if I was going to have a smart baby, somebody to go to the lawyer and say, 'We could get a lot of money for this one.' No one seemed to care about me."

At 15, she had the baby. Her parents secured a lawyer to draw up adoption

The 'Illogic' of Jim Nichols

Spectrum *often runs editorials
that don't enjoy the full support of
the editorial staff. Usually the
dissenters just shut up about it and
mope around the office, but
sometimes they feel impelled to
respond to the offending item. In
June 1989, after* Spectrum *had
editorially affirmed a woman's right
of sovereignty over her own body,
associate editor Jim Nichols used
his column space to argue that the
arguments espoused by pro-choicers
were "illogical" and could not
withstand scrutiny.*

*"While I'm no logician, I was
trained in college to evaluate
arguments within a logical
framework," Nichols wrote. "And
when you get right down to it, the
arguments in favor of legalized
abortion are little more than
arguments of convenience, not
logic."*

*The column drew heavy fire.
Olivia Farrell of the* Arkansas
Times *responded with a lengthy
letter that took Nichols to task for
emotionalizing the issue ("His
remark that he won't dwell on the
issue of little hands and feet allows
him to neatly inject just that issue
while claiming to eschew it.") and
for sloppy logic ("If Nichols wants
to believe in sanctity upon
conception, that is his right. But to
claim that such a belief is the result
of irrefutable logic ... is the worst
sort of sophistry. He offers no
proofs; he simply offers statements
of emotional belief, then hides
behind a cloak of dispassion.")*

papers under which her child became their child. "I never had legal representation myself. They never told me a thing. I gave up all rights to my son."

Today, with the emotionally distant relationship between herself and her parents, she is lucky to get to see her son occasionally, but he doesn't know she is his mother. Today, she channels her anger and pain into counseling the children of friends who find themselves in similar circumstances. But not all of the anger is used up. She would be the first one to admit it. "I didn't finish high school. I left home when I was 15," she said. "I lived on the streets in New York, and I told a lot of lies to survive."

Some women in the Arkansas delegation were moved by the urgency of preserving abortion rights to become active for the first time. It was Barbara Ann Middleton's first major demonstration. She also became pro-choice after making early choices in her own life between having a child or abortion.

On Monday afternoon, after lobbying Arkansas's congressional offices in Washington earlier in the day, Middleton split off with a few others from the rest of the travelers and made her way to Union Station to eat and shop for souvenirs for her family. Dressed in white pants and a brown tweed jacket, she looked very tired but still animated as she sat in a hard-backed chair at a Chinese short-order bar in Union Station and told her story.

"I married at 17. I had a baby at 18. And I divorced at 19," Middleton said in a voice that implied that she had gone over these facts many times. "And [I] found myself in a situation where I had to do something quick to survive, so I learned to do secretarial/clerical work because for me that was the easiest quickest way for me to earn a buck to support my son." She had moved from Louisiana to Tulsa, Oklahoma, after the divorce, "looking for greener pastures — don't ask me why Tulsa."

"So, I find myself 500 miles away from momma and daddy and, uh, with Tony — who was very young at the time — trying to carve out some kind of existence for us. And I find myself pregnant. I was using birth control. But I found myself pregnant. That was in '74, yeah, 1974, the year after *Roe v. Wade.*

"I was shipping my son back and forth between Tulsa and Monroe, Louisiana, at times when I could not bring enough food into the apartment to feed both of us. I said, 'Well, I'm going to send him home. I'm not going to go running back to Louisiana because if I do, I'm never going to escape again. So, I decided to have the pregnancy aborted at six weeks, very, very quickly. But it was a heartbreaking decision for me to make because I am very maternal — I have three beautiful, wanted children. But at the time, it seemed the only thing I could do. It seemed very unfair to that life that I already had in this world to take care of him. And I had to be separated from him for long periods of time.

"I remember the worst that it got, two days that I went without food so that I could feed him. So I could not see where it would be anywhere near feasible that I could bring another life into this world to take care of. And I might add that the father of the — I don't know what word to use there — flew the coop. Said bye-bye. So I knew I was going to be left with no support from him."

A couple of women who had moved into the apartment next to her in Tulsa, coincidentally, worked at an abortion clinic. "That's where I went. And my employers — who were very conservative — were very supportive of me. I don't know why, but I felt I could go to her, the female half of the husband-and-wife business, I felt I could go to her. You've got to understand I was straight from the woods. I was from Calhoun, Louisiana, and no family, so I went to her. She checked out the abortion physician and made sure that he was alright and took me to the abortion counselor." Middleton's father paid for the abortion.

"I felt that he would understand about it and he did," Middleton said. "My mother didn't know about it until a long time later."

During the Washington march, Middleton discovered that she made a great spokeswoman after several national broadcast reporters gravitated to her in crowds and asked her for comments.

"I don't know why they always come to me," she laughed. Maybe because she had that anger-in-the-eye, I-could-really-say-something look. On camera, she always gave articulate, logical answers. Back on the bus, Middleton invited everyone to come to her house two weeks later for a reunion picnic and promised to join others in a counter-protest April 15 at an abortion clinic in Little Rock where pro-life demonstrators had threatened to picket.

The Washington trip seemed to give most participants a taste of social activism that they were ready to continue. One woman, Joan Morris (who carried her pet poodle with her in a plastic mesh bag on the march) vowed to return to Arkansas and organize grass-roots letter-writing campaigns. Those plans were echoed by most people riding back to Little Rock.

Another woman who was moved to activism by her early experiences, Frances Grace Block, 57, was the designated "Bus Mom" of one Arkansas bus. Block looked no-nonsense in her pastel sweatsuit with a whistle hanging around her neck. She works as a receptionist for Planned Parenthood, but about 30 years ago, she had two illegal abortions.

She was living at home still with her family, a socially prominent Little Rock clan. Her father arranged the abortion with an out-of-town physician, using a fake name. Block had no anesthesia during the procedure.

"I remember I held that nurse's hand real tight," she recalled. "We never mentioned it again."

That abortion was clean and quiet. The second time, her boyfriend set things up with an abortionist in Hot Springs. A taxi picked her up at a particular street corner in Little Rock, drove her to an unknown address, unloaded her and left. The abortionist "stuck something up inside me and told me to go home. Two days later I had the abortion on a toilet in my parents' bathroom. I had to pull it out. I started hemorrhaging on the bathroom floor. My parents called our family doctor — that's back when they still made house calls. He just put me in bed and I guess they thought it was just a heavy period. He told me to keep my legs elevated for two days."

When she later married, she found she was unable to bear children. She skirted around the question of whether the abortions caused her infertility. "I guess it's a good thing because I know I'm not the maternal type. I'm just not. You might as well face it," Block said. "The fact that I went to a back-alley abortionist the second time I guess demonstrates how scared I was and the fact that I was willing to die rather than let my parents know I was pregnant again."

While she sat in her seat at the front of the bus, staring ahead into the oncoming traffic, a young woman picked up the microphone on the public address system. She was a counselor at a Little Rock abortion clinic. When her voice came over the system, it was choked with emotion.

"Little 12-year-old girls come in our clinic. Women come in there and they don't want to get an abortion. Nobody wants an abortion. But they can't have a baby. They make that decision. I marched Sunday for each and every one of those girls."

The bus erupted in applause. And the talk continued. Trees whizzed past in the windows. People began to think of home and the little wars they would wage there.

(May 1989)

Jim Nichols

The Rescuers

Sometime this summer, Dr. Doty Murphy will begin to serve his jail sentence.

Murphy, a 47-year-old obstretrician and gynecologist in Springdale, Arkansas, seems unlikely to boast and he certainly doesn't brag about a criminal record. Nonetheless, there is a certain pride in his voice as he talks about his conviction in March on a misdemeanor criminal trespassing charge stemming from a protest at a Fayetteville abortion clinic.

"These little unborn babies are very valuable and they're human," Murphy said in his office, which he calls Immanuel Clinic. "It needs to be addressed by the American people, and since there's no one to defend them, we need to stand up."

Murphy and seven other pro-life activists stood up on the steps of Dr. Bill Harrison's clinic at 9 a.m. last October 14 and chained themselves to the clinic doors. They wanted to block young women intent on having abortions, if only for a moment, until the police inevitably arrived. In that moment, they hoped, maybe one woman might reconsider, and a fetus might be saved. Harrison called the police, and all eight were arrested on misdemeanor charges of trespassing and failure to submit to arrest.

No one misses the irony anymore: the pro-life movement, populated heavily by political and philosophical conservatives, has adopted the ways and means of the left in its protests. Protest marches, picket signs and "passive resistance" sit-ins lifted from labor organizations, the civil rights movement and leftist environmental activists have been incorporated into the language of the right.

For that reason, however, the movement is sometimes portrayed in the media as a bunch of women-hating radicals — or so its members argue, at least. Consider, for example, this charge, brought by author Meredith Tax in the May 8 issue of *The Nation*: "The right-to-lifers are more up-front; even while they use the language of social needs, their hatred and fear of women is plain on their faces ... [T]he motor power of this campaign is not love or compassion but rage — the rage of the repressed, who think sex is sin and must be punished."

"People try to categorize and criticize these people as evil," James Howe, editor of the *Pro-Life Action News*, a Springdale-based monthly bulletin, said of his fellow pro-lifers. "I was one of 'em — I actually used to heckle the picketers. But now I'm one of the people out there picketing."

Philosophy-major Howe adopted a pro-life stance when he came to the conclusion that pro-choice arguments were logically untenable — before deciding on religious grounds that abortion is morally wrong. Others — including "liberals," he said — share his conclusion. The pro-life movement, Howe argued, is not just right-wing ministers and Catholic conservatives any more.

"We have all kinds of people. We have men and women, students, lawyers, doctors — we have everybody, all kinds. It's a true grass-roots movement."

AT THE HEAD of the most highly activist wing of the Fayetteville-Springdale pro-life forces is Dow Pursley, a psychologist described as "fanatical" by his critics and "very motivated to make a difference" by his allies. Pursley is president of the Pro-Life Action League, a loosely knit and conservative collection of Christian anti-abortionists. By his own count, Pursley has been arrested "17 or 18" times outside Harrison's clinic, and has gained a reputation as something of a rabble-rouser.

Asked how he felt about the label of fanatic, Pursley chuckled: "I'm certain people think all sorts of things."

A big man with the shoulders and chest of a football lineman, Pursley laughs easily. That might come as a surprise to a lot of people, intimidated by the sight of his frame and fiery-eyed determination on a picket line or chained to a clinic door. Pursley finds some amusement in his image as a crusading John the Baptist, but says it's not entirely true. "People have the perception that my whole life revolves around fighting abortion — it doesn't," he says with calm humor. "I coach soccer, I teach my kid to throw a baseball ... I hang-glide, I skydive a little.

"I've got three goals in life: be a good father, be a good husband and someday be a good grandfather."

Pursley says he has "a tremendous amount of friends" who favor the pro-choice position. Some tease him about his zealotry. He does, however, take his mission as an activist seriously — as seriously as he takes his fundamentalist Christian beliefs. The San Diego native-turned-Springdale-resident said he had been largely apathetic about the abortion issue for years; although he'd long held pro-life convictions, he hadn't acted on them. It took a string of women seeking counseling at his clinic for emotional fallout, which he attributed to earlier abortions, to prompt him to act.

Their problem, he said, was post-abortion syndrome, a psychological disorder often likened to the post-traumatic stress disorder experienced by some Vietnam veterans. "I saw so many of them — it just kept coming up — that I started keeping stats," Pursley said.

"In one nine-month period, which I thought was an appropriate time frame, I saw 17 women having significant problems with post-abortion syndrome — women who couldn't run a blender, women who couldn't run a vacuum cleaner, women who had slit their wrists."

Finally, he said, a 17-year-old girl he knew committed suicide on the one-year anniversary of her abortion. Pursley decided to present his concerns to Harrison, the sole physician at the area's only clinic performing abortions. Harrison, Pursley said, was less than receptive. Pursley recalled Harrison saying that with the number of abortions he performed he expected some percentage of the women to suffer post-abortion syndrome.

"I thought if I'd take this information to the guy, he'd relent, that he'd see," Pursley said. "But he just acted like, 'Big deal'."

It was then that the psychologist became the activist. Pursley said he started out a few years ago trying to give "sidewalk counseling" to women entering Harrison's clinic. He claims the traffic noise on College Street forces him onto Harrison's property, where women can hear him. Walking on that property has earned him arrest after arrest.

Further, Pursley has graduated from mere picketing and "sidewalk counseling" to become active in "Operation Rescue," a form of passive resistance in which participants actually block the entrance to an abortion clinic — sometimes, as Pursley has done, by chaining themselves to the doors. He was with Dr. Doty Murphy when the two were convicted earlier this year and is now awaiting a June trial on another trespassing count and a charge of failure to submit to arrest.

Carl Staff was there, too. Months later, Staff sat at a desk in the Christian bookstore and library in downtown Springdale, downstairs from Pursley's office, stuffing audiotapes of Bible messages in envelopes to mail to believers. Bespectacled and wearing a thin moustache, the 28-year-old spoke gently but sincerely about getting arrested last fall.

"I don't know if scared was the word — I wasn't personally scared," he

The Terror of Jihad

A Little Rock fundamentalist social-action group, the Family Council, declared holy war on Spectrum _in the spring of 1990. In a letter sent to all of the paper's advertisers, dated June 1, the organization declared that_ "Spectrum _not only runs conventional advertising, such as yours, but also ads that solicit homosexuality, adultery and other forms of misconduct and perversion."_

The letter demanded that advertisers "encourage those responsible for Spectrum_'s content to conform the paper to community standards. A respectable_ Spectrum _can have a place among Arkansas periodicals. We urge you as emphatically as we can to do your part in 'cleaning up'_ Spectrum." _In closing, the Council issued a thinly veiled threat in its reminder that "collectively we are those who patronize the merchants and businesses of Central Arkansas."_

It was the beginning of a campaign that soon spread among local zealots and included such highlights as the verbal harassment of business owners and the theft of entire stacks of the paper from newsracks. (These good deeds were never linked with the Family Council.) As Samuel Richardson's Pamela _taught, though, "Virtue" is always rewarded, and_ Arkansas Business _columnist Carrie Rengers subsequently recognized the Family Council as having made the "most frightening" local media move of 1990._

Where Will It End?

Spectrum's classified advertising was not the only target of the morality watchdogs at the Family Council. In the August 1990 issue of The Arkansas Citizen, *the organization's newsletter, a story headlined "Homosexuals Plan Programs for Arkansas Schools" suggested that "pro-homosexual forces" were at work in the public schools.*

Family Council director Jerry Cox warned in the article that these forces "are planning to go into every school district in Arkansas and place a staff person there to help homosexual students feel good about being gay while encouraging other students to become homosexuals."

Larry Page, a Little Rock attorney and secretary/treasurer of the Council, was quoted as saying, "If we accept homosexuality now, what will we be accepting in the future? Will we someday be asked to approve of incest, or child molestation, or activity with animals? Where will it end?"

It didn't end there. The intemperate actions of the Family Council led one loose affiliation of free-thinkers to run the above ad.

said, pausing. "It's hard to describe the feeling. I guess I was just doing what I thought was right, and I was willing to accept the consequences."

For Staff, like most activists, his involvement was one of degrees. Reared a Baptist, he had always been taught that abortion was wrong, he said. But it wasn't until about four years ago, when a friend took him to a pro-life meeting, that he decided to take a stand. First it was occasional picketing. Then, last summer, he became active in Operation Rescue when a woman he knew called, emotionally distraught, to tell him her daughter was going to Harrison's clinic for an abortion.

"I decided to block that door and try to save that baby's life," he said. "Really, that's the whole goal — not to make a statement or to buck the system. It's to save lives."

HATE THE SIN, not the sinner. Such is the philosophy proffered by the leaders of the activist movement, each of whom denies any animosity toward Bill Harrison whose clinic is at the center of the maelstrom — he's the only physician in the area who performs abortions outside a hospital setting.

"I don't hate the man," said Staff. "I don't spite him or wish him evil. I just wish he'd change his ways and stop."

Pursley echoes the refrain. "Far from hating Bill Harrison, I feel sorry for him," he said. "He may see me as the enemy, but I'm not — I'm his best friend. I'm trying to help him ... I pray for him every night."

Harrison isn't buying it. And, he said, neither is he going to bow to the pressure.

"It makes me tremendously angry," he said of being targeted. "I'm really surprised no one's been punched out out there."

Virtually every Friday since 1984, when Harrison's colleagues stopped performing abortions, the picketers have been outside his clinic doors. Sometimes there's one or two; sometimes dozens, carrying signs lumping Harrison together with Hitler, Himmler and Herod. Three times his clinic has been the target of minor vandalism — once by a small and ineffective firebomb thrown by a teenager who reportedly was later treated for an emotional disturbance.

Still, he says, he won't be deterred from, as he puts it, "providing a service I feel the public wants" because of the protests.

"This is a form of flashing. It's like a flasher jumping out from behind a tree and showing his little dinky. And when they actually come into my clinic or chain themselves to the door and harass women, it's a form of psychological rape."

City Prosecutor Terry Jones said there were four rounds of arrests from May to December 1988, on charges ranging from trespassing to fire code violations when protesters chained themselves to the door. Jones worked out plea bargains with four of the defendants who were to go to trial last month, and a University of Arkansas law student, Melissa Rust, successfully prosecuted Pursley, Murphy, Alan Wagner and Jane Lawrence for trespassing. Each is to serve 14 days in jail and pay a $100 fine.

Jones personally opposes abortion, which he says puts him in an awkward position. "I'm probably personally in favor of their position," he said. "It makes it difficult because I actually like the people I'm prosecuting ... The people who are the heads of the anti-abortion movement up here seem to be very, very level-headed."

Nonetheless, "It's kind of an irritant to the police department, with limited manpower and resources available. They have to take all that time and expense to process and prosecute cases every time there's an arrest," Jones said. He then added a note of concern: "I haven't seen anybody draw swords going after one another, but that's always a potential problem."

The pro-lifers discount that possibility. Every one professes only nonviolence — saying they draw the line where violence is involved. Still, their belief is that God's law, that man shalt not kill, supersedes man's laws against trespassing. Thus, short of violence or inflicting suffering on people, it is their responsibility to act.

"We live in a unique society — a free society," said the Rev. Paul Sagan, pastor of Fayetteville's Covenant Presbyterian Church. "Therefore it's incumbent on us to take advantage of that freedom by protesting injustice.

"I rank [abortion] as the number-one issue. In fact, I rank it above the issues that brought about the American Revolution — they're small in comparison. I'd rank it right next to slavery — but I'd put it slightly above slavery. They're very similar, because in the Dred Scott case the court declared that blacks were not fully men in the eyes of the law."

Jeannie Champagne, a mother of five and an active participant in Rescue protests until her arrest early this year, likens the movement to the civil rights movement, and to the underground network that saved Jews from the Nazis in World War II. "I hope that I would've done that," she says.

She and Pursley spearheaded one of the most controversial actions in the high-profile conflict over abortion in Northwest Arkansas: _Operation Blitz_, a mass mailing on April 10 through which 17,500 Fayetteville residents received brochures graphically depicting aborted fetuses in various stages of development. That action spurred a wave of letters to the editor at the _Northwest Arkansas Times_ that still continues a month later, along with charges of below-the-belt tactics aimed at its initiators.

To Champagne, it was simply an effort to counter a steady stream of misinformation — information that holds that a fetus is only a part of a woman's body, a simple glob of tissue that is dispensable. She said so many women told her that they'd wished they'd seen the graphic photos before they'd had an abortion that she got the idea for the mass mailing.

Pursley is pleased by the results. Several women, he said, called to thank him for saving their babies when they decided, looking at the pictures, that fetuses are people. "Blitz is probably the most effective single thing in the fight against abortion in Northwest Arkansas," he said.

For him, the fight will be a long one. He has no fear of being arrested for what he believes, and says even if he had to spend his life in prison to save an unborn baby, the trade-off would be worthwhile.

"I'm not going to break laws of the state or nation capriciously simply because I have some theological point to make," Pursley said. "We're people who believe abortion is killing a child, and that's a big issue. I have to compare it to the Holocaust — there's nothing else to compare it to.

"It's the issue of our age: are we going to kill off our posterity, or are we going to live? The Supreme Court's going to decide that. I'm fearful for our future if they don't come to some rational decision on this."

(May 1989)

SMUT PATROL

Not only did the fundamentalist Family Council object to Spectrum's _classifieds, so did a group calling itself the National Socialist American Workers Party. In the August 1990 issue of their broadsheet, the_ People's Observer, _the neo-Nazis allowed that they weren't troubled by_ Spectrum's _"discredited dogmatic liberal content" or "anti-Christian, pro-secular Humanistic Worldview," but they wanted to make certain that their readers got the point that "SEX ADS are more appropriate for the SEX ARCADES or ADULT BOOKSTORES."_

We had always wondered where they bought those KINKY LEATHER JACKBOOTS.

Philip Martin

Crime and Punishment

On the Wednesday afternoon they sent Terry Taylor to prison for the rest of his life, a rally was underway in downtown Little Rock.

About 150 people gathered in the shadow of the Henry Moore sculpture on Metrocentre Mall last October 26 to celebrate "Wear Red Day," the midpoint of National Drug-Free America Week. Banners fluttered and placards danced in the hands of school kids while two "recovered drug addicts" played "God Bless the USA" as the sun poured down. Small red ribbons bearing "Just Say No" messages were on sale for 50 cents.

Red ribbons were everywhere that week, as people publicly demonstrated their opposition to drugs, drug users and especially drug dealers. Even among the pool of Taylor's potential jurors, a couple of strips of scarlet flashed.

Soon after that jury was selected, 22-year-old Terris Lynn Taylor was on his way to the state pen. After a brief trial and just 14 minutes of deliberation, a Pulaski County Circuit Court jury made up of six men and six women found him guilty of conspiracy to deliver cocaine. It took the jury just 27 minutes more to decide that the sullen, stunted young black man before them, a "habitual offender" with three previous nonviolent felony convictions, should be given the stiffest penalty possible.

Taylor was sentenced to life imprisonment for selling officers one-eighth ounce of cocaine, an "eight ball'' in street parlance. That is not an inconsiderable amount — worth about $350 on the street — but it wasn't the kind of deal to make a drug "kingpin" take notice either. And, as the evidence showed, the investigators actually received only about half that much cocaine. Taylor's criminal record spans five years, but all the crimes he has been convicted of haven't involved more than $1,000 in total contraband. He's never been accused of doing violence to another person. He's certainly never been accused of being a criminal mastermind, or even a high-profile hood. The cops in Jacksonville, Arkansas, weren't familiar with him before they arrested him — he wasn't among their usual suspects. Terry Taylor was small time.

Thus, there was no reason to believe *State of Arkansas v. Terris Lynn Taylor* would be anything but a routine case.

Taylor's attorney, James E. Smedley, settled upon a jury he was happy with — one he thought represented "a cross-section of the community" and wasn't "rigid in their attitude about drugs." He weeded out the ribbon-wearing jurors before the trial. "I got rid of that bullshit right away," he recalled.

But it didn't help. Smedley chose not to put Taylor, a three-time loser, on the stand in his own defense. That would have permitted prosecutors to introduce information on his past convictions which Smedley had worked to exclude. What remained wasn't much of a trial. Smedley characterized it as a "swearin' match" between two police officers and Taylor's 17-year-old girl-friend, Michelle Akins.

Akins testified that Taylor couldn't have sold the coke to a Highway Patrol investigator and auxiliary Jacksonville police officer at the time they said they purchased it. Akins said she and Taylor were on the phone for five hours discussing the possibility of her having their baby aborted.

"What it came down to is that Michelle just wasn't a good witness," Smedley said. "She just wasn't believable, and I didn't know she was going to start in about an abortion — I thought, 'My God, anything but that.' And she's white and he's black ... it just wasn't a good situation."

Still, Smedley said, he tried to make the best of it. Through procedural motions, he was able to keep the jury from hearing the bulk of the circumstantial evidence against Taylor. The jury never learned the police had a phone number that they said Taylor had given them if they ever wanted more coke. They never found out the police had the license number of Taylor's brother's car, the same brother Taylor shared a house with in the Sioux Trail area of Jacksonville.

All the state really had was the sworn testimony from a handful of police officers and a few grams of white powder. But all Smedley had to work with was an alibi supplied by his client's high-school-aged girlfriend who said Taylor was chatting on the phone with her for five hours about her abortion.

Smedley knew his case was a loser. But he thought the jury might be sympathetic toward his client, that maybe they would recognize Terry Taylor for the pathetic, petty hoodlum he was. If convicted, there was no question Taylor would do time. He was running out of second chances.

Nothing, however, prepared Smedley for that sentence — a sentence Circuit Judge John Langston later called a message to drug dealers.

"I was shocked, the prosecutor was shocked and the judge was shocked," Smedley said. "We couldn't believe what had happened, but there's no way a judge is going to ignore a jury's verdict. That's just not done, not when that judge is going to have to run for re-election."

It was stupid to be in that courtroom in the first place — the same brand of stupidity that led Taylor to give out his home phone number when dealing cocaine. Taylor, Smedley thinks, should have jumped at the deal the prosecutor offered him — 20 years in prison in exchange for his guilty plea. With credit for good behavior, he could have been paroled in less than seven years. But Taylor left him with no choice.

"I tried to get him to take the plea bargain," the lawyer said. "But he wouldn't do it; he thought it was too much time. He wanted his day in court. Well, he got it. He sure got it."

JACKSONVILLE POLICE weren't really looking for a cocaine dealer when they started their investigation, but two guys in the Jackson Square apartments were dealing a lot of nickel and dime bags of marijuana to school kids. That was an intolerable situation.

So Mike Davis, at that time a member of the Jacksonville Fire Department as well an auxiliary police officer, and Investigator Ronda Byrd went under-cover. On February 17, 1988, at about 12:45 p.m., a 34-year-old Vietnam veteran named Olliver Arthur Clark fished his hand inside a purple Crown Royal bag and pulled out two clear plastic bags partly filled with what lawmen sometimes call a "green leafy substance." Davis handed Clark a $20 bill, took the Baggies and stuffed them in his sweatshirt pocket.

In his report, Davis wrote that Clark said he "sure appreciated" the officer's business and that he could come back anytime.

Davis and Byrd came back several times during the next few weeks, and on the afternoon of March 7, they asked Clark and his partner, Mitch Neely, if they had any cocaine. Clark said they didn't, but could get some from a man named

"J.T."

Clark dialed J.T.'s number, explained the situation, and soon an older-model white car cruised into the apartments' parking lot. The officers made a note of the license plate. Davis and Byrd, Clark and J.T. drove to a house near the Wagon Wheel Restaurant, and J.T. went inside and came back to the car with the purported three-and-a-half grams of cocaine.

They drove back to Jackson Square, but before J.T. left, he gave the officers a slip of paper with a phone number written on it.

On April 19, Clark and Neely were busted. Sgt. Robert Baker and Sgt. William Shelley led the raid on unit number 401 of the Jackson Square Apartments. They found a few bags of dope, a couple of scales, a bone pipe, with what appeared to be marijuana resin in it, and a few roaches scattered in the ashtrays.

Neely made a statement to police. He admitted selling marijuana and said that "90 percent" of his customers were junior-high and high-school students. Ollie Clark made a phone call for the police. The call, officers insist, was to J.T. to set up another cocaine deal.

Terry Taylor says Ollie Clark — a man he had met only once before — called him to ask for a ride home from McDonald's.

ANYONE WHO THINKS prison is a state of mind has never been inside the whitewashed cinder-block walls of the Cummins Unit. This is a warehouse for the poor and the mean. Though the ceilings are gymnasium-high in the open cafeteria where visitors wait to meet with prisoners, there is a stale dimness that hangs in the air like a stain. Everything here is institutional green. A crude sign on the caged-up, closed-down snack bar warns that only "free-world" persons are eligible to purchase Snickers bars.

While you sit there, waiting for your inmate to appear, something wild, blind and pale rolls over in the black waters of your gut. The instinct is to bolt.

But then Terry Taylor is led in, walking proud, pulled up to his full height of about five-foot-eight. He is compact and delicate all at once, like one of those natty lightweight fighters who can't punch worth a damn but are harder to hit than a Roger Clemens fastball.

His banty chest strains against his prison shirt, the top buttons open to reveal a small triangle of tight chocolate chest. His face is hard and angular — you could cut your knuckles on that face. When Taylor levels his eyes at you — bracketing you in his sights — there is something weirdly dignified and somber about his demeanor.

Like all the other inmates, Taylor is dressed in white. White stands out well against the morbid khaki earth that surrounds the prison. If a man took a notion, well there's an awful lot of open field to cross, and, up in the tower, the guards wouldn't have any trouble picking up that color.

Like a lot of men in prison, Taylor is soft-spoken and innocent.

No one will tell you Terry Taylor is a saint, except maybe Terry Taylor. He never sold cocaine, he barely knew Ollie Clark, and he really was talking on the phone to Michelle, his "fiance," for five hours on the afternoon of March 7. He is a garrulous sort, who says he's been known to talk on the phone for eight hours straight.

"We were talkin' about our child," he says quietly. He pauses and looks down at his cheap new prison-issue boots. "She eventually lost it."

This is not Taylor's first stint behind bars. Between September 1984 and April 1988, he was arrested at least three times. In February 1985 he pleaded guilty to a charge of criminal conspiracy to deliver marijuana. Later that same year, he pleaded guilty to charges of selling a few ounces of marijuana. In November 1986, Taylor was convicted of burglary and theft of property after he broke into a neighbor's house and stole a .22-caliber rifle and a lamp. With parole violations, the tab for the burglary was seven years in prison. Still, by September 1987 — 11 months later — he was out on parole.

Taylor maintains his innocence in the break-in, and he says the other charges were the result of his being in the wrong place at the wrong time. Still, he will admit he's had some trouble. When he was a "young" man, he had a couple of scrapes with the police.

"They had me up in the jail in Jacksonville a few times," he says. "I used to occasionally get high, and I've been places where people have sold and used drugs ... But I've never delivered no drugs. I've never sold drugs."

The record is a little fuzzy. Like all juvenile records, Taylor's is not a matter of public record, and he will not volunteer much.

A counselor who worked with the teen-aged Taylor remembers him as a bright, "cunning" youth who had a problem with alcohol and, possibly, drugs.

"I couldn't be a character witness for him," the counselor, who spoke on the condition of anonymity, said. "He wasn't exactly a bad kid. It was just that he didn't seem to be able to follow rules. As far as I know he never hurt anybody but himself."

Taylor was born in Little Rock on March 9, 1966. He describes his early life as structured, his mother and stepfather as "decent."

"I was taught all the basic things that a child would be taught — discipline, respect ... I was taught to go to school. I was taught to treat people the way I wanted to be treated," he says. "My mother was very religious and very strict, as was my stepfather.

"As a teenager, I became the type of person who is real easy-going and I wanted to help everybody," Taylor says. "Most of the time it only seemed to get me in trouble."

Taylor said he met his real father, Willie Everett of Star City, for the first time when he was nine years old. From that time on, he split his time between the streets of Little Rock (later North Little Rock and Jacksonville) and south-central Arkansas. He says he dropped out of high school after his first child was born to "live up to my commitments." By the time he was 20, he was the father of three children.

Now, he says, he gets letters from those children wondering where he has gone.

IN THE FRONT ROOM of her brother's clean but modest ranch house in suburban North Little Rock, Michelle Akins grants an interview. The reporter is met at the door by a tall, fit young man who sits silently on the couch as introductions are made, then leaves abruptly, apparently satisfied the visitor is neither a narc nor a prankster. Akins explains her bodyguard by saying she has received some "funny" phone calls in the past few weeks.

Akins's version of Taylor's upbringing is somewhat different. "It was hard for him," she says. "He was really raised by his grandmother — that's why his last name is different from everyone else in his family. I get the feeling his whole family was pretty rowdy. His cousins were always in trouble; and I think his mom had a lot of boyfriends. He has some aunts who used to work the street. He'd been more or less on his own for a real long time."

Akins is a pleasant, mildly babyfat girl, big-boned and effervescent. She wears a peculiarly mature hair style — a swept-up, dark mane streaked with silver. In her black sweater and fringed, studded leather boots she could be 13 or 30. Beneath a touch of blue eye makeup, there is something tired about her eyes.

Akins can still remember the date of her first meeting with Terry Taylor.

"September 26, 1987 — that's when we started going together," she says. She met him at his brother Robert Burnett's house on Sioux Trail. She and some friends stopped by to visit Burnett and found Taylor there, sitting on the couch. He was quiet, shy and he treated her nice.

Blind Justice

In September 1987, Jane Wood reported that the state used a seldom-enforced law to confiscate a saving account and monthly social security payments from an 85-year-old inmate whose eyesight was failing. Roy Beverls was the first inmate taken to court under Act 715 of 1985, which allowed the state to recover costs of incarceration from inmates. Though he wanted to use part of his $4,800 savings account and/or his monthly $43 to pay for a routine cataract operation that could have restored his vision to near-normal levels with glasses, the state prevents inmates from paying from operations with their own money. Instead, operations are provided at no cost when the state deems them appropriate which it declined to do in Beverls's case.

Then-Attorney General Steve Clark attacked Correction Board member Bobby Roberts as a "bleeding heart liberal" for suggesting that Act 715 be studied. The attorney general claimed the Beverls case had been taken out of context, but, at the time the money collected from Beverls — in a hearing in which the inmate was not provided counsel — represented more than two-thirds of the total monies collected under the act. In fact, the Beverls case was the only state victory under the act. In the only other unchallenged judgment an inmate settled out of court and was allowed to pay a $5,500 judgment in $100-a-month installments.

Beverls died blind and in prison.

He told her he had just got out of jail. Akins knew he had some problems with the law, but he seemed so sensitive, so calm and quiet. He seemed almost poetic to her. Now she reads the poems he sends her from prison over and over.

"I know he didn't sell them any cocaine," she says. "There's this other guy who calls himself 'J.T.' — I never knew Terry by that name."

She hesitates; like a fawn listening to a snapped twig, some instinct is disturbed.

"I know he didn't sell them cocaine on March 7. I was with him that morning. I had just found out that I was pregnant and we were talking about getting an abortion — we talked about it all afternoon on the phone. On March 12, I had the abortion."

Softer now, she continues.

"He just couldn't have been selling cocaine. He never had any money. For a long time, he and Robert were having a real hard time of it. I was giving him my paycheck every Monday — I used to work at Sonic. Just signing it over to him. And this other girl — Belinda Liggins — she was also helping him out financially, buying them groceries and stuff. I think she's trying to get a lawyer for Terry now. We don't speak anymore."

Akins knows she wasn't a good witness for Taylor. She thinks the turning point of the trial might have been when she forgot her boyfriend had just started working as a dishwasher at the Holiday Inn. When the prosecutor asked Michelle if Taylor was working, she says she slipped and said he wasn't.

"When he finally made bail and got out of jail, he couldn't get his job back," she says. "But he was doing so good, trying so hard."

Though Akins was not surprised when the jury found Taylor guilty, she said she expected him to be sentenced to 20 years — the lightest sentence for which he was eligible. Life in prison floored her.

"Terry really got a raw deal. For an eight ball. I mean, there's people out there who murder and rob people and they don't get life in prison. The day he was sentenced, some other guy, some guy they caught with 200 pounds of marijuana, was sentenced to 15 years. To me, 200 pounds of marijuana is a lot bigger deal than an eight ball."

(On the same day Taylor was sentenced, 42-year-old Domingo Lope of Houston was sentenced in Pulaski Circuit Coùrt to 15 years in prison and fined $50,000 for possession of 200 pounds of marijuana.)

Once while Taylor was in jail — he spent three and a half months in the Jacksonville city jail before finally posting bail — Michelle came to visit him. After she left, she said, officers found a small amount of marijuana on the floor. She was arrested and eventually fined $300 for misdemeanor possession of marijuana.

That was something else James Smedley kept Taylor's jury from hearing.

THERE IS MORE KAFKA IN TAYLOR'S STORY than Dostoevsky. Taylor was offered several opportunities to cut his losses and do his time, but he seems to maintain a stubborn, almost arrogant, aloofness from reality. An observer in the courtroom during Taylor's trial said that the overwhelming feeling one got from watching the defendant was one of smugness — that Taylor seemed unconcerned, confident that Akins's testimony would deliver him.

"It was like Terry was trying to beat the system, that he would stick his girlfriend up on the stand and she'd lie and he'd walk out a free man. The jury didn't buy that: they didn't like that attitude. They made him pay for it. Juries don't like drug dealers, and they don't like guys who think they can beat the system."

Smedley wouldn't speculate on why the jury took such an apparent dislike to his client. For that, he said, "you'll have to ask the damn jury."

For their part, the jurors seemed to regard Terry Taylor as a punk and

Michelle Akins a liar.

Dale Gossien, a Little Rock engineer with the state highway department, served on the jury. He was fulfilling his civic duty. He followed his conscience and the judge's instructions. He was not surprised at the verdict.

"He didn't go on the stand in his own defense," Gossien said. "I think the jury wanted to see what he had to say for himself. We figured he was proven guilty in the courtroom — there wasn't much to the case. It was open and shut."

Gossien said the jury may have been aware of the anti-drug demonstrations going on that week, but he doubted it had as much effect as the jury's collective perception that drug dealers often got off "with a slap on the wrist."

"I think we were determined not to do that," Gossien said. "I think — like it said in the paper the day after — the judge said he thought the jury was trying to send a message. Sure, it might be unfair to this guy who gets life while people who have maybe done worse things don't get as much time, but I don't really see that as our problem. We followed the law."

Obviously, it wasn't a hard decision for the jury. Gossien said the two black jurors were perhaps the most vehement in their desire to put Taylor away for a long time.

"I think people like him may be a lost cause by the time they're three years old," he said. "That's sad, but I think it's the truth. It's got to start even before they get to school. Our society has got to make some basic changes."

Besides, Gossien believes that even though the jury sentenced Taylor to life, about "seven or eight years" is all he'll serve.

"That's all anybody serves," he said.

IN ARKANSAS, life in prison *means* life in prison. Pulaski County Prosecutor Chris Piazza said the habitual offender statute that Taylor was sentenced under was designed to keep "sociopathic criminals" off the streets.

"Psychiatrists, psychologists have shown that you can't reform a sociopath," Piazza said. "The rate of recidivism is such that they just commit crime after crime. What you can do is take them out of circulation, remove them from society. Sooner or later they may burn out, and decide that it's not worth it to keep banging their head against the wall. That may take 50 years: it may never happen."

Piazza said the sentence given Taylor was "harsh," but said that it reflected society's attitude toward drug dealers.

"I think it's good," he said. "I think juries are showing people they're not going to put up with this sort of behavior. We're going to go after a lot tougher sentences. We're going to use the habitual offender statute to get these people off the streets."

Though the crimes Taylor was convicted of were relatively petty crimes, at least one of his former acquaintances described him as a career criminal.

"What you have to understand is that Terry's world is not like your world, not like my world," he said. "I imagine there hasn't been a day in his adult life when Terry hasn't broken the law, has stolen something or another. He's not going to get rich doing it. He's always going to have to struggle to get by. That's the way he survives — he doesn't have a steady job, he may never hold a steady job. That's just not the way he thinks."

David Pinkerton, the neighbor whose house Taylor burglarized in 1986, doesn't believe Taylor deserves another chance.

"I sent him to prison; he had his parole once," Pinkerton said. "Now I hear he's doing life. Good — that's the best place for him."

Smedley says the only chance for Taylor to gain his freedom is for the governor to commute his sentence. For that to happen, Taylor would have to make an application to the state Board of Paroles and Pardons. The application would be reviewed by a screening committee, then the full parole board would

Reading and Righting a Wrong

In October 1987, as part of a report on adult illiteracy in Arkansas, Anthony Moser profiled Marilyn Allen, who had spent 13 years in public schools without learning to read. Marilyn, who had a talent for drawing, looked forward to going to college and perhaps pursuing a career in an art-related field.

At Philander Smith College, though, it soon became clear that her professors wouldn't provide social promotions. Dropping out, and unable to get any kind of work that required reading skills, Marilyn became a maid at a motel. But one night, while watching television, she saw a public service announcement offering help for adult illiterates. "When I saw the number on TV," she said, "I knew I just had to call."

The next day she was referred to the Literacy Council of Pulaski County, which set her up with volunteer tutor Jan Spann, a sales executive for Southwestern Bell Telephone Company. The two couldn't have been more different. But as they met twice a week for two-hour sessions, a close friendship formed.

Six months later, Marilyn was still working toward reaching a fifth-grade level. Yet she was displaying a talent for narrative, creating an alter ego in a short story that she brought her tutor one evening as a gift. "Marilyn is a budding artist," Spann commented, "and now she's a budding writer."

make a recommendation to the governor.

"They used to do that fairly regularly, but not anymore," Smedley said, referring to the hard line Governor Bill Clinton has taken on pardons since returning to office in 1983. "And you've usually got to serve seven years before the board will even hear your case. Then they make their recommendations to the governor, and its completely at his discretion. He's not bound by law to grant anything."

Smedley said there was no basis on which to appeal the case. There have been similar life sentences handed down under the habitual offender statute — not a lot, but a handful — and they've all been upheld by the higher court.

"I don't know a damn thing we can do about it," Smedley said. "I'm hopeful that somewhere down the line we can get a commutation for him, but in this political climate it's not a sure thing."

Terry Taylor says Smedley is no longer his attorney. He says he is sure that his case is going "to the Supreme Court" and that he will be exonerated. But no appeal is before the court, no wheels are turning in his behalf: time has run out for Terry Taylor. The woman who answered the phone in Kansas City — at the number that Terry said was his mother's — says she doesn't know him.

Michelle Akins paid James Smedley's legal fees. She has since quit her job at Sonic, however, and doesn't make enough money from babysitting to hire another attorney.

Belinda Liggins — a woman Taylor says he sometimes lived with and who provided him with emotional and financial support — did contact another lawyer on Taylor's behalf. Little Rock attorney Josh McHughes said that after Taylor was sentenced he contacted him about possibly filing an appeal.

"I agreed to do it if they paid the cost for having a transcript [of the court proceedings] prepared," McHughes said. "After talking with her and the attorneys involved in the case, it didn't look like there was much basis for an appeal, but I would have filed the motion if they could have put up $800. I checked with the stenographer and she told me to transcribe it would cost between $700 and $900. Last time I talked to Belinda, she was trying to raise the money. She said she had about $300 or $400 raised and she was going to go to his parents to see if they could help. That was about three day before the deadline for the appeal."

A defendant must file an appeal motion within 30 days of sentencing. Terry Taylor didn't make it.

Oblivious to his predicament, or maybe just naive, Taylor is making plans for his post-prison life.

"First thing I'm going to do when I get out is go to my children, with Michelle — because I love Michelle — and try to compensate them for the time I've lost," he says. "I'll try to live up to society, like I always have, and I'll try ..."

His voice tapers off into nothingness. He sits and looks straight ahead. In the months he has been here in Cummins, he has had one visit from his family. They all live far away now, and he says it's painful for them.

Michelle Akins doesn't think she will ever see Terry Taylor freed.

"He's gone," she says. She shuffles his letters, folds them together and puts them away in a crinkled envelope.

"It's not something I like to think about."

(February 1989)

Stephen Buel

Will Gannett Campaign in the Newspaper War?

Two days after the Gannett Company announced its plans to buy the *Arkansas Gazette*, a half-page ad on the cover of a newspaper trade magazine offered this update on the communications empire's first 1986 acquisition:

"*News* Posts Largest Circulation Gain In 25 Years!" the blue headline boomed. Below was an account of how *The Detroit News* had increased its circulation lead over a rival by 370 percent in the two quarters since Gannett acquired it. "The latest figures are in," the red and black text boasted, "and the *Detroit News*, Michigan's #1 newspaper, is now even more #1." Lower, it bragged: "Now that's dominance."

Gannett is known for nothing if not dominance. With 93 daily newspapers and about 40 semiweekly or weekly community papers, it is the nation's dominant newspaper chain. It owns the nation's dominant billboard company, Gannett Outdoor, as well as eight television stations, 18 radio stations, the Harris Poll and *USA Today*, the splashy feature paper which makes disputed claims to be the nation's dominant daily.

Gannett recently applied its dominance to the Little Rock newspaper war by paying $51 million to the descendants of Judge Carrick White Heiskell for the 167-year-old *Arkansas Gazette*. Although few serious changes are yet apparent, the company's arrival in Little Rock instantly changed the face of journalism in Arkansas. Because it is now likely that there won't be two competing Little Rock dailies in a few years, Gannett's presence here will produce lasting and perhaps detrimental effects.

It is hard to predict what strategy Gannett will use in its battle for dominance with the *Democrat*, because dominance has typically come easily for Gannett. Aside from the competition in Detroit — which the company is seeking the federal government's permission to end — only one of Gannett's 93 dailies operates in a truly competitive market. That paper is the *Arkansas Gazette*.

That's what makes Gannett's purchase of the *Gazette* so interesting. News accounts of the *Gazette* purchase have almost all asked whether *Arkansas Democrat* publisher Walter E. Hussman, Jr. will be able to survive the onslaught of Gannett's deep pockets. (And a headline in *Arkansas Business* — "So Long, Walter Hussman?"— perhaps put it best. Hussman later said of the headline: "I hope everyone will remember that five years from now. They'll probably say we were lucky.") Equally or even more valid, however, is the opposite question: Can Gannett compete, or more to the point, will it choose to? It never has previously.

Little Rock and Detroit are just two of the four cities that the nation's most profitable newspaper group has entered in the last 18 months in an effort to shake the perception that it is an efficient but editorially uninspiring collection of minor-league papers. In a year in which Gannett chairman Allen Neuharth has made much of his desire to enter into journalism's "major leagues," Gannett's entry into Little Rock may be designed to counter the belief that it is either unable or unwilling to operate in a competitive, two-newspaper town.

This topic is clearly a sore point with Neuharth. Asked at his company's debut Arkansas press conference about the strategy behind its first entry into a competitive situation, Neuharth evasively replied that Gannett has plenty of

Newspapers have always been a favorite Spectrum subject. Issues 40, December, 1986; 12, November 1985; and 82, August 1988.

Send In The Clowns

Chronicling the trials and tribulations of the Gannett-era Arkansas Gazette *and its ongoing "war" with the* Arkansas Democrat *has long been a favorite* Spectrum *theme. In August 1987, an editorial headlined "The Gannett Company Sends In The Clowns" observed that the company's "rainbow-brite" propensities were beginning to surface in the pages of the "gray Old Lady." In an effort to promote the Ringling Brothers Barnum and Bailey Circus, the* Gazette *printed color photos of four prominent Arkansans made up as clowns above their page one masthead.*

In August 1988, a long story by Anthony Moser observed how the struggle between the papers had graduated "into the journalistic equivalent of an all-out nuclear exchange," with both papers sinking money into their operations at an alarming rate. Moser's story also revealed that Democrat *publisher Walter "Boo" Hussman was considering filing an antitrust lawsuit against the* Gazette *(the pre-Gannett* Gazette *had filed a similar action against the* Democrat *in 1984). While that lawsuit never materialized, the ill will between the two competing dailies has never abated. And Moser has since moved on — to the* Arkansas Democrat.

experience in competitive markets — through *USA Today* and its chain of 10 suburban newspapers on the fringes of New York City. Despite this somewhat disingenuous response, the fact is that Gannett has never chosen to operate for long in a truly competitive newspaper market. A July 6, 1986, *Los Angeles Times* article, included as part of the press kit that accompanied Neuharth's visit, described Gannett's strategy this way:

"In every Gannett town where there is a second newspaper, Gannett arranged or inherited a joint operating agreement to share profits and stop competing financially — with Gannett invariably in charge of the joint operating agency."

In the case of Detroit, where Gannett's *News* and the competing *Detroit Free Press* are theoretically still foes, the company initiated efforts to enter into shared operations even prior to its acquisition of the *News*. Under such an agreement — which, as an exemption from antitrust law, must be approved by the federal Justice Department — one of the two newspapers would revert to afternoon delivery so that both papers could be printed in the same plant on the same presses.

All business operations are typically merged under this type arrangement, leaving two, usually enfeebled news staffs locked in lukewarm editorial competition while servants to the same master. Once operations are merged, news coverage can be reduced and advertising and circulation rates can be increased without fear of competitive recrimination. Total profits — and newspaper monopolies are always profitable — are then divided among the two owners according to some prearranged formula.

Few would seriously suggest that Gannett cannot compete. Its performance in Detroit against another chain-owned paper seems proof that Gannett can compete and win. But, Detroit illustrates Gannett's unwillingness to compete. Even while boasting of a 370 percent increase in its circulation lead, the company is seeking to end the contest simply because the road to victory is too long and arduous to deliver the kind of profits the company's stockholders have come to expect.

Gannett's stockholders have ample reason to expect profits. Wall Street's most respected communications company has a reputation of streamlining its newspapers' operations and boosting their pre-tax profit margins to twice the industry norm by gradually trimming news budgets and sharply increasing advertising and circulation rates.

Gannett's commitment to profit outshines its commitment to news. The uneven quality of *USA Today* amply demonstrates this, but nothing makes the point better than Gannett's 1986 "Best Of Gannett" competition. Among larger newspapers, the chain's "best overall work" award was recently won not by a long-standing Gannett newspaper, but by *The Des Moines Register*, an independent paper in the *Gazette* mold that was acquired by the company in the last 18 months. It says a lot about the nation's largest newspaper chain that the way it has entered the "major leagues" is by buying major-league newspapers rather than building them.

What changes can readers of the *Gazette* expect to see under Gannett? Thus far the new ownership has been playing its cards close to its vest no doubt aware that its competitors across the mall — newly dubbed "Arkansas's Newspaper" — are eagerly looking for any sign the *Gazette* is under the leadership of carpetbaggers or scalawags. For this reason alone, Gannett's selection of William Malone, publisher of its two Springfield, Missouri, papers, was masterful. Malone, a native of Marked Tree, Arkansas, spent 21 years across the Mississippi with the Memphis newspapers and spent his freshman year at Arkansas State University. Also indicative of Gannett's savvy is the decision not to prominently identify the *Gazette* as a Gannett paper on its masthead.

Gazette readers have already seen a variety of innovations on the business side of things, but few editorial modifications so far. The exceptions have been a greater willingness to use its pages for self-promotion, as when the *Gazette* recently boasted of printing their largest newspaper ever, and the occasional appearance of upbeat articles by or about national Gannett luminaries — speaking to charity organizations or expressing their earnest commitment to the people of Arkansas.

Indications are that less subtle changes are in the works. A few weeks back, employees reported to the newsroom to find a *Gazette* newsrack almost directly across from the desk of news editor William Rutherford, the man usually responsible for designing the *Gazette*'s serious-minded front page. How much longer will the *Gazette* remain Gannett's least-splashy newspaper?

Another likely innovation will be more frequent turnover among the paper's staff, as the best young salesmen, circulation managers and reporters move on to bigger Gannett papers, opening the door for recruits from smaller ones. System-wide Gannett job openings are already being posted on the paper's bulletin-board.

New publisher William Malone, interviewed last Saturday after a full day's work, said the *Gazette* is a fine paper he is proud to be associated with. Malone said no operation is so good that it cannot be improved, but after just six days on the job, he understandably admitted that he had few concrete ideas about how such improvements will be executed.

The personable new publisher did confirm that the *Gazette* has begun using its new color presses to print various feature sections, the first of which evidently appeared last week.

"We will be using color quite extensively," he said.

Malone also indicated that hirings are probably in the works. After all, cutting costs might serve Gannett well in a monopoly market like Springfield — where the afternoon *Leader & Press* will soon be merged with the morning *Daily News* — but that would obviously play into the *Democrat*'s hands in Little Rock. Pledging that any staff additions would be long-term, Malone said that he will be looking at every department to see whether its present staffing levels are sufficient. He said that, based on a cursory evaluation, the reporting staff looks like it may need to be enlarged.

"It's really too early to say what we will do or if we will turn a profit in 1987," he said.

Malone said criticism of Gannett's commitment to news may once have been valid but is not today. Yet, even if reporters are added to the *Gazette*'s staff, Gannett history would seem to indicate that the real battle with the *Democrat* will occur on the business side of the operation. This skirmish is already underway; in just two short two months, we have seen dueling Sunday supplements, the celebrity battle of the philanthropic newspapermen, cut-rate home delivery rates, stepped-up television advertising, full-page newspaper promotions and front-page press releases. The major editorial innovation at the two papers has been new chairs in the newsroom — six at the *Democrat* and enough for the whole newsroom at the *Gazette*.

Is a joint operating agreement in Little Rock likely after several more months of such behavior — despite the present earnest denials? *Democrat* publisher Walter E. Hussman, Jr., has already demonstrated the depth (and some would say irrationality) of his commitment to maintaining an editorial voice in Central Arkansas. Faced with a foe so committed — a man who has almost cheerfully lost about $40 million in pursuit of this goal — how long can Gannett be expected to rummage around in pursuit of meager millions if there is more money to be made in joint operations?

Hussman and the *Democrat* have been counted out of the picture too quickly by most observers (but not by Malone, who lunched with his rival last week). Despite what one thinks of Hussman's paper or methods, his success

Paying the Piper

In its second issue, in June 1985, Spectrum *reported that a funny thing happened to the* Arkansas Democrat *after its Sunday real estate section ran a story about a man who was encouraging people to sell their own homes without a Realtor. It seems that a sizable number of Realtors suddenly declined to buy display ads in the following week's section. Indeed, the number of display ads from Realtors declined by about 20 percent.*

Two weeks later, Spectrum *subsequently reported, though, things appeared to be back to normal. The paper ran a lengthy article about the pitfalls of selling your own home, and ad linage was again up to par.*

with the *Democrat* has been near phenomenal by industry standards. In eight years, he has brought it back from near death to the point where he claims he can strike a profit if his paper's circulation climbs by one more percent.

Perhaps more to the point, in the arena of crass competition that the *Gazette*'s sale has opened in recent months, Hussman seems to have won the two major battles:

■ The *Democrat*, after all, was the first to initiate cut-rate Christmas subscription rates in which a portion of the proceeds went to charity — in its case, the Salvation Army. Nashville publisher John Siegenthaler, head of the Gannett team that inspected the *Gazette* while the sale was being finalized, admitted in early December that the *Gazette*'s subsequent United Way subscription deal was a response to the *Democrat*. "One good idea deserves another," he said.

■ The *Democrat* was also the clear winner in the duel of the Sunday magazines. After the *Gazette* used page-one space to explain it would be replacing the popular *Parade* magazine with the Gannett-owned *USA Weekend*, Hussman responded with the detail omitted from the *Gazette*'s account — that Hussman's newspaper group had actually stolen *Parade* from the *Gazette*. This scenario also demonstrated the *Democrat*'s willingness to match the *Gazette*'s front-page press releases one for one.

YET, FOR SOMEONE WHO conclusively won rounds one, two and three of the newspaper war, Walter Hussman's response to all this has been strangely subdued. Having increased his circulation and advertising almost to the point of profitability, having repelled the *Gazette*'s deadly antitrust lawsuit and then having forced the Pattersons into selling their paper, one would think Hussman would be happier than he seemed to be in a recent interview.

Hussman wouldn't come right out in our interview and say he thinks Gannett wants to put him out of business, but he came close. He's been doing his reading on Gannett, and when asked what that consisted of, he forwarded a copy of an article about Gannett's Salem, Oregon, operations entitled: "The Newspaper That Was Murdered."

By the same token, as publisher of the weaker newspaper, it would also be unstrategic of Hussman to act incautious or to make any indication that he desired a joint operating agreement because he feared for the *Democrat*'s future. (Malone said that he and Hussman did not discuss joint operations during their recent lunch.) Hussman said he would throw in the towel and walk away from the *Democrat* in defeat if his paper's circulation and advertising linage were to decline steadily while the *Gazette*'s increased. Still, he continues to maintain that Little Rock is capable of supporting two profitable daily newspapers. On the whole, he said, Gannett's entry into the market should actually make this easier because the *Gazette* will now benefit from Gannett's greater buying power in areas like newsprint.

Assuming that Gannett were to choose to compete with Hussman, Malone's challenge would be to see whether he could pare down some of the operating inefficiencies hinted at in the antitrust suit, while at the same time making amends with the many advertisers the *Gazette* offended over the years.

For the *Democrat*, the challenge would be greater — to improve the quality of its news and editorials so that the paper could resume the circulation growth it enjoyed for several years until last September's new *Gazette* subscription drive. Probably the greatest skepticism about the *Democrat*'s ability to do this comes from within the *Democrat* newsroom itself. Hussman recently took to a desktop and asked reporters to resist whatever financial enticements the *Gazette* might throw at them. While no doubt intended to draw the troops together, numerous *Democrat* employees say it actually had the effect of alienating them. Simply put, many employees of the *Democrat* newsroom say they aren't sure the

Democrat could survive a serious run with the *Gazette* if Gannett indeed opts to compete and boosts the *Gazette*'s approximately three percent before-tax annual profits up to the 20-30 percent rate common at its other papers.

Would Little Rock really suffer from an end to competition? Yes, but I'm not sure how much. The sad fact is that there are already many days when readers don't benefit much from competition. The *Democrat* employs many fine people, and there is probably not a day that goes by when some *Democrat* reporter doesn't provide a more detailed account of some story than his *Gazette* counterpart. Yet, on many other days, reading the *Democrat* is hardly worth the effort.

Take, for instance, the two papers' coverage of the Iranian arms crisis. Almost without exception, the *Gazette*'s play of the story and selection of wire service stories has been superior to that of the *Democrat*. Although many of the key stories on this have been written by reporters for the *Washington Post* or *Los Angeles Times* — and thus available daily to the *Democrat* by wire — most days the only way to discover this has been by reading the abbreviated rewrites of their stories available in the *Gazette*. The *Democrat* has, however, managed to pick up on a *Post* story suggesting that Gannett chairman Allen Neuharth makes monthly payments to support an illegitimate child, and it devoted an entire half-page to a *Post* item about the chocolate "sheep turds" that apparently can be found under chairs in the waiting room of Neuharth's office.

Hussman seems aware of these problems. In response to a series of questions about how he would respond if the *Gazette* were to hire more reporters or commit *itself* to printing Arkansas's fatter newspaper, Hussman said, "Our problem is not the space but the quality of the space."

Ultimately, though, I don't look for the competition to manifest itself in the news pages of either paper. The department that seems to have been working hardest at both papers since the sale is promotions. In fact, the final installment of the newspaper war looks like a battle that will be waged through advertising media other than newspapers. Perhaps this explains why most cities no longer support two.

(December 1986)

More than four years later, there can be no denying that Gannett indeed campaigned in Little Rock's newspaper war. Nor, however, is there much question that the Democrat *has managed to gain the upper hand. Although both papers reportedly lose millions of dollars each year, the* Gazette *is believed to be posting losses far in excess of those suffered by the* Democrat. *Ad linage and circulation have appeared to increase steadily at the* Democrat, *while the* Gazette *has lost several of its largest advertisers. Turnover at the once-stolid* Gazette *has also increased markedly, with several of the paper's most visible columnists defecting to the* Democrat. *By the beginning of 1991, most observers were holding their breath to see which paper would cry uncle first.*

Wishful Thinking

In June 1988, Spectrum's *Jim Nichols — in a story headlined "Is There A New Editor In The Democrat's Future?" — reported that flamboyant* Arkansas Democrat *managing editor John Robert Starr might be out in favor of former* Arkansas Gazette *managing editor Bob Douglas. Nearly three years on, Starr is still at the* Democrat's *helm and still waiting for a apology or a correction or an acknowledgment that we made a mistake. Well, this is it, John Robert, and on archival-quality paper, at that. You're still there, and we were wrong. In the words of* The Book of Common Prayer *(Rite II), "We are truly sorry and we humbly repent."*

'Outing' A Friend

It was not lightly that Anthony Moser and Stephen Buel decided to write about Patrick Kelly and identify his exact cause of death. The editors' decision was influenced largely by the last two pieces that Patrick wrote for Spectrum *before his death.*

Patrick's last full-length piece concerned Darel Clark, a friend to several Spectrum *employees, who killed himself as his diabetic condition worsened. Kelly's other piece was a short editorial in which he expressed revulsion for supposed gay rights activists who chose, despite their words, to remain closeted.*

Anthony Moser

With Death, an Awakening

I first met Patrick Kelly about three years ago, when he came to work for the *Arkansas Democrat*, where I was employed as a reporter. He was already very ill at the time — he walked with the help of a cane and had lost the use of one arm, which he kept in a sling.

When Patrick was asked about his condition, he told most people he was the victim of a serious automobile accident. Among friends he was more truthful and said that he was recovering from a viral infection of the brain. This explanation was technically correct, albeit incomplete. The toxoplasmosis that afflicted Patrick's brain was one of the rare, opportunistic infections that Acquired Immune Deficiency Syndrome allowed to invade his body. So far as I have been able to determine, however, he never mentioned AIDS to any of his co-workers.

Friend, colleague and former associate editor of Spectrum, Patrick died at a Dallas hospital earlier this year of a disease brought on by his AIDS. He was 28. His death is a case study in the implacable nature of this tragic disease.

In retrospect, it is amazing that Patrick was able to continue working as long as he did. He was frightfully thin and frail. Once, after we had attended a press conference at the Coachman's Inn, he collapsed while trying to walk down a flight of stairs. His legs began shaking involuntarily, and he was unable to get back on his feet.

"You're gonna have to carry me, Tony," he said. I picked him up, and he was so light that it shocked me. I realized then that he was very, very ill, but I never added it all up. Strange, opportunistic infections; profound emaciation; constant fatigue — it had AIDS written all over it but neither I nor anyone I knew realized it then. Patrick went to great pains to shield his friends from his suffering. He asked me not to tell anyone about his collapse, and I never did.

He survived much longer than the average patient with an active, diagnosed case of AIDS — almost four years, in fact. He made two trips to the University of California at Los Angeles Medical Center seeking new, experimental treatments, and they may have helped some. But in the final analysis, Patrick had a death sentence from the day of his diagnosis, and he knew it.

"Pat fought a hard battle, and he was very courageous," his mother said in reflection. "The cards had just been stacked against him. Four years ago, when this first happened to him, I don't know how he accepted it. But somehow, he managed to keep on living his life. He kept his problems pretty much to himself."

A former roommate of Patrick's said he at times became "very scared of people in some respects; very cautious about his handicaps. This made him seem aloof, when really he was just scared."

Ultimately, it was not toxoplasmosis but simple pneumonia that killed Patrick. His immune system was all but destroyed and his body was unable to fight the infection. Within three weeks of its onset, he was dead. His sudden death was a merciful one. Had the pneumonia or some other opportunistic infection not taken advantage of his weakened condition when it did, he might have died a slow and extremely painful death from the toxoplasmosis that had already left him in such a debilitated condition.

Of all the ways a man can die, death from toxoplasmosis — a very rare condition in the absence of AIDS — is among the most relentlessly hellish. Thousands upon thousands of parasitic microorganisms called toxoplasmas invade the brain and central nervous system, slowly eating away at the tissue. As the infection worsens, the patient lapses into what physicians describe as a "descending fugue state," now known as AIDS Dementia. Reasoning, as well as motor skills, abandon the infected person, and he is racked with fever, chills, swelling of the brain against the skull, and severe pain. He may linger for hours or days in the "agonal" region of existence — the cusp between the living and the dead. By the end, death is a welcome visitor.

On a very personal level, Patrick's death suddenly made AIDS real for me, transporting it from the vaguely abstract to the hellishly concrete. As a political conservative and heterosexual, I had never really given AIDS or homosexuality a second thought — until Patrick died. I was not even aware that Patrick was homosexual until about a week after his death. For me, the lesson of his life and death is simple: that we are all human beings first, and whatever else second.

Although Patrick apparently never told any of his professional colleagues about his battle against AIDS, Nyma Benner — an *Arkansas Democrat* photographer and close friend of his — came to a conclusion about the situation prior to his death.

"Patrick would say things without saying them," Benner said. "He was like that in his ability to communicate."

About a year before he died, Patrick took a friend of his who was also suffering from AIDS to Mexico for experimental treatments. "He was always thinking about someone else," Benner said. "He was calm. Sometimes people who are facing death seem to handle it better than those around them."

Ultimately Patrick faced his final battle by himself. The loneliness and isolation this disease compelled him to finish his life in are terrifying to imagine. Thomas Hobbes described the life of man as "solitary, poor, nasty, brutish and short." That may be hyperbole when applied to man in general, but it rings true for the life and death of an AIDS victim.

(December 1986)

Pit Of Hell Comix

Pit of Hell *was* Spectrum*'s
first, and arguably most controversial comic strip, a slice-of-afterlife
chronicle of a perfectly nice and
normal-seeming young man named
Tom who just happened to be
consigned to the fiery lake for all
eternity. Drawn, after a fashion, by
bull dadaist Janor Hypercleets with
assistance from James Neff, and
punctuated with naturalistic yelps of
anguish,* POH *ran from the first
issue of the newspaper until — in a
very un-comic strippish turn — the
damned found a back exit and
escaped. YEEEARRG.*

Oft-Told Tales from Old White Gentlemen

On the 30th anniversary of the occupation of Little Rock's Central High School by the 101st Airborne Division, the University of Arkansas's Center for Arkansas and Regional Studies held a three-day symposium in Fayetteville to explore the political, social and historical implications of "The Crisis at Central High."

It went pretty much like you'd expect: Orval Faubus got the blame. He was blamed for calling out the National Guard to keep nine black students from attending Central High. He was blamed for allowing a segregationist mob to grow unmolested in front of these troops. He was blamed for pulling the troops out and letting the mob riot. He was blamed for creating a situation in which the federal government felt the need to send the 101st Airborne to occupy Central High for an entire school year.

Of course, Faubus denied it all. He claimed that he was just trying to prevent violence, that he called out the Arkansas National Guard to raise certain philosophical and constitutional issues, and bragged that he hadn't needed Central High back then to further his political future. He even took credit for the fact that nobody was seriously injured and no property was damaged. Nobody bought it: not Wiley Branton, the civil rights attorney who filed the original Little Rock desegregation lawsuit; not Judge Henry Woods, a mere lawyer at the time; not old *Arkansas Gazette* warhorses Hugh Patterson and Harry Ashmore; and especially not the panel of three reporters who covered the "crisis" as it happened. To a man, they blamed Orval. They said he whipped up the segregationists for his own political purposes, and testified that if only the governor had left things alone back then, integration would have gone forward without violence, and without becoming an international spectacle. *Arkansas Democrat* Managing Editor John Robert Starr, who at the time was an AP reporter, said Faubus's actions created the crisis. Bob Douglas, a former *Gazette* editor, went even further, saying that Faubus brought on "an atmosphere of hatred that hovered over Little Rock like a toxic cloud. Governor Faubus made racism and racial hatred respectable."

Bob Douglas is no orator, but that statement was about as close to eloquence as anybody got in this symposium. The restrained indignation, the bitterness and sadness in his voice, turned his words into a eulogy for broken hopes and a distant time. From this high point, though, the session devolved into a series of anecdotes — oft-told tales from old white gentlemen, stories about the days back when they fought that rascal Orval. All of this was fine as far as it went, but it ignored an important point. The issue at Central High was not Orval Faubus. The issue was racism. Faubus did not create racial hatred — he simply exploited what already existed. In 1957, race relations in Arkansas were described by one speaker as "relatively good," but there were no black reporters working for the *Arkansas Gazette*. The "toxic cloud" that Bob Douglas described had been hanging over black people in the U.S. for 200 years or more, but most whites didn't notice it until Little Rock, and then only because the smell started sticking to them.

Central High was the first occasion for many Americans to take a good, close look at racial hatred. They had a chance to see it twist the faces of ordinary people, see it transform the girl next door into a monster. The new miracle of television brought it right into their living rooms. It was a shocking experience, and with the horror came denial. People around the world said it wasn't the white race that was at fault, it was America. People in the Northern states said it wasn't

Palefaces

In a September 1985 issue, a brief item mentioned that the Jacksonville Chamber of Commerce had printed a slim booklet designed to attract industry to the city of 25,000 some 20 miles north of Little Rock. Pertinent Data About Jacksonville *carried a curious statistic — it unabashedly emphasized that 83.5 percent of the people who resided in Jacksonville were white, as compared to a 74.8 percent paleface rate in the county as a whole.*

Editorials

Spectrum's editorials are known for their schizophrenic tendency to shift from the left to the right, depending on the subject and the writers on board at the time. Spectrum *editorials run unsigned, but to avoid slighting any of the contributors to this section, we identify them following their pieces.*

Issue 34, October 1986.

America, it was the South. Progressives in Arkansas said it wasn't them, it was all those rednecks and their leader, Orval Faubus.

This evasion of guilt was on its way to being enshrined as history by the university symposium when Ozell Sutton spoke up. Sutton — who had been the first black reporter on a major white Southern newspaper when he worked for the _Arkansas Democrat_ in the early and mid-1950s — was actively involved in the integration struggle at Little Rock. He said very little about the events of 1957. What he did say was that the "crisis" was racism, and the crisis is still with us.

"We sit here smugly and say we're not racist, [that] we would not have been around Central High School. But we do nothing to correct the structure that continues to grind out discrimination."

Ozell Sutton looked at the scholars and administrators who were hosting the symposium and told them that the University of Arkansas's record of recruiting black students and faculty was "totally disgusting." He said racism is a system, and until people are willing to change the system, to make it include people rather than exclude them, the "crisis" will continue. The difference between Ozell Sutton and most other participants in this symposium was the difference between a soldier and a spectator. It's hard to begrudge Hugh Patterson, Harry Ashmore and the others their place in history — after all, Central High was the central event of their public lives. Still, for them, it was the whole war. For Ozell Sutton and other blacks, Little Rock was just the opening skirmish. Sutton didn't share his war stories like the others, partly because his best stories were of other times and other cities, of courage and death, of victory and frustration. But you don't tell your war stories until the fighting is done. For Ozell Sutton, and for blacks in Arkansas and America, the "crisis" and the struggle continue.

(Steve Voorhies, October 1987)

Why It's Too Bad About Bill

And so it is that the road towards the Democratic Party's 1988 presidential nomination is growing ever more littered with the withdrawal speeches of the best and the brightest the party has to offer. Forced to choose between taking a realistic shot at becoming the leader of the free world or remaining a good and attentive father to his seven-year-old daughter Chelsea, Governor Bill Clinton chose the latter last week. New York Governor Mario Cuomo, who mesmerized the 1984 Democratic National Convention with his "Shining City on a Hill" speech, has already said that he will not be a candidate. Arkansas Senator Dale Bumpers, widely regarded as one of the finest orators in national politics, is also out. So is New Jersey Senator Bill Bradley, and, at least for now, Georgia Senator Sam Nunn. Among the Republicans, Illinois Governor James Thompson, a solid Midwestern sort, and New Jersey Governor Tom Kean, a rising GOP star, have made it known that they too will be on the sidelines.

In their announcements of non-candidacy, most of these men said they were leery of the deep personal sacrifices and time spent away from their families that a modern presidential campaign requires. They are men who want to be president but who do not want to forfeit their own personal values to reach that goal.

American democracy has always been filled with dichotomies and idiosyncratic quirks. But perhaps the most inexplicable and contradictory of the lot is the manner in which we chose our presidents. Like all Western democracies, we expect our leaders to be able, ideologically palatable, personally resourceful and ambitiously driven. But unlike the parliamentary democracies of Western Europe, the President of the United States is both chief of government and chief of state. The latter, more ceremonial role, combined with the general "cult of personality" which both informs and distorts so many facets of the American Mind, creates an additional requirement for American presidents.

Respecting and trusting our presidents is not enough. We want to *love* them and to embrace them as paragons of our own national virtue and humanity. We want real people — *their* political agenda. Thus FDR became a paradigm of paternal assurance to a nation ravaged by war and economic chaos. Eisenhower, during a sleepy time of postwar contentment, became the golf-playing Grand-dad so dear to our hearts. JFK was the dashing, romantic older brother.

And yet, over the past two decades, the process of running for president has become a dehumanizing, debilitating ordeal that requires presidential candidates to sublimate their most humanizing instincts — love of family, the preservation of a domestic life of reasonable tranquility, personal privacy — to a myopic obsession with an insanely elongated campaign process.

The Carter administration ushered in two salient features of the post-Watergate presidency. While the American public has always maintained a healthy interest in its first family, Carter was subjected to a scrutiny even intense by Kennedy standards. And by rising from less than one percent in the opinion polls in 1974 to winning the nomination in 1976, Carter institutionalized the two-year campaign as a staple of American presidential politics. This trend seems to be so open-ended that, in the near future, we will become gridlocked into a perpetual presidential race, one that begins as soon as the last one has ended, with no privacy for the candidates' families at any time.

The news media must bear a large part of the blame. As was illustrated in the case of Governor Clinton, any potential candidate who wants to test the waters will instead find himself washed away by a torrential flash-flood. For weeks, indeed, for *months* prior to his decision not to run, Clinton was asked by almost every reporter he saw, each and every time he encountered them, whether he was running or not. It was as if Clinton had no right to contemplate the issue in peace, at his own pace and on his own timetable. He was late, we were told, he was very late to be entering this race. Because he wanted to make up his mind before opening his mouth, Clinton was said to be indecisive and wishy-washy.

Returning from an education convention in Denver the week before he made his announcement, Clinton was met at the Little Rock airport by a horde of reporters. Once again, the question was asked, "Governor, are you running?" Clinton repeated that when he made up his mind, he would tell them. When asked why he was taking so long to make up his mind, he answered, "This is ridiculous ... I might even take longer if you all weren't doing this." Ridiculous indeed, that we do not want a man whose hand might be on the button to make decisions with care and deliberation.

There is a certain sad irony to what the process does to someone like Clinton, forcing him to choose between his powerfully kinetic and almost consuming sense of ambition, or the genuinely moral and humane qualities that can cause a person, especially one in a position of power, to focus his presidency to preserve his own humanity. His political talent and intellect made it possible for him to consider the race, but his regard for old-fashioned values like "love" and "obligation" made it impossible for him to follow through.

"I think there are worse things than going to your grave knowing that you lived putting your child first," Clinton said.

In the long run, there may be few things worse for the health of American democracy than a system so cynical that running for president and caring for your child have become mutually exclusive.

(Anthony Moser, July 1987)

The Tree Truth

One of the most durable myths of Arkansas politics is the Bill Clinton Tree Story. Versions of the tale vary, but they all involve the future governor climbing a tree on the University of Arkansas campus during the spring of 1969 to burn his draft card or otherwise protest the war in Vietnam and staying for several days. Political opponents and other detractors of Bill Clinton periodically bring up the apocryphal story.

As recently as the 1990 gubernatorial race, the story was circulating in some parts of the state and many people even claim to have seen a photograph. They're mistaken. But, as Spectrum *reported in July 1987, there* was a tree incident in Fayetteville in 1969. A non-student named Steve Pollard, a Boston native who claimed to be a Vietnam veteran, hoisted a mattress and other provisions into a willow tree across from the UA Student Union and stayed until he was arrested a few days later.

Sound Familiar?

In an apparent effort to affirm its solidarity with the United States Congress, the Chinese government — those enlightened folks who showed the world in 1989 how to deal with unpatriotic protesters — enacted a flag desecration law in the last week of June 1990 (shortly after the United States Supreme Court had struck down its American model). Willful damage to the star-flecked banner of the People's Republic would get you up to three years of imprisonment, detention, surveillance or deprivation of political rights. While they were at it, the Standing Committee of the National People's Congress also banned the use of the glorious red ensign as a trademark or in advertising. "Now there's an idea!" a July 1990 Spectrum *editorial observed.*

Old Glory's Evil Twin

As flag burning became a hotly debated issue around Independence Day 1989, Spectrum *offered this modest proposal as an addendum to a proposed anti-flagburning constitutional amendment:*

"The public display of any flag or symbol, or any representation of such a flag or symbol, used or associated with insurrection or rebellion against the United States, is hereby prohibited."

This provision, the editorial continued, would apply only to those flags and standards which signify treasonous activity and "attack the very existence of the American Flag, such as those carried by the Symbionese Liberation Army, the Weather Underground and the Confederate States of America."

The Wonder Year

Two centuries after 1789, that watershed year for the political and social future of Europe and the United States, the anniversaries of the French Declaration of the Rights of Man and the American Bill of Rights have been commemorated by truly breathtaking events abroad. From the tragic democratic uprising in China to the joyous breaching of the Berlin Wall, history — and, in recent weeks, hope — have filled the pages of newspapers and the broadcasts of television and radio networks.

Throughout Central and Eastern Europe, signs of the demise of the statist distortions of Marxism are rapidly accumulating. Just when you recover from your elation over the news from Poland, along comes the latest development in Hungary and then — hardest to believe — in East Germany, that bastion of Communist orthodoxy. It seems that 1989 is destined to be recalled two centuries hence as another *annus mirabilis* — a year of wonders.

In contrast to the optimism on daily display in Europe, the mood of the United States in this historic year appears to be one of uncertainty and even fear. As we join Philip Morris, Inc., in observing the bicentennial of the Bill of Rights, our devotion to the First Amendment guarantee of freedom of speech is being compromised by political opportunism and public indifference.

What is happening in this country? The pilgrims' "city on a hill" has been exchanged for a locked-and-bolted apartment. Our traditional sense of self-assurance, noted long ago by Tocqueville, is giving way to a defensive, mean-spirited narrowness of vision. Perhaps it is the consequence of eight years of institutionalized supply-side selfishness. Or it may be a reaction to the ambiguities of the Vietnam-Watergate-Iran-Contra period: Americans seldom relish ambiguity. Whatever the factors, our nation is, in the military euphemism, advancing toward the rear.

While peoples long subject to totalitarian rule are experiencing the heady sensations of relative or total freedom, Americans are revealing their ambivalence toward their own 200-year-old First Amendment. Despite the fact that flag-burning has never — even during the Vietnam War — been a favorite domestic pastime, the President and other cynical politicians have appealed to the viscera of those still nursing grievances against draft dodgers and the Warren-era Supreme Court. Burn, if you must, the Bill of Rights, they rail, but spare your country's flag. How, one wonders, do they regard the "desecration" of the Hungarian flag by the citizens of Budapest who cut out the Communist emblem at its center?

In the meantime, that estimable friend of South Africa and tobacco, Republican Senator Jesse Helms of North Carolina, has turned art critic in an attempt to impose his provincial world view on the National Endowment for the Arts. That agency now moves with fear and trembling, uncertain whether to disburse funding to art exhibits that might contain naughty pictures or catalogue statements that could be construed as — gasp — political. (Wasn't it Judge Robert Bork, culture hero of the right, who conceded that the First Amendment protects, if nothing else, political expression?)

Closer to home, the good folks at Watson Chapel have celebrated the benefits of the Bill of Rights in their own fashion, possibly as a reminder to the rest of us that 1989 is also the year of Salman Rushdie's *Satanic Verses*. Offended by John Steinbeck's use of "God damn," "crazy bastard," "Jesus Christ" and other terms their students presumably have never heard nor used, the school board has removed his 1937 novel *Of Mice and Men* from their classrooms. It's too bad they didn't act a couple of decades sooner — they might have been able to influence the decision of the Nobel Prize committee. And, of course, earlier this year —

soon after Rushdie had gone into hiding — the Conway school board distinguished itself by banning William Manchester's *Glory and the Dream.*

None of these symptoms of insecurity portend the collapse of the republic, although the national drug-war hysteria carries with it the real potential to induce a siege mentality and a willing acceptance of police-state restrictions on freedoms now taken for granted. (An ABC News-*Washington Post* survey indicates that 52 percent of the American public approve of warrantless searches of homes to combat drugs.) At this point, however, it is clear that the United States, at the end of the short-lived "American Century," is philosophically adrift, farther away than we should be in this year of transformation from the expectations of those hopeful architects of a "more perfect Union." It is ironic that we must be reminded of our 18th-Century ideals by 20th-Century East Germans, Hungarians, Poles and Chinese.

(Bill Jones, November 1989)

The Uptown Backlash

They say the rather stunted life-expectancy of the average man in Bangladesh now exceeds the brief span of existence achieved by the composite black man of New York's Harlem. We should be shocked by this, they say. Shocked because *our* prematurely deceased are, for the most part, victims of poor character as opposed to the much more common victims of poor economies.

The principal character flaw in a black man's constitution is his inability to perceive the difference between healthy habits and unhealthy ones. This has been hinted, listed, spelled out by black leaders on nearly every news show within the last month. At issue is a proposed brand of cigarettes, aimed through the few marketing venues still left open to the tobacco companies—directly for those with a higher billboard "susceptibility": black males.

The cigarette is called "Uptown." Intense market research has prompted R.J. Reynolds, the manufacturer, to fill the niche left by newly abstemious white males, tailoring new cigarettes to meet a black man's preferences. For instance, the Uptown 20-pack, when peeled open, reveals 20 fuzzy ends staring upward. This gimmick, paired with super-elegant print advertising, has caused black leaders nationwide to decry the cynical motives of our nation's marketing barons.

Unfortunately, however, a business is financed by offering products to consumers, and they must choose whether to consume or not. Insinuating that black men haven't the intelligence to choose, nor the stamina to resist, temptation seems to be overtly offensive.

RJR spokesmen have rightly criticized this call for protection from target marketing as a creepy sort of "paternalism," suggesting that black leaders, characterizing themselves as being made of strong moral fiber, intend to protect their weaker brethren from themselves. These self-appointed monitors would force advertisers to limit marketing aimed at the black community to "positive" products — in effect controlling the images, ideas and choices allowed blacks. RJR, bowing to pressure, has dropped plans to test market "Uptown."

No one can be shocked by the revelation that advertising is manipulative. Could any child have watched the fun-loving, respectful and egalitarian family-mannequins who push, say, board games without desiring the same attention and admiration every fourth turn? This particular broadcast fantasy involves all people, regardless of age, in a situation requiring judgment, intelligence and

Examining the Test

In June 1985 the Arkansas Department of Education released aggregate scores for Governor Bill Clinton's much-heralded basic skills test for teachers. The results indicated that 10 percent of the state's teachers had failed. Of the 27 counties in which more than 10 percent had failed, 20 employed more black teachers than the state average of 13 percent. Moreover, at least 25 percent of the teachers in the five counties where more than 20 percent did not pass were black. Yet the D of E, wary of further controversy, declined to compile statistics indicating performance by race.

Spectrum *contended that disclosure was necessary so the public could assess the reasons for the apparent racial disparity in test results. "Was the test culturally biased?" the paper asked. "Or does this indicate an unequal commitment to public education in the southeast Arkansas counties where the failure rate was highest?" It fell to* Spectrum *to provide the information, based on census data compiled from records submitted to the federal Equal Opportunity Commission. The figures suggested that the approximately 4,500 black teachers who took the test failed at a rate of about 35 percent. "This is not exactly the kind of thing one remedies in one-on-one training sessions with teachers," an editorial lamented.*

action wherein common rules divest one's parents of the power to make decisions for their children. Board games are sold. In reality, those with little power will always incur parental guidance. Whether that is in the best interests of the black community is debatable. But power is undeniably tied to economic clout, and blacks must be allowed to play in America's capitalistic game to achieve financial independence, and thereby achieve freedom from their protectors. Designing products that recognize this vastly underutilized economic clout is a positive step, as is target marketing. With the freedom to choose, blacks may one day be able to light their pipes and smoke them.

(Philip Martin, January 1990)

Delta Blues

In April 1990, Clay Hathorn wrote: "The Delta is a land both fertile and blighted. Straddling that big mean river, stretching from southern Illinois to the Gulf of Mexico, it is the cradle of the first blues we know much about — the land of the sharecroppers. It is a stunningly flat, stunningly green plain. ... [T]he Delta can seem picturesque, with its unpainted wood shacks gone to silver, its tin roofs and whitewashed tires gleaming and quaint. Even poverty can look romantic when the light hits it right."

Though Hathorn's story — which was subsequently reprinted in The Nation, The Dallas Morning News *and* Southern Exposure *— anticipated the findings of a federal commission appointed to study the region and make recommendations on how to turn the Delta's economy around by the end of the century, it wasn't the first time that* Spectrum *had focused on the region. In June 1988, associate editor Anthony Moser detailed the pathology of poverty in the region, which Arkansas Senator Dale Bumpers likened to a "third-world" country.*

Gerrymandering Is Gerrymandering

There can be no denying that our state's existing legislative boundaries were drafted in such a manner as to keep blacks out of the Arkansas legislature. That much should be apparent simply in the observation that the current system manages to send only six blacks as representatives or senators to the Capitol out of 135 — four from Little Rock, one from Pine Bluff and one from Crittenden County.

Thus, it is long past due that these boundaries were redrawn by the federal courts, even if they are due to be redrafted again in 1990 after the new census. That much of the recent news from the federal courthouse is welcome.

Unacceptable, however, is the notion that black-majority districts must be at least 60 percent black because black candidates are not likely to prevail in districts with a lesser racial majority. This argument — advanced by the plaintiffs in the case and recently adopted by a three-judge panel — holds that black-majority districts should be gerrymandered in this manner to make up for the fact that blacks of voting age are less likely to participate in the electoral process than their white counterparts. U.S. Circuit Judge Richard Arnold wrote in his majority ruling that federal civil rights law does not require "that black political superiority be ensured by artificial means." Yet Arnold's opinion elsewhere makes a mockery of this principle, arguing that the extraordinary majorities are justified due to the history of low voter registration and turnout among blacks of the Delta.

To accept this misguided argument is to redirect the focus of civil rights law from its proper aim — ensuring equal opportunities to all voters — to that of predetermining the outcome of legislative elections. It's one thing to require that governmental boundaries mirror the populations they represent. That much is not only just, but long overdue. But to argue that black districts need to be heavily black is to accept the idea that the court, and not the voters, should have the final say in determining who goes to the statehouse.

Stacking the deck with the intention of guaranteeing the election of a candidate of one particular race — even a race long under-represented in the General Assembly due to discrimination — is to commit the very same sin the court was supposedly remedying. The rights of minorities ought to be protected, but not enhanced.

(Stephen Buel, February 1990)

Displaying Little Regard for the Mysteries of Life

There are many simple questions for which science has no simple answers, and some of the simplest involve life itself. Two of those questions pertain to current events. One is "When did the human species come into existence?" and the other is "When does the life of an individual begin?"

Science does not have the answers to these questions. It does not have the answer to the former because a definitive pattern of human evolution has not been established. To the latter, science has no answer because it is not able to answer a more fundamental question: What is life?

This pair of simple questions is of current interest because of the points of view espoused by the creationism and pro-life movements, both of which have received considerable political attention and are about to receive more. Creationism arguments emanating from Louisiana will be heard later this year by the United States Supreme Court. In Arkansas, as well as several other states, the pro-life movement has helped put an anti-abortion amendment on the November 4 ballot.

Both the pro-lifers and the creationists have experienced setbacks in Arkansas in recent years. In early 1982, U.S. District Judge William R. Overton ruled against the equal-time teaching of creationism with evolution, saying that "creation science" is a religious point of view, not a scientific one. Two years ago, the Arkansas Supreme Court disallowed the ballot title of the Unborn Child Amendment, saying the title was misleading. The amendment was renamed "The Limitation of Abortion Funding Amendment" by the Unborn Child Amendment Committee and will appear on this year's ballot as Amendment 65.

The people responsible for the creationism and pro-life movements share a common belief concerning the time scale of the beginning of life. Creationists say the human species appeared virtually instantaneously, and pro-life proponents say that the life of an individual begins in the same fashion. The pro-life movement's point of view was stated a few months ago during a KLRE interview, when the vice-president of the Unborn Child Amendment Committee at one point said, "Life begins at conception." Not "We believe life begins at conception," but "Life begins at conception," as if the statement represented an unquestionable fact.

Those of us who will admit to not being sure when life begins must ask of the pro-life movement, "How do you know that?" The only thing science has to offer in this regard is that there is a unique set of DNA present after fertilization occurs. But uniqueness and the existence of life are not the same thing.

More satisfactory from a scientific standpoint is the view that life does not begin at a certain moment, but rather that it evolves from one stage to another — from separate and living sperm and ovum to fetus, and from there to a full-fledged human being. Such a point of view does not imply that there is nothing wrong with abortion. On the contrary, it says that abortion is very disrespectful of the mystery of human life. However, by stating unequivocally that human life begins at conception, the pro-life movement is also disrespectful of this mystery.

Creationists have also shown little regard for the mystery of human origins. There is validity to the creationists' criticism that some people falsely accept evolution as a fact. That is not a problem with evolution but with people's understanding of science. This problem is only worsened by the arguments put forward by the creationist movement, because the creationists have created the perception that people must accept one theory or another, when in fact people do

Issue 42, February 1987.

not have to accept any scientific theory as fact. That includes such now-obvious theories as Newton's theory of universal gravitation.

It is appropriate to mention gravitation at this point, because it, like evolution, can be said to contradict the Book of Genesis. Before Newton, it was imagined that celestial bodies moved in accordance with divine law, not in accordance with any natural law that could be described by humankind. What Newton did for physics, Darwin did for biology. Newton discovered universal gravitation and described it with a simple equation, and Darwin discovered the evolution of the species, which he described in terms of the law of natural selection.

To put the scientific viewpoint in its proper setting, the late UCLA astronomer George Abell, who gave an energetic lecture at the University of Arkansas at Little Rock one afternoon not long before he died, included a section called "What science is and is not" in the first chapter of his highly-regarded astronomy textbook. Abell wrote, "One could argue, technically, that the sun and moon do not exist at all — that we are dreaming the whole thing. Most of us accept the existence of a real world; moreover, we accept many scientific theories as fact — such as the rotation and revolution of the earth. But in this acceptance we are going beyond the rules of science into religious belief. Science does not dictate as fact that the earth moves, but only that its motion is required by Newtonian "theory."

In light of Abell's words, it should be reiterated that some people's acceptance of evolution as fact must be regarded as scientific naivete or as a pseudo-religious belief. But even if one chooses, for the sake of argument, to consider the latter case, there is still no credence warranted for the creationists' claim that the theory of evolution is itself the equivalent of a religious belief. Evolution, including human evolution, is no more and no less godless than the theory of gravitation.

The creationists apparently are not satisfied with such a separation of religion and science. They wish to take the literal translation of the Book of Genesis and pit it against evolution in the arena of scientific theory. In doing so, they force people to make a choice between evolution and Genesis, much as the pro-life movement forces people to choose between the belief that life begins at conception and the belief that abortion is perfectly proper. In short, the creationist argument equates evolution with atheism, and the pro-life argument equates abortion with murder. That these two arguments do not have any scientific validity hardly matters if they are given political validity in the coming weeks.

(David Trulock, October 1986)

Vultures Over Barnhill

The feeding frenzy has officially begun. The journalistic vultures are flying so thick and furiously over the University of Arkansas at Fayetteville's Barnhill Arena they may need an air traffic controller to prevent mid-air collisions. The object of their appetite is Razorback basketball coach Nolan Richardson, whose Hogs, after a disastrous season in his maiden 1985-86 campaign, are struggling once again this year.

In a period of five days a little over a week ago, the sportswriters and editors of Little Rock's two daily newspapers lined up against Richardson in a nearly unanimous formation. It is now clear that Arkansas's first black head coach in any major sport is well on his way to being slam-dunked, although he may get one more season before being thrown overboard.

The opening salvo was fired by *Arkansas Gazette* "Senior" Sports Editor Orville Henry, who emerged from his early season polka-dot euphoria to pronounce Richardson's coaching of the road game against Texas "awful," and to pummel the coach's tactics from beginning to end. Richardson's quotes were placed in the sort of context that made him sound like a simpleton, and Henry concluded by sarcastically remarking, "Now that would be a lick — Richardson taking these guys to the Final Four [former coach Eddie] Sutton envisioned for them."

Since Henry's comments on such sensitive subjects are generally regarded as carrying the imprimatur of Arkansas Athletic Director Frank Broyles, *Arkansas Democrat* Managing Editor John Robert Starr announced a few days later that fans should regard Henry's column as the official "kiss of death" for Nolan. Starr also repeated the rumor that Broyles has been going around the state telling the big-time money-men behind the Hog program that he made "a grave mistake when he hired Richardson, but he couldn't afford to fire the university's first black coach." Starr all but endorsed the Dump Nolan campaign, referring to him as a "poor coach," and chiding him for making excuses, especially the one he evidently made after the Texas loss:

"We just can never get any breaks [from the officials]," Richardson reportedly said. "This league isn't ready for a black coach. I told my players that I'm sorry I'm their coach right now. I'm hurting their chances because of it."

Henry's column appeared February 6; Starr's on February 10. On February 7, Kane Webb, one of the *Democrat's* two Razorback beat men (and that's "beat" as in regular assignment, not "Beat" as in Kerouac; the *Democrat* has none of them), delivered perhaps the most stinging criticism of the lot. "They've had enough chances and, Lord knows, we've heard enough excuses," Webb began, adding this descriptive sentence to sum up the Hogs: "They are, in a word, bad." After quoting Richardson's comment about the officials' reaction to his race, Webb ended his piece by saying, "If Richardson is correct and the SWC isn't ready for a black coach, that's a shame. If Richardson thinks the officials are responsible for any loss, that's a crock."

The next day, *Democrat* Sports Editor Wally Hall strongly suggested in a unique "sports editorial" that it was time for Nolan to point himself in the general direction of the state line. Hall reported that Richardson was not even in Broyles' top five choices back in 1985, and was hired, more or less, by default. He accused Richardson of using on-court profanity (!), and chastised Richardson for raising the specter of racism.

Webb's column in the *Democrat*, including Richardson's controversial quote concerning racism, was a scoop the *Gazette* didn't have. So, several days later, Henry lamely responded by attempting to portray the Democrat writers as irresponsible, asserting that Richardson's comment was a confidential aside not intended for publication. He blasted the competition's lack of ethics. This is rubbish. If reporters reported only what the principals wanted the public to hear, readers would be misinformed indeed. Henry is grasping at straws; his frustration at not being allowed to act as exclusive kiss-of-death dispatcher for Broyles was evident in the fury he directed against the *Democrat*, abandoning his normal, condescending reference to it as "another newspaper," and this time naming the *Democrat*, Webb, Hall and Starr all by name. Anyone notice how personal all this is getting?

During this entire siege, Richardson's only stalwart defender was the *Gazette*'s Nate Allen, a longtime Fayetteville correspondent who, much to his credit, had the gumption to issue a rebuttal to Henry, his former boss. But, quite tellingly, the *Gazette* played Henry on page one. Allen, whose column often appears on the front of the sports section, was shunted inside this time.

Take This Job ...

In an interview with Anthony Moser in November 1987, Little Rock's Channel 7 "Live at Five" co-anchor Deborah Mathis lashed out against the personnel practices and editorial judgment of the city's television news departments. She was particularly unsparing toward her own station's drift toward favoring "fluffy, soft features" over hard news.

As a black woman, Mathis said, she had found a "barrier out there" unconsciously erected by management: "They've come from a background where black people are not the mainstream." When the "Six and Ten" female co-anchor left Channel 7, Mathis thought she might have had a chance at the principal slots. Instead, the ABC affiliate imported two young, white, blond-haired reporters from out of state, and Mathis remained at her post on "Live at Five."

Mathis acknowledged that "I don't come across ... as the warm, all-loving anchorwoman. I don't think my job is to make people feel soothed and comfortable." Someone somewhere evidently felt uncomfortable, and several months after the Spectrum *article appeared, Mathis left Channel 7. She now writes regular columns as a member of the* Arkansas Gazette *editorial board.*

Gaze Of An Assassin?

Whodunit?

In January 1990, Spectrum published a story by two British journalists, John Sergeant and John Edginton, which revealed new information on the assassination of the Reverend Martin Luther King Jr. A convicted murderer serving time in a federal prison in Oklahoma claimed to have been intimately involved in a widespread conspiracy that resulted in King's death, and he seemed to have intimate and encyclopedic knowledge of the details of the case.

Jules "Ricco" Kimble, asserted that the conspiracy involved Central Intelligence Agency agents as well as members of the Memphis Police Department and organized crime figures. Sergeant and Edginton did the bulk of the reporting on the story while preparing a documentary on King's murder for the BBC. Their program, Who Killed Martin Luther King?, was broadcast in Britain in September 1989 and aired in the United States in the summer of 1990.

Should Nolan Richardson get the axe? Let's look at the facts. The Porkers were 12-16 last year; and a dismal 4-12 in the Southwest Conference. They aren't doing one heck of a lot better this season. They are almost hilariously inconsistent, and downright pitiful on the road. Richardson's a great recruiter, but his X's and O's on-court coaching seems a little nonsensical at times, and his inability to settle on a starting lineup way over two months into the season is downright flabbergasting. But his absence from the team during the tragic illness and death of his daughter Yvonne no doubt contributed to the squad's lack of cohesion and chemistry, and no one would dispute that family comes first.

Just who are these sportswriters to knit Nolan's name into the roster of those to be guillotined? They are all behaving like some sort of demented Madame DeFarge with a word processor. All last season and through much of this season they treated the Razorbacks with kid gloves, instead of pointing out their manifold sins and weaknesses on the court. The build-up they supplied was so big that a letdown was inevitable. We were going to see a new breed of "Hawgball," for which the *Democrat* sponsored T-shirts. We were soon to be "Rollin' With Nolan." And let us not forget that just a few short weeks ago, after Arkansas beat then-No. 6-ranked Kansas in Barnhill, Henry exhorted us to "Run the Polka-Dot flag up the flagpole!" — a reference to Richardson's distinctive speckled sartorial splendor. Now a *Democrat* headline asks us: "Are Polka Dots The Right Image?"

Richardson's racial comment was regrettable, but there is indeed more than just a hint of racism within all of this. Anyone who hasn't been living on a mountain top in Tibet has heard the slew of Richardson gags going around, most of which are out-and-out darkie jokes, as Gene Lyons of the *Arkansas Times* so aptly put it. And the word on the street is that the heavyweight Razorback Club types have instructed Broyles and UA President Ray Thornton, to wit: "Never, under any circumstances, hire a black head coach, *ever again.*"

It will be a sad day for the University and the state if Richardson is fired. Hiring him was the single most courageous thing Frank Broyles has done in his official capacity. It sent out a message, that we as a state have outgrown Faubus-era hatred, the racial acrimony of 1957 and Central High, the Jim Crow pettiness and the cancerous prejudices that diminish us all.

Wally Hall is wrong. We do not "owe" Richardson another year. He deserves another year. Three years is the standard length of time most successful coaches are given to rebuild when they take over a program in decline, and the Hogs were definitely in decline, even before Sutton left. Richardson has been successful every place he has worked, including a national junior college championship and a five-year record of 119-37 at Tulsa. He can make us winners, too. We hope the Razorbacks pull it together in time for the Southwest Conference tournament. It's not impossible. And if they could win the tourney and get into the NCAAs, who knows, they might win a game or two, if they play as they did against Ohio State and Kansas. Richardson's definitely on the ropes, but he's still swinging. And that we are glad of.

(Anthony Moser, February 1987)

Nolan Richardson led the Arkansas Razorbacks to the NCAA "Final Four" national championship tournament in the spring of 1990. As this book went to the printer, the 1991 Razorbacks were ranked number five in the nation.

Taking Another Bite from Free Speech Guarantees

In early July, the United States Supreme Court took another chunk out of First Amendment freedom of speech guarantees.

At issue was the power of government to prohibit gambling advertising in Puerto Rico except where such advertising is directed at tourists. The court upheld the right of the state to ban advertising of an activity as a power included in the right to ban the activity itself.

Instead of shuddering, many citizens, seeing the decision as a step toward banning cigarette advertising, greeted the gambling advertisement ruling with glee.

This sort of narrow perspective is regrettable, as are the current efforts in Congress to restrict cigarette advertising itself. The gambling decision has opened the door for wholesale restrictions on all types of commercial speech which could go far beyond banning cigarette advertising, which itself should not be restricted. Of course, as would be the case in outlawing cigarette ads, these restrictions would be the children of good intentions.

The basic argument used by the court in upholding the advertising ban is spurious — and dangerous. The court contended that the lesser power to ban advertising of an activity is included in the power to ban the activity itself. Here the court confuses regulation of speech with regulation of action — an essential constitutional distinction that previous courts have spent years defining. The two activities of government are distinct, separated by the First Amendment's increasingly threatened protection of speech and expression.

The court has long followed the "clear and present danger" doctrine for restricting the freedoms of speech guaranteed by the First Amendment. This means that expression can only be prohibited if it presents a definite and real danger to the public.

Since prior courts did not find clear and present danger in publication of works as diverse as the Pentagon Papers and plans to build an atomic bomb, advertisement of gambling in Puerto Rico cannot be considered as much more than a clear and present irritant.

Furthermore, if there were a real danger from the advertisement of gambling, it would be just as dangerous to advertise the activity to tourists as well as residents. Elsewhere in rulings of the court, such discrimination between classes of citizens has been prohibited. But in the Burger Court's attempt to walk the fence between moralism and public plunder, it has fallen gracelessly into an indefensible muddle of legal contradictions.

This is a very bad decision. But when delivered by the Supreme Court, even an opinion as shaky as this becomes an almost unshakable precedent. More spurious legal reasoning is bound to be constructed along the same dangerous lines.

(Jess Henderson, August 1986)

Dr. Leo Buscaglia vs. Andre the Giant

James Neff

James Neff, the most frequent contributor of art to Spectrum, *has a surgeon's hand when it comes to satirizing the "touchy-feelie" elements in society.*

Philip Martin

Against the Democratization of Education

Issue 107, July 1989.

In this age of egalitarianism, it is perhaps illiberal to suggest that the Republic might be better off if fewer citizens elected to go to college. It would be elitist to suggest that the democratization of higher education — one of the great American experiments— has failed.

Call me elitist. Bring back the meritocracy.

The question of who is fit for college brings to light all of the confusing and conflicting notions Americans hold about such things as equality, excellence and the encouragement of talent. Some, among them Arkansas Governor Bill Clinton, like to believe that the more people are exposed to the university, the higher will be the levels of public competence, understanding and culture. Traditional liberal thinking accepts the power of the university to reduce the gap between wealth and poverty.

Unfortunately, the true fruits of democratic education have been an erosion of intellectual standards and the steady devaluation of the college degree. College graduates are everywhere, and no one seems capable of critical thought any more. Anyone who interviews applicants for entry-level jobs knows about the preponderance of semi-literate college graduates. Best-sellers such as Allan Bloom's *The Closing of the American Mind* have been written about how stupid we have become, and though Professor Bloom's book is flawed by an incomplete understanding of the youth culture he so abhors as well as by a general lack of generosity, his arguments are difficult to refute.

We have become a nation of philistines. Most of our state universities have been corrupted into trade schools that seek merely to provide students with a rudimentary understanding of the rules of the game — be the game accounting, management, journalism or engineering — and four years of decently played football in exchange for their tuitions. In a radio address a couple of weeks ago, Clinton suggested that although "the college-going rate" of Arkansas's high school seniors has increased from 38 percent six years ago to 45 percent last year, if the state wants to compete with other states for good jobs, then it would have to make strides toward approaching the national average of 55 percent. Clinton is right when he says we need to do a better job of educating our people. He is wrong when he suggests that putting more people in higher education is the way to go about it.

What we need to do is increase the quality of the product that comes out of our colleges. The only way to do this is to constrict the flood of unprepared students. Our colleges are swamped with indifferent students — the bored stupid youth of a nation in intellectual decline. Somehow the idea of continued education has been muddled with the idea of college. In our minds college has become some kind of magical key that opens the door to the good life — a requisite to decent work at a decent wage. We do our children a disservice when we lead them to assume useful learning and growth come only from attending college, from listening to tweedy men talk from behind lecterns and reproducing required information on occasions called examinations.

Forced continuance of education may simply prolong a situation in which an untalented student is doomed to fail. Countless students have been pointlessly injured in schools that did not prepare them to earn a living and undermined their

Columns

In Spectrum's *columns, the institutional schizophrenia of the editorial staff is given even freer rein. Name your hobby-horse (feminism, elitism, libertarianism, whatever) and you're bound to find someone riding.*

Also Sprach Allan Bloom

The surprise best-seller of the summer of 1987 was Allan Bloom's diatribe, The Closing of the American Mind. *In his review of the book, Bill Jones applauded the University of Chicago professor for his refreshing "refusal to mouth the ritual pieties" but termed his uniformed rant against rock music a descent "to the visceral level of a crank." The greatest value of the work, in Jones's view, was that "in the heyday of the M.B.A., [it] brings [Cardinal] Newman's concept of a liberal education [as 'an end sufficient to rest in and pursue for its own sake'] back to the center of the debate."*

confidence beyond repair. Other clever, though uninterested, students glide through an overcrowded system with their intellectual character and fitness untested. It is no wonder that expectations have diminished — if everyone in a society must be "above average" to be considered of worth, the "average" must go underground.

We need to scale down our emphasis on college and legitimize alternative forms of higher education. Properly understood, a college or university merely offers one kind of specialized education, a brand suited to the needs of a relative few. Aristotle said democratic education was not education that blindly embraced the masses, but the education that worked to preserve democracy. It is a cruel mistake to regard college as a necessary component of the American Dream, and it is wrong-headed to regard a college education as a right.

(May 1989)

Stephen Buel

A Logo is Worth a Thousand Words

I love that scene in *The Wizard Of Oz* where the scrawny guy behind the curtain stops pretending he's a wizard. Once his charade is revealed, he suddenly gets friendly and tells his visitors how they can get more out of life. The Scarecrow doesn't really need a brain to get ahead. Heck, brains are a dime a dozen. What the scarecrow needs is a degree — something prestigious-looking that will make him stand out in a crowd.

I've got a similar piece of advice for people or organizations craving news coverage to help legitimize their events. Don't make the mistake of assuming news will catch the media's attention. Dozens of real news events don't receive any attention each and every day. If you really want to get front-page coverage or make the evening news, you need a logo.

Take the case of those five Soviet women who barreled through Arkansas last week. From my limited understanding of the event, I'm told that its purpose was not to sign any treaties or negotiate any trade agreements, but to forge a few "peace links" between our women and their women. Women, after all, have a greater sensitivity to issues like peace and friendship because they're more nurturing than us guys. Just ask Margaret Thatcher.

To me, it looked more like a vacation. But did you ever see such news coverage? I bet I had a better time during my New Year's Eve visit to Key West a few months ago, but damned if I could get one bit of news coverage of my trip. Not even a five-minute interview on "Live At Five." Reporters there were all too busy commentating about the suspicious demise of *The Miami News*, the only competitor to *The Miami Herald*. Too bad, because I'd have had a few things to say about that.

My problem down there in Florida was that I didn't have a logo. Those Soviet women sure did — a nice two-color one done up by Jim Johnson of Cranford Johnson Robinson, the state's largest advertising agency. Johnson's logo said far more about East-West relations than any of the news stories I read about the Soviet women's vacation. It featured the outline of two women's heads, each staring at the other in profile. Both faces were outlined by twin, Barbara Walters-style hairdos, each concealing a national symbol — a hammer and sickle in the Soviet woman's hair and the Stars and Stripes in the American's. The clever thing about it was how the two women's faces were mirror images of each other — as if to drive home the point that underneath it all, Yanks and Commies are really just plain folks.

Because they had such a groovy logo, anything those women did was news. Alexandra Schevchenko pets a piglet and it makes page one of the *Arkansas Gazette*. (Of course, piglets are also logos in Arkansas. Ms. Schevchenko's encounter with a water buffalo could have been far more interesting, but it only made the feature section. Oxen don't make good logos.) In typical commie-bashing fashion, the *Arkansas Democrat* didn't pay much attention at first. But then somebody dared to mess with a logo that the *Democrat* respects, and even flies on its front page — the American flag. Once *Democrat* reporters got wind of International Paper's decision to fly the Soviet flag over its Pine Bluff paper mill in honor of the women, they cut loose, devoting more than 40 inches of newsprint to the affair. After all, this was news; three anonymous callers had complained to the *Democrat* about this brazen use of the communist logo.

I wonder whether those poor Soviet tourists ever wished they didn't have such a nice logo. Because they did, they were subjected to 11 straight days of news media treatment that seemed to imply they were a different species of life than you and I. TV did its part too. One local reporter went so far as to volunteer, in an interview, how he wouldn't even try to pronounce one of the women's last names because he'd probably mess it up. Maybe women *are* more sensitive than men.

(April 1989)

Anne Neville

Giving in to Fear

The three men walking toward us looked bigger in the dark.

We were three, as well, young and collegiate; three white girls out on the town, trying hard as we knew to be grown-ups. The men walking toward us were about our age — only boys, really, though we didn't see it that way then. In our wide eyes, they were the urban denizens we hoped to pass for that night in our tight black and glossberry lips. Lanky and easy as they walked alone in the warm evening, they laughed among themselves as we drew near on the narrow city sidewalk.

Drawing ourselves up tall and tense on our shaky heels in that suddenly dead quiet street, we smiled — so cool — as we passed the three young men. We nodded. They nodded. It was a stylized, civil moment and once it had passed brief glances of relief and self-congratulation flashed among the three of us as we continued along the quiet night street toward the well-lighted restaurant where we would order our sweet, colored drinks and let our breath out completely.

We hadn't walked 10 feet further when we heard it. One voice, louder than the rest, floated back from the group of young men we had just passed.

"Sheee-yit, they're *scared* of us!"

Political Correction

Stephen Buel's column, "A Logo Is Worth A Thousand Words," provoked response from several quarters. Terre McLendon, the events chairman of the Soviet-American Women's Exchange, characterized the piece as "an ill-organized jumble of sentences that purport to criticize an event" about which Buel knew very little. On the other hand, Jim Johnson, of Cranford Johnson Robinson Associates, the firm which designed the logo in question, wrote to thank Buel for his "fine comments" about the Soviet Women's logo.

On still another hand, former Spectrum associate editor Anthony Moser, who had moved on to the Arkansas Democrat, checked in with a letter criticizing the media for fawning over the Soviet visitors. "Those were not ordinary peace-lovin' Russian proles who were tromping around our state. These were the hired henchmen — pardon me, henchwomen — of one of the most repressive regimes in the world."

Moser's letter also drew a response, from Kelley Bass, then the assistant features editor at the Arkansas Gazette: "Now Tony Moser's gone and done it! He's uncovered the truth about the Arkansas Gazette ... We at the Gazette are a bunch of Commie sympathizers. In fact, we covered the Arkansas visit of our comradettes from the motherland in hopes that the entire state would see the superiority of the Soviet way."

He was amused, incredulous. And he was right.

And I was ashamed.

We were frightened that night because three other humans happened to be male, happened to be black, and happened upon us when we were vulnerable. They showed no hostility, meant us no harm. But we knew our statistics, had read for years the advice that told us to cross the street, to hail a cab, to ring a doorbell, to be safe rather than sorry and to ask questions later. The young men were Other to us, and Other was enough to trigger our fear.

That fear was legitimate, though its object that evening was mistaken. Another night, another three men — or three women or three large dogs — might well have harmed us, and there was no way for us to know a harmless encounter until the moment had passed. Because we had no means of intuiting intent, our caution was as reasonable as our knee-jerk suspicion was ugly. All of us had been threatened and harassed by strangers; all of us understood that our security was a fragile thing, resting almost entirely upon the independent decisions of millions of strangers not to harm us.

The worst thing about fear is that it corrodes the finest part of the soul. Fear knows neither charity not benevolence. It is an unthinking, irrational emotion, making the random stranger its focus, an enemy by definition. Like some wild jungle thing, it tenses at an unfamiliar step, at a silhouetted bulk in a doorway.

Fear makes us less than we are. It makes us quick to slander in our minds, to generalize from single horrors and focus our gut terror upon strangers, upon Others who are of necessity guilty until proven innocent. One of the finest things that makes us human is a desire to trust without proven reason to do so; to believe in a community of man and to do and receive good within the context of that idea — to depend, in short, upon the kindness of strangers.

In a society where Others are ever more numerous and the reasons to fear multiply with each day's newly reported atrocities, that ideal becomes ever more elusive. The sadness and the correctness of my unmerited fear of three young men one dark urban night long ago bothers me to this day. My reaction would be the same if I saw them tomorrow.

(March 1990)

A NORML Boy

Spectrum profiled the 17-year-old president of Arkansas NORML in issue 75 (May 1988).

Philip Martin

On Narcing

In the long-ago time before St. Mikhail rehabilitated the Soviet character, our grade school teachers periodically impressed upon us how horrible it would be to live in that land of gray steppes and crummy concrete. In Russia, they told us, all allegiance is due the state. In Russia, they told us, children often turned their own parents in for acts of disloyalty. Our teachers allowed us to imagine Khrushchev pinning heavy medals to the kids' chests as their ragged parents huddled in the cattle cars that would take them to Siberia.

While some of us — probably those who grew up to live messy, mismanaged lives as serial killers or talk-show hosts — may have relished a chance to turn our parents in, the American psyche generally detests a rat-fink snitch. I know I do.

In junior high school there was nothing we hated more than "narcs." The word wasn't strictly applied to undercover narcotics agents — in fact, the few of us who weren't unrepentant "heads" by the time we were 13 probably thought an undercover narcotics agent was a pretty groovy thing to be; you got to shoot guns and stuff. We used "narc" as a slightly more adult synonym for "tattletale," and we knew that our first loyalties were to each other. If there was trouble among us we would work it out. Involving the authorities was unthinkable.

Of course, as we grew older we realized there were some situations where the authorities had to be notified. We grew to understand the need for police and we were grateful for their presence. But they were to be held in reserve. We believed that people should be tolerant with other people's behavior up to a point. Sometimes that point coincided with the law, but most of the time the law was a little less forgiving than our own particular scheme of justice.

And therefore I don't think I'll be phoning the number on the billboard that, according to the hype, every Arkansan will see in the next three months. I don't think I'll drop a dime on this particular aspect of crime. It's not that I'm for drugs exactly — I've seen a lot of people with a lot of problems that they've compounded by using drugs — it's just that my allegiances and priorities lie elsewhere. And I don't understand the need for a special "turn-your-drug-addict-neighbor-in" hotline. The whole thing strikes me as Un-American. Are there really people who don't know they can call the police if they witness some wrongdoing? If I see someone committing a major crime I'll probably call the police. If I see someone using or selling drugs I'll probably mind my own business.

I guess that strikes some people as basically unpatriotic. I'm sorry, but I believe it's possible to love one's country without being overly fond of its *apparatchiks*. I will grant that there is a drug problem, though I'll debate whether it's any worse than it was three or five or 10 or 20 years ago. And I'm not sure, given the other problems facing this state and this country, that the current emphasis on The War on Drugs is entirely warranted. Call me a conscientious objector. Hell no, I won't go.

If I'd wanted to fight the War on Drugs I had my chance in 1982. That was the year Ted Gary, the Chief Deputy of the Jefferson Davis Parish Sheriff's Department way down in South Louisiana, tried to recruit me to work as a real narc. I just said no.

Like Ted, lots of people who want you to dial that hotline number have good motives — a lot of them think we're in the midst of a crisis that calls for extraordinary measures. I think they're wrong. It's no worse than it was.

What really bothers me, I guess, is that there seems to be no one saying "wait a minute, there's more at stake here than putting bad people in jail and ridding our country of an awful scourge." What bothers me is that we're creating a drug hysteria that will make it easy for our legislators to do things we'll later regret. I'm troubled that there seem to be so few dissenters, so few who seem to think that we at least ought to step back and think about what we're doing.

(November 1989)

Stephen Buel

Reporting Rape

When I was a student at the University of California, a Berkeley cop was charged with raping a San Francisco woman. Berkeley was suffering through an unrelated series of rapes at the time, and the case received wide publicity. The

Enemies List

1	Rating This Week
1	Weeks On Chart
☛	With A Bullet

1   Ron Fuller
1   The state rep from Pleasant Valley scored big points on the Republican double-speak scale at a UALR student rally October 12 by urging students to support a tax increase for education, which Fuller said he couldn't support himself until fat is cut from the state budget.

2   Beryl Anthony
1   House Ways and Means Committeeman Anthony voted to deprive Arkansas ratepayers of the $200 million in refunds owed them by utilities. The utilities collected ratepayer money for taxes they now don't have to pay because of tax reform; instead of insisting on a prompt refund, big-biz pawn Anthony allowed them 30 years to do so. Coincidentally, Beryl the Squirrel got $22,000 in campaign funds from utilities.

3   Bill Clinton
3   The governor, now a legislative follower instead of a leader, has given up on education and is letting the constitutional experts in our legislature draw up a paranoid anti-drug agenda. Looks to us like Bill's joined the race for governor.

4   Tommy Robinson
13   Our bloodlusty congressman gripes that no one has been executed in Arkansas in 20 years, promising to be *the lethal-injection governor* if elected. He forgets, or perhaps just doesn't know, that he has no control over the appeals process, and that Clinton has signed his share of death warrants.

5   Wally Hall
1   The Democrat's sports editor and resident homophobe referred to the San Francisco-Oakland World Series as "the fairyland feud" not once, but twice, on his low-brow call-in show on Channel 4. What's that dead animal on your head, Wally?

6   The Arkansas Gazette
☛   For stealing away newly bourgeois Spectrum associate editor Jimmy "The Weasel" Nichols, who leaves us now to fight for his share of the Gazette's shrinking newshole. Spectrum's loss is Gannett's gain. Good luck Jim; call us when the dailies merge.

Enemies List

The "Enemies List" was exactly what it said it was — a vicious, unfair and vindictive list of mostly local people and institutions Spectrum *deemed worthy of derision. It was great fun while it lasted.*

Double Standard?

Responding to "Reporting Rape," Fran Jansen of Little Rock wrote: "If Buel truly believes that the 'failure to identify rape victims is responsible, in part, for the strange stigma attached to its victims,' then why did he not do his part to erase the stigma by revealing the name of his friend who was raped?"

Buel replied: "To argue that rape victim's names should be revealed in news stories ... is not to suggest that they should be casually bandied about whenever it suits a writer's purpose," noting that only three sentences of his column dealt with the incident involving his friend.

In a February 1990 story, "Rape Crisis," Spectrum reported that in 1988 Little Rock recorded 27 more rapes than Washington, D.C. The article quoted several rape victims by name.

police officer, as I recall, was suspended from duty pending a verdict. I couldn't wait to see him jailed.

Operating under a policy that governs most media, area newspapers did not report the name of the alleged victim. Although the name of the accused officer was used so frequently as to become a household word, the name of his accuser was never revealed. Then the *San Francisco Chronicle* accidentally printed the accuser's name, and a remarkable story unfolded. Witnesses suddenly turned up to dispute the woman's story. It became clear the officer had been innocent all along. Far from being the aggressor we'd imagined him to be, he was the victim of a compulsive liar with a history of pressing false charges.

Because I'd believed the cop was guilty, his case intrigued me. I was taking a journalism ethics class at the time, and I argued that newspapers should publish the names of both the accused and the accuser in cases of rape. It was an unpopular position. It still is.

Nonetheless, I believe it is irresponsible for the news media to report an accusation and print the name of the accused but not the accuser. That's why I oppose the use of unnamed sources in most cases. If such reporting could almost cost this man his reputation, allegations of rape should either never be reported or both names should be published.

I don't mean to suggest that most people accused of rape are innocent victims. Rape is a brutal, violent crime, and I'm inclined to believe most any woman brave enough to go public with her story and risk the firestorm of notoriety that her actions may bring down upon her.

Society probably holds more misconceptions about rape than any other crime. The failure to identify rape victims is responsible, in part, for the strange stigma attached to its victims. By withholding victims' names, the media unwittingly perpetuates the myth that they are "bad" or "careless" girls who have asked to be victimized.

Because rape is portrayed as a sexual act as opposed to a violent crime, the victims of rape are often treated as if they were the aggressor. All too often, the victim, and not the rapist, ends up being the person whose credibility is questioned. Society treats rape victims this way because most people, particularly men, do not have a clear picture of who rape victims are and how pervasive this crime is.

At the time of the Berkeley case, I encountered a statistic indicating that one in every three women are raped during their lifetimes. This number startles me as much today as it did then. If this is true, then all of us know women who have been raped. And yet — without a clear portrait of the real victims of rape — society clings to the media image of rape victims as willing victims. In reality, they're our neighbors and loved ones.

The concept that rape victims get what's coming to them is perhaps the most abhorrent idea in modern criminal justice. Think of rape as a violent crime — and not a sexual act, as is it usually portrayed in the media — and the repugnance of this attitude becomes even clearer. Would anyone even momentarily suggest that the victim of a non-sexual assault asked to be assaulted? Of course not.

A friend of mine was raped last month. I have great sympathy for her. Because the courts don't take rape any more seriously than the rest of society, the teenager she has accused of raping her was released from jail because the jails are "too full." Strange, but there was plenty of room in the Jacksonville jail on June 1 to detain me for forgetting to pay my fine for fishing without a license. Such are our priorities.

A probable rapist walks the streets today because someone doesn't consider rape to be as important a crime as failure to pay a ticket. We protect people like this by cloaking the identity of their victims.

(June 1989)

Anne Neville

Killing Joke

One of my favorite books when I was young was a coffee-table collection of classic *New Yorker* cartoons. By the hour, I would flip through the pages of the large volume, enthralled by the straight-faced, line-drawn *New Yorker* sophisticates, with their funny, angst-ridden view of the universe.

One cartoon I never understood, though. It was a jolly piece entitled "The Rape of the Sabines," featuring fat, happy and toga-ed women being toted off by fat, happy men in soldiers' helmets. One woman was winking largely at another. All was merry conspiracy.

Though I didn't care for this drawing — it made no sense to me but still seemed vaguely offensive — I turned to it often. Sufficient examination, surely, would reveal it to be as funny and sophisticated as those in the rest of the *New Yorker* collection.

The main thing I couldn't understand was why everybody in the picture was so happy. Too young to be clear on the specifics, I did know that rape was not a cheery thing. It was a species of assault on women, and my child's mind had registered that it carried with it a deep shame.

And this cartoon bore little relation to what I knew of the rape of the Sabine women — except for the togas and helmets. The Sabines, my non-cartoon reading had informed me, were an ancient Italian people, whose women were appropriated by the Romans in about 200 B.C. Legend has it that Romulus, needing wives for his men, lured the Sabines to Rome for a specially designed festival of games. At a prearranged signal — Romulus raised his cloak — the Roman soldiers were free to help themselves to the virgins. When the Sabine men fled, the Romans seized their marriagable women and carried them off to various parts of the city. This struck me as pretty grim stuff. Ponder it though I might, I never did understand all the cheeriness of the sly drawing.

I understand now that the artist meant to take a tongue-in-cheek look at the scene, to show how all those virgins the Romans thought they were abducting were really pretty hot mamas, well aware they were pulling one over on these callow youths.

I understand too that I was right as a child. The cartoon is offensive.

Set aside the objection that it had almost nothing to do with the legend that is its taking-off point, a legend having far more to do with legal questions of the possession of women than with sexual violence. It suffices to say that the artist associated rape with sexual attraction and portrayed his Sabines as smiling accomplices to their own assault.

In a society still struggling to come to terms with just what rape is and precisely how a rapist or a victim should be treated, the fact that such a cartoon should have been printed in an otherwise intelligent, fine-grained venue indicates dramatically the extent of our confusion on the topic. Neanderthals don't sketch for *The New Yorker*; nor do they edit it. Certainly nobody intended to offend, to belittle or to harm with this lighly conceived "alternative history." It was meant as silliness, and probably widely perceived as such.

There is, of course, no question of banning cartoons like this one. Extremists would call them conceptually dangerous and would advocate censorship on the grounds that their concept encourages an unacceptable view of rape and of women themselves. These zealots have their intellectual roots in the ugliest of history's repressive regimes, no matter how early and often they vote liberal.

Rather, it is important for us as a society to clarify our thought on the very tricky, very touchy subject of rape. Problems of definition abound, and have for centuries; historically, the word "rape" covers everything from abduction to unhappy or pre-arranged marriage to non-consensual sexual relations under the threat of violence.

The one thing rape is definitely not is sexy.

Perhaps, as Susan Brownmiller has suggested, rape is a political weapon by which all women are kept in a state of fear. Perhaps its increasing incidence is a result of the tension between assumed macho male and glamorized, objectified female roles in our culture, and the realities of a social existence which does not easily accommodate those assumptions. Perhaps rape is nothing more nor less than another way in which one person can damage another, part of a great and tragic arcade of harms.

But rape isn't funny, it isn't erotic and it's not a fit subject for jokes and cartoons. To play lightly with the topic is to misunderstand it, and thus to perpetuate it. Those winking Sabines did not appear in a vacuum; they were supposedly amusing because they fit somehow into a world view shared by the *New Yorker* cartoonist, his editors and presumably the magazine's literate, educated readership. That realization is far more disturbing than any single incidence of a questionable illustration, for it suggests that an entire frame of reference must be shattered and reconstructed.

To blame *The New Yorker* would only be killing the messenger.

(February 1990)

Stephen Buel

Let's Get Art off the Dole

Government funding of art perpetuates the myth that art cannot exist without public subsidy. That art is sickly and endangered. That, somehow, art is like cod liver oil; it's good for us, but we wouldn't really put up with it if we weren't forced to.

I don't buy the argument. Good art is scrappy. It speaks to a need in us, creates a market for itself and then fills that market. My art friends may regard this as heresy, but art is just another commodity, like toasters or free newspapers. Some of us happen to value art more than we value toasters, but others prefer toasters.

Who is to say that those who don't value art are wrong in objecting to the expenditure of their tax dollars on art exhibitions? Misguided though they are, those poor slobs who would rather view a televised football game than attend a musical or stage performance have a legitimate right to ask that their tax dollars not be squandered on displays from which they derive no benefit. (For exactly the opposite reasons, I think it's reasonable that Razorback football take no tax dollars out of my pocket.) The recent decision by the Corcoran Gallery of Art in Washington D.C. to cancel a scheduled exhibition of photographs by photographer Robert Mapplethorpe is certainly cowardly for a major arts institution, but who can fault those taxpayers who don't wish for their tax dollars to be spent underwriting sexually explicit art they don't approve of?

Then there is the troubling business of just how the government selects the art that it does choose to underwrite. Government funding of art inevitably leads to the establishment of an official, and somewhat sanitized, state artistic style. When I debated this point last year with some friends from the Arkansas Arts Council, our state's official arts welfare agency, they conceded that one of the problems they were trying to rectify was their agency's historic preference for Ozark crafts over other Arkansas art forms. It is to their credit that they viewed this as a problem. Still, our government should not be in the business of ranking art forms. Working artists have enough problems selling their work without having to compete for room in the marketplace with the sanitized "art of state."

Besides, if a work of art cannot come into being without taxpayer subsidy, who needs it? Like the maker of any other product, an artist is strengthened by the need to stay in touch with the marketplace and receive the democratic feedback of potential customers. The need to survive in the marketplace forces you to do a better job or go away. If there is no demand for an artist's work, that's the artist's problem, not mine. I reject the notion that artistic inspiration is somehow too pure to sully with "crass" commercial considerations.

It would certainly hurt at first, but the Arkansas Arts Center would be better off in the long run without public funding. It would have to do a better job of marketing itself to the public, which it could. In an interview in *Spectrum* a few years back, Arts Center Executive Director Townsend Wolfe explained how his institution was able to replace the loss of a third of its government funding in the early Reagan years by seeking more private contributions. That's something to be proud of. By pursuing more money in its own back yard, I suspect that the Arts Center also ended up involving more people in its activities than it had previously.

One potential source of funding is business. I'm impressed by the extent to which local business institutions support the arts in Little Rock. One notable example is First Commercial Bank, which has underwritten a number of worthwhile exhibitions at the Arts Center. One particularly memorable show funded by the bank last year was a series of multiple exposure nudes and street scenes by Arkansas photographer Marcia Wallace. There was nothing timid or sanitized about this impressive exhibit. That work as challenging as Wallace's can secure corporate underwriting speaks well for the marriage of art and corporate philanthropy.

Clearly, art won't die if we get it off the dole. And it's better for the arts to have artists rolling around in the mud along with the rest of us. It's better for society too. It keeps us closer to art.

(July 1989)

What Is Art's Problem?

During its first five years, Spectrum *carved out a special niche for itself in the often-infuriating genre of counter-intuitive commentary. Erik Pierson provided an example in May 1988, with an article entitled "What Is Art's Problem?" Pierson's former conviction that the "best art was truer than science, holier than religion, more enriching than economics and more essential than political philosophy" had been shaken by both the contemporary "art merchants" who pander to the "shallow tastes of a conspicuously consumptive market" and the "self-serving academic establishment."*

"Worse still," Pierson wrote, "is the unholy alliance that art has formed with government and with tax-motivated foundations." He blasted Richard Serra's "Tilted Arc," a "slightly curved wall of unevenly rusted steel" commissioned for a federal plaza in New York City, as a work that prompted the question "not only how much art matters, but whether it matters at all." Letters from readers wanted, in essence, to know: "What is your art writer's problem?" Jeff Kessinger of Little Rock contended that "The surface of the article is didactic and its theme reactionary," and asked, "Are quick conclusions the answer?"

TUESDAY PROMISED TO BE AT THOMAS' DISPOSAL, IF HE COULD ONLY FIGURE OUT THE SIGNIFICANCE OF HER DRESS.

©1989 JLOUCKS

Jeff Loucks

With his starkly graphic line drawings and sometimes inscrutable, always evocative cartoons, Jeff Loucks has helped defined the Spectrum *aesthetic. Comprised of but a few, tightly controlled lines, Loucks's work is instantly recognizable, and informed by a sense of the absurdity of the mundane.*

Michael Jukes

Culture

Spectrum's *cultural criticism covers a broad, well, spectrum — from Salman Rushdie to Tanya Tucker, from political style to personal quirks.*

Philip Martin

Common Drunks

Sometimes I drink too much. Not that I've ever backed the Volvo over anybody's kid or anything, but I admit that sometimes — not every day, or even every month — I do drink too much. *Occasionally*. As in every once in a while.

I don't happen to think this is a bad thing, though there are plenty of people out there who have charts and graphs and slabs of documents designed to show you where I'm wrong. There are plenty of people who will say bad things about drinking. I will concede that alcohol is a crutch, but sometimes — like when your legs are broken, for instance — a crutch is not such a bad thing to lean on.

Alcohol affects people in different ways. Some people probably shouldn't drink. Some people probably don't need to. But one of the most delicious pleasures available to sophisticated people is the giddy afterglow that comes from consuming adult beverages (we're not talking about flavored vodka or wine coolers here). Like those Japanese connoisseurs who risk paralytic death by eating blowfish, some people decide a few dead brain cells are worth the moments of fuzzy, heart-bursting inexactitude. Sobriety, after all, is no guarantee of quality thought — no more than drunkenness is a guarantee of enlightenment.

What getting drunk might allow you to do is to explore an otherwise unavailable part of yourself. Some nights the wine might lead you to something brutish, some nights something wanton, and on the best nights something still and tranquil. A man who likes himself drunk is a man at peace.

Usually, I like myself a little drunk, when I've let my shield slide down my arm to rest on the ground. I like it when I realize I'm saying things I wouldn't say without the encouragement of alcohol. Sure, it allows you to make more of petty things than you should — to see the evil motive in innocent gestures. It heightens your state of mind. It can allow you, like Mies van der Rohe, to see God (or Satan) in the details.

When I drink I believe that alcohol *can* make me smart, and it *can* make me dashing and it *can* put me in touch with something inside that is always drunk and closer to the spirit realm than I can let myself be otherwise. Holy men have their own kind of intoxication, lovers have their own — I refuse to see the sadness in a mild buzz. The Sufis say wine gets drunk with us, not the other way around. All I know is that drinking can keep me honest.

Liquor is like DMSO for the mind — it can be either a lovely solvent, or a superb binding agent. I have seen it dissolve a few stolid encounters. I've seen it bring fast enemies to the brink of reconciliation, fast friends to the threshold of brotherhood, fast women to the verge of sanctity. For the most part, alcohol has been a positive influence in my life.

All right, so I beat up a men's room once — broke and ripped my meat hand on this glinting brass fixture above a urinal — but I had a reason for that. That was the summer I thought I was Pete Townshend and all I would drink was Remy Martin champagne cognac. It was about the time *Empty Glass* was released. I had my first real girlfriend (her name is Kim and if she reads this she really should give me a call) and she let me know it was all over by coming into this bar where I hung out in Shreveport with this sad-eyed, black-banged med student she'd been dating before she took up with me, which in all probability she had done just to make him jealous.

Funny, I can't recall why exactly, but I'd been drinking that night. Medicating myself against some injury, real or imagined, when she swept in with him in tow. It set me off. I lifted the snifter and redoubled my communion with the dark, aromatic spirits. I didn't even look at them, though I knew she was watching me. Watching me drink. When the band went on break I slipped off to the men's room and busted up a couple of mirrors and an oak stall door before the flushworks finished me. I'm glad I was drunk. Otherwise it would have hurt like hell. Especially the second time I punched it.

My friends hustled me out of the bar through the kitchen, before the management realized what had been done and who had done it. I wound up at a party with a lot of people I didn't know (someone drove me there) and I met a lawyer who was about ten years older than me who took me to her home and made me coffee. She sat me in her kitchen and wrapped my wounded hand in gauze. We talked — just talked — until daylight, and then she fished her keys from her bag and drove me to where I had parked my car the evening before. I felt beautiful and tragic as the spell wore off. I slept long into the afternoon and if when I woke up there were sulfites lapping at my brain, I embraced the dunning bastards. Right, I know I owe this — I will pay for my memories like a man.

Later my drink was Scotch, primarily because it mixed best with water and ice and saved me from having to trudge back and forth to the concession stands at college football games. Generally my dates thought me sophisticated — most boys spilled cheap rum or V.O. into Coca-Cola — and put up with the smoky sweet bite of Chivas (unfortunately, back then I got my taste from advertisements in *The New Yorker*) on the rocks. I had my following among some sorority women — I imagined they took my shyness and fear of them as gentleness, my eccentricities for quiet decadence, my long soft gazes for soul. I drank both to give the impression I had doom in my blood and to lubricate a reluctant tongue.

There was a collegiate morning when some friends of mine and I stole a couple of cases of champagne — I'm still afraid to say where from, though the pilferage was hardly noticed — and handed out bottles to girls we hardly knew. In our wake the campus might have sounded something like Beirut under siege, with the irregular "pwap"of corks being launched into the just-blue sky before 7 a.m. classes. We shared our own tepid bottle on the golf course that day, a few of us, swigging right from the foil-draped neck between snakekilling five-irons and skulled wedges. That day we were drunk on something other than alcohol, maybe on the residual vapors of fading boyhood.

In law school my roommate would drink all my beer and never replace it. He would drink the medicinal brandy I bought to soothe my blistered throat, he would buy himself Boone's Farm Strawberry Hill and finish a quart of beer each night before bedtime because that was what he said Huey Long used to do. I drank generic beer because the cans (white with the word BEER stamped on them in large, *sans serif* letters) were cool.

I had only a few beers with my father because he died before I really got comfortable with the idea of drinking with him. But I can remember cementing the myth, a few games of roadhouse pool, the grim smile of a man looking past the bounds of his own mortality. And there was a night in Rio de Janeiro, in a hideous crowded place called New York City Disco, when our table got too loud (it was the Australians) and the waiter replaced our Cuba Libres with an awful drink made from Coke and gin. If rum tastes like pain — like a fastball in the teeth — then gin can taste like retribution.

I remember my closest friend and I sitting on the rickety balcony of the Café Sbisa in New Orleans, drinking a satiny *premier grand cru* Médoc moments before we were rescued from our bill by a group of marauding Cajuns who discovered we were newlyweds and decided we must accompany them on their Gold-Carded rampage through the Vieux Carré. Wine still tastes like love to me, and even last week's routine chardonnay echoes faint and sweet in the back of my mind.

Most of what you read now about alcohol leaves out how full of wonder, how sensible it can feel to be drunk. I know alcohol doesn't solve my problems. And I know how annoying and dangerous drunks can be — I speak only for myself. I haven't made rude belching noises in public, or accosted strange women or even explained to some helpless bartender why Shoeless Joe Jackson was — despite all the sentimental claptrap — guilty, guilty, guilty.

I drink martinis and I forgive the bartenders at the Capital Hotel for making them with Absolut instead of my called-for Stoli. I drink beer when I've a mind to, and wine when the company is good. My experiences with alcohol have been primarily decent experiences. Like all friends, sometimes we disappoint each other, but not past the forgiving point. I wouldn't presume to tell anyone what to do, but I might gently remind those who believe moral superiority can be attained through strict attention to what we put in our bodies that Hitler was a vegetarian. And Christ lifted up the cup.

Volvo Liberals

In a letter to the editor, Rex Nelson, communications director for U.S. Representative Tommy Robinson during his Arkansas gubernatorial campaign, complained about a December 1989 column by Philip Martin which criticized Robinson (once a Democrat but by then a Republican) in passing. In part, Nelson's letter read:

"Anyone else around here would tell me I'm wasting my time writing Spectrum, *since the holier-than-thou, look-down-on-the-average-Arkansan, Volvo-driving, granola-eating crowd that reads* Spectrum *is not likely to vote for TR anyway."*

Scant hours before the letter arrived, the wine-sipping associate editor had purchased a previously owned Volvo. Honest.

James Neff

Anthony Moser

Uncle Sam, Famous Deadbeat

We've been on a national bender for almost a decade now — a protracted "Lost Weekend" of the American conscience. Living beyond our means, awash in the giddiness of our Gold Card, we've run up $200 billion annual budget deficits and a national debt of almost $2 trillion. Long after last call, when we were tapped out and busted flat, we kept pounding on the bar for one more round, charging it all at the plastic altar of credit.

But now it's dawn on a rainy Monday, and reality has thundered its wake-up call. It's Morning in America all right, and we've got a four-alarm hangover that just doesn't know when to quit. Our wallet's empty, our credit cards have all been canceled and we've bounced half-a-dozen checks down at the bank.

Welcome, America, to the very real consequences of your very surreal actions.

The meltdown on Wall Street — culminating in the 508-point free-fall of the Dow Jones industrial average October 19 — was not, as President Reagan said under the roar of whirring helicopter blades, "purely a stock-market thing." To ask how the Crash of 1987 is going to trickle down and affect the economy as a whole is an inversion of the real situation. It's the economy as a whole, under the burden of massive budget deficits, a spiraling debt and a hopeless trade deficit, that was living a lie. Finally, when Congress and the Gipper wouldn't do anything, the results of our wicked ways trickled up to Wall Street.

Forty-two years after the United States defeated Nazi Germany and Imperial Japan in World War II, it is the West Germans and the Japanese who are getting the last laugh. Keynesian economists were once fond of saying that deficit spending was okay because we were borrowing the money from ourselves. This is no longer the case. In the process of financing our deficit-fueled national expansion, we've stretched our domestic money supply to the limit and pushed private foreign investors far past the threshold of skepticism.

In the past year we've instead borrowed $80 billion from the central banks of foreign potentates, most prominently Germany and Japan, to keep the value of the dollar from falling through the floor and our *papier-mache* economy from collapsing. It's the Marshall Plan in reverse, folks — the vanquished have come back to bail the drunken victor out of debtor's prison. Once the world's greatest creditor nation, we are now the world's largest debtor.

Suddenly, the dead-in-the-water Reagan administration and Federal Reserve Board Chairman Alan Greenspan seem to have become Keynesians themselves, announcing they will print money to keep interest rates and the value of the dollar down, thereby attracting more foreign investment and avoiding recession. But with more dollars chasing a limited supply of goods and services, this will, in all likelihood, undo the one great success of the past seven years: the victory over inflation.

To some extent, of course, Wall Street and its Yuppie-Greedhead investment bankers are to blame. Institutional investors, such as insurance conglomerates and pension fund managers, no doubt began to sense that something had gone mortally awry: that the bulls in the market had become berserk cannibals, feeding on one another. There was always the lurking suspicion, bolstered by frequent headline-catching arrests, that the stock market boom was fueled more by pharmaceutical-grade Bolivian Marching Powder than by the forces of macroeconomics. The zany calculus of arbitrage, where a split-second difference in the execution of a computer-generated trade can make millions of dollars of difference, had stopped making sense. And many of the safeguards built into the system after the crash of 1929 — such as requiring at least 50 cents in cash for every dollar's worth of stock purchased on margin — were being unraveled.

The most glaring example is on the Chicago Merchantile Exchange, where, for seven cents on the dollar, investors can buy "futures options." These options, quite simply, are bets on what the Standard & Poor's 500 is going to do between the present and a particular point in the future. So, an investor who buys heavily into blue-chips on Wall Street in the hope that they will soar, can hedge his bet by gambling on the Chicago exchange that the S&P as a whole will drop. You make money on one, you lose on the other. This is a less responsible form of gambling than that practiced at the racetrack. On a horse, you can hedge by betting your nag to win and show, but you can't bet him both to win and to collapse in the home stretch.

Structurally, the price-to-earnings ratio on many stocks, including blue-chips, was completely out of line. For instance, Apple Computer, one of the hottest stocks of the 1980s, was trading at $23 for every $1 of Apple profits. Ratios of this magnitude, now common, are twice the size they were five or six years ago. At such a level, stocks become tools of speculation first and investments in a company second.

It's too easy, however, just to blame coke-snorting Yuppie stockbrokers who screamed "buy, buy, buy" at their customers simply to increase their own

Voodoo Doo-doo

In December 1988, Bill Jones recalled George Bush's 1980 description of Reagan's supply-side economic plan as "voodoo economics," noting that Poppy had now "embraced the tenets of Reaganomics with all the fervor of a true believer." After eight years, Jones observed, "the Reagan-Bush administration has left the country stranded, as the president-elect might say, 'in deep doo-doo' — with a record federal deficit approaching $2.6 trillion and a new status as the world's largest debtor nation."

Three books dealing with the consequences of the "Reagan Revolution" seemed to support the assessment. Benjamin M. Friedman's Day of Reckoning *explored the impact of the transition from "tax-and-spend to spend-and-borrow," making the case that under Reagan the United States had mortgaged its economic future by "running up our debt and selling off our assets."*

In Falling From Grace, *Katherine S. Newman studied "downward mobility" among middle-class Americans and called for a stronger, more compassionate community response to those affected by the "broken covenant."* The Great Divide *by Studs Terkel focused on working-class frustrations but detected hopeful signs in grass-roots movements. The three works, Jones wrote, "raise pertinent questions [about] what sort of nation we have become ... and what kind of country we want to have in the future."*

commissions. A disaster on Wall Street would indeed be "purely a stock market thing" if the underlying economy was sound. The problem is that it is anything *but* sound.

Is there a way out that will avoid both recession and inflation, at least in their most extreme manifestations? Is there an answer that will restore confidence in America? This, after all, is the most important question. The markets were not reacting to an anticipated "global economic collapse," as some pundits have been suggesting, almost comically. What Wall Street was saying is that we're in over our heads, lost in bad craziness of the most pathological variety. We pretended that the old guy with the hearing aid was "The Gipper," Drake McHugh or all those other never-say-die tough guys he played in his movies. Although his accomplishments in reshaping the national agenda should not be underestimated, he has now become, well, simply the old guy with the hearing aid. The president's clout has vanished into the ether, but the job still must be done. And it will require one of the most significant bipartisan coalitions of the postwar era.

The job, to boil it down to three words, is *cutting the budget*. Not trimming it or paring it down or meeting the Gramm-Rudman targets, but rather bringing the Texas Chainsaw Massacre to Capitol Hill. The American people, staggering under an Inquisitorial array of local, state and federal levies of every sort and description — including the heinously regressive Social Security tax — should summarily vote out any congressman or senator who even speaks the words "tax increase" before at least $60 billion is cut from next year's budget.

The much-vaunted "budget summit" now being held by members of Congress and the administration is a cruel hoax. The summit's goal is to cut $23 billion, which is the same amount that will be automatically cut November 20 by the Gramm-Rudman law even if nothing is done. This "summit" is simply looking for easier, softer places to make the cuts than the across-the-board, 50-50 split between defense and domestic programs that Gramm-Rudman would exact.

Where to cut? Well, the federal budget for 1988 is $108 trillion. Of that, $291 billion is defense, $204 billion is Social Security, $302 billion is "entitlement" programs, and $150 billion is to pay *interest* on the national debt. This leaves only $130 billion of non-defense "discretionary" spending.

Clearly, this area — which is where all those nightmarish boondoggles like $2 million programs to study the mating habits of frogs are always found — is not the real problem. We must take our chainsaw to defense, Social Security and the so-called "entitlements," only 20 percent of which are actually aimed at reducing poverty.

How? Let's start with defense. Reagan's proudest accomplishment is that he's made America "stand tall" again, and that's all well and good. But in doing so, recently departed Secretary of Defense Caspar Weinberger took us down an expensive and wasteful path that has institutionalized the thing President Eisenhower warned us to avoid — "the Military-Industrial Complex." Weapons systems are being deployed for no better reason than to placate a constituent contractor who wants to stick his hand in our pockets.

Two shining examples are the MX missile and the B-1 bomber. Both are high-tech extensions of antiquated ideas — big, lumbering first-strike weapons that are highly vulnerable. The B-1 is a hopeless turkey that has never worked, and two have crashed on test flights. It has never met its performance specs and should be killed. Meanwhile, the vast majority of defense experts not owned by the weapons barons agree that it would be far better to scrap the MX — which is now being installed in old, sitting-duck Minuteman silos — and move directly to the Midgetman mobile single-warhead missile.

Traveling about on trucks and conveyors, many Midgetmen would survive even the most massive nuclear assault, thus making such an attack unthinkable. Serving a similar purpose is the D-5 missile on board our efficient Trident

James Neff

submarines. These, along with the radar-evading Stealth bomber and the ground-hugging cruise missile, combine to form a credible triad of air, ballistic and sea-based nuclear forces that will survive well into the 21st century.

Domestically, the farm subsidy programs, which maintain a "way of life" for a handful of agrarians while bringing on higher food prices for the rest of us, should be eliminated. There we would save $26 billion a year. Similarly, the time for tax-free "entitlements" for the middle class has passed. Social Security, as well as federal and military pensions, should be taxed for all recipients who are above the poverty level. Medicare recipients should receive benefits on the basis of financial need. We should also limit federal cost-of-living benefit increases to 60 percent of the consumer price index, which would save $150 billion annually within 15 years.

These three measures would chop out about $200 billion a year. The budget would be balanced, and we'd have a *surplus* with which to start paying off the principal on the national debt. Moreover, there would be no need for artificial trade barriers. The rebounding strength of the American economy would restore our place in the world markets.

The only real argument economists make against this chainsaw scenario is that, by restricting the flow of public dollars into the economy, it would bring on a recession. That may be true, but any Western economy that depends on public largesse for its basic lifeblood hasn't long to live anyway. The administration has tried to economize with smoke and mirrors, selling off public assets and pushing paydays into the next fiscal year. That's not going to cut it. We can only sell off our property once. Our debts go on forever.

It's almost impossible to get the public mobilized on an issue as seemingly arcane as reducing the deficit and attacking the debt. But the hard, cold fact is that it is arcane no longer. Your job, your checking account and your children's futures are next in line to take the hit. The old cliché still holds true — what goes around comes around.

It's come around.

(November 1987)

Old and Not-So-New Politics

Means of Ascent, Robert A. Caro's account of Lyndon B. Johnson's 1948 Senate race against Coke Stevenson, glorified the former Texas governor as much as it vilified the future U.S. president. The author turned the two men into symbols of traditional and modern campaigning — Stevenson's leisurely courthouse-lawn conversations and handshakes stood in marked contrast to Johnson's radio and helicopter blitz, which, along with votes from the quick and the dead, gave LBJ a narrow victory.

In an April 1990 review of the book, Bill Jones observed that "Stevenson is the real subject of Means of Ascent, *just as Brutus is the main concern of Shakespeare's* Julius Caesar. *Indeed, both [figures] shared a fatal confidence in their own virtue and the public's perception of it." Caro's second installment in the projected four-volume* Years of Lyndon Johnson, *suggests, said Jones, that "the 'new politics' of the sound bite and the hard sell is not so new, after all, and it implies that the 'old politics' of stolen votes and stuffed ballot boxes may have simply evolved into something more sophisticated and, perhaps, sinister."*

Randal Seyler

Government by Media Event

On Friday, May 13, 1988, the Bolivar County Port at Rosedale, Mississippi, is the site of a historic economic event. The event is historic, according to press aides from three states, because the cooperative agreement to be signed by the three governors will toss the first shovelful of dirt onto the prone, twitching face of old-style Southern politics. Like the ending of a typical Hong Kong Kung Fu movie, where the young guys gang up on the bad old master, the three young governors are going to tag-team Grandmaster Economic Wo and kick butt.

At least that's the plan, as Arkansas Governor Bill Clinton, Mississippi Governor Ray Mabus and Louisiana Governor Buddy Roemer join forces. The governors are here to make their marks on the "Governor's Agreement/ International Cooperation Initiative," a vaguely titled piece of paper declaring that the three states will work together to improve their economies and attract foreign investors.

To get this historic tag-team action underway, however, there must be a requisite amount of pageantry. In this case, pageantry demands a barge, 150 guests, about 50 media types, several potted plants and breakfast pastries. The three chief executives sit behind a large walnut veneer table. Behind it there are four flags; one from each state and, on the governors' far left, a Japanese flag in honor of His Excellency Nobou Matsunaga, Japanese Ambassador to the U.S. His Excellency will be on board for the ceremonies, although no one ever really finds out why.

To the governors' left there are about 150 seats for visiting dignitaries and guests. To the right, sits the block of media seats and a small platform covered with television camera tripods. The platform is covered with sulking cameramen even before the first guests arrive. To the right rear of the barge are the Porta Potties, and just in front, members of the Delta Jazz Combo from Delta State University in Cleveland, Mississippi, are tuning up with groovy Hugh Wilson faves "WKRP in Cincinnati" and "Do You Know What it Means To Miss New Orleans?"

By 9 a.m., the governors' aides have transformed the barge into a floating Holiday Inn lounge. The Delta Jazz Combo is honking out whitebread Dixieland as the first guests wander aboard, while several school buses unloaded the first herds of what will eventually become 1,200 flag-waving, hooting Mississippi school children.

The serving table soon opens, and the media descend, ravenously gobbling up cinnamon rolls and slurping down RC Cola as men in white, pinstriped plantation suits with highwater pants roam the boat shaking hands and slapping backs. Out on the river, a speed boat carrying two blue-suited, mirror-shaded FBI types buzzes by, flying the Mississippi state flag and Old Dixie. By the time a crowd of black children from Martin Luther King Elementary School in Pace, Mississippi, crowd the gangplank carrying a banner reading "Don't hesitate, open the gate, negotiate," the speedboaters thoughtfully lower their Confederate flag.

As the zero hour nears, aides break out boxes of miniature state flags and begin distributing them to the children while another spokesman hands out press kits, including a pre-written news story on the event. When the governors finally arrive, press aides usher the guests forward to welcome them. Then Clinton's head towers over the ambassador, and it's time to witness history.

The mayor of Rosedale, Dr. J.Y. Trice, opens the ceremonies by asking

Jesus to help the local economy. Then moderator John Maxwell of Cleveland, a man chosen for his historic job because of his good voice, takes the podium and introduces Clinton.

"We are here because our people have a vision of how their future should be, and they have hired us to make sure it comes true," Clinton says. Then he notes that while the Delta has fallen behind the rest of the country economically, it continues to top the charts in illiteracy, teen pregnancies, unemployment and infant mortality.

"I long for the day that there are so many boats on the river between Memphis and New Orleans that it looks like tourism on the Rhine," Clinton adds, perhaps a bit fancifully.

After Mabus and Roemer offer similar platitudes, the Three Amigos break out the ink. History is made, and the crowd dutifully responds with gratitude, before returning to the serving table for more RC.

(June 1988)

Anne Neville

Bush League

Say goodbye to Hollywood. George Bush, perhaps the only man in history to have actually worn the seal of the vice presidency on his blazer, is in the Big House now, and things are going to be changing around here, but good.

Forget all that "kinder and gentler" business, forget education and let the poor fend for themselves (after eight years of Reagan, they're used to it anyway). We're talking rep ties. We're talking Return of the Preppie.

After eight years of Reagan glitz and glimmer — the "let them eat cake" ostentation of the self-made-and-still-proving-it couple whose hearts never strayed far from Tinseltown even when their ambitions did — the nation is ready for a style change. George Bush promises to deliver: good grammar and good taste.

His credentials are impeccably prep, of course: Andover and Yale. Even his running off at 18 to enlist in the Navy in World War II and winning the Distinguished Flying Cross bespeak his properly, tastefully upper-class origins. He was, after all, a Navy aviator — the youngest of the brightest and the best. And he's married to Barbara, the white-gloves finishing school grad who gifted him with her first kiss and who now encourages her English springer spaniel to sleep between them at night in the best asexual preppie tradition.

The shift in White House occupants promises to be all the more significant because of its inherent cultural drama. Bush isn't simply assuming the mantle of the presidency, he's taking it from Ronald Reagan — a man to whom he would almost certainly have nothing to say at a party were it not for their shared political ambition. For where Bush is upper crust, Ronald Reagan is strongly, identifiably and unabashedly what cultural critic Paul Fussell calls "high proletariat" (or, at best, bottom-rung middle class).

After all Reagan went to Eureka College in *Illinois*, for heaven's sake. Why, they probably don't even have a scull team there. And need we mention that the man married not one actress, but *two*? In George Bush's circles, the only thing worse would be to have been married to them simultaneously — and that wouldn't have been *much* worse.

Even way back in 1984, when *Class,* his funny, incisive examination of American society, hit the shelves, Fussell had this odd couple down. While he never directly contrasted president and vice president, he made free use of them as archetypical examples of their classes.

"If you're skeptical that looks give off class messages, try conflating ... Mayor Daley with George Bush." In a later passage touching on personal grooming, Fussell notes that upper-class men sport "moderate-length hair, never dyed or tinted, which is a middle-class or high-prole sign, as the practice of President Reagan indicates."

All of this is significant because White House denizens have Serious Style Clout, even when their own tastes might best be stashed beneath the nearest handy bushel. Need we remind you of Billy Carter?

Serious Style Clout, in the case of the Reagans, meant that for eight years Americans, in the best *nouveau gauche* tradition, just said no to understatement and dashed headlong, *en masse,* into the valley of debt.

Greed was good, taste was out and what you couldn't buy, you leased. In a frenzied show of conspicuous consumption, Americans paid big bucks for things like Rolex watches and a mystery called *nouvelle cuisine,* which most often consisted of three string beans and half a kiwi floating in a lukewarm pool of something yellow.

People hopped on the bandwagon to prove they could afford to — or at least to make others think they could. The poor were poor because they wanted to be, Reagan told us. And who wanted to be cast as a misfit? Money could buy happiness, and wealth meant its possessor was doing something right.

So America ate microwaved "goor-may" food indifferently served by abusive waiters in restaurants catering to climbers too ignorant to know they were being had. It snapped up overpriced jewelry designed for Tiffany's by the inimitably vulgar Paloma Picasso. It embraced a fashion aesthetic that allowed only for This Year's Model, which meant no aspirant could appear in anything but brand new, hot-off-the-racks clothing. Were the dresses ugly? Who cared? They were new and they were expensive and they were Designer — Oscar, LaCroix, Galanos — just like Nancy's dresses. And it quickened the national pulse when we learned that she couldn't afford hers, *either,* that Nancy differed from her emulators only in that she didn't have to lie about whether or not a gown had been worn when she returned it after the gala.

Enter a new president with nothing to prove (except, perhaps, that he's not a wimp). He wears old clothes because he likes them and feels no need to prove he can afford new ones. Bush — unlike Reagan, who never got beyond the high-school full Windsor — knows how to knot a tie. In timeless prep tradition, he knows that Oxford cloth trumps broadcloth and that collar stays are, well, just not done. That's the sort of thing you just don't learn at Eureka College.

Sure, they're rich, but preps don't have to keep *shouting* about it. They assume everybody knows already. So Barbara wears fake pearls and doesn't discuss designers. And George wears frayed shirts, plays stupid jokes (a favorite is a prep-school oldie involving a "dropped" dollar bill and a length of invisible fishing line) and doesn't worry about that front lock of hair that won't stay combed right.

Look for the rest of America to follow suit. Suddenly, it won't be enough to give the impression of simply having money, even if it's lots and lots of money. To make the grade now, the money will have to seem old, which means it will have to shut up and behave itself. Look for a Lacoste revival (if you can dig out the old, holey ones, so much the better — new *anything* will be suspect) and the return of Glen plaid, old tweed and lots of navy for both men and women. Watch for a decline in college business and science majors and the renewed popularity of humanities courses, which can be considered practical preparation for nothing whatsoever and are therefore highly desirable.

Other trends to watch for include a revival of straight-on drinks like vodka with a splash of water *(never* tonic), scotch and water *(never* soda) and Bloody Marys *(never* after 3 p.m.); the renewed popularity of bland, hearty WASP food, consumed at home; and a spate of nondescript, possibly unwashed autos cruising the streets. That's what people with old money drive: Plymouths and Dodges in the least interesting styles and colors imaginable.

To those exhausted by the excesses of the past few years, the simpler style of the White House will probably come as a great relief — but one big *caveat* should be kept firmly in mind. A president's style is *only* his style — underlying substance may be very different. Ronald Reagan, with his air of the Sun Belt proletariat dressed up for church, drew the political support of dissatisfied workers. This traditionally Democratic voting group defected to Reagan in 1980 believing he would both stimulate the economy and leave its social services "safety net" untact. Even when unemployment increased and social welfare programs were cut, Reagan remained popular with workers, in large part because he seemed to be just another wage-and-hour guy who happened to make good. So what if he never seemed to let his job interfere with his leisure? What working stiff wouldn't do the same, given the opportunity? Reagan said the opportunity was there for the taking.

The Radicalism of Robert Bork

In the heat of the 1987 debate over President Reagan's nomination of Judge Robert Bork to the United States Supreme Court, Spectrum *ran an editorial appeal to Arkansas Senators Dale Bumpers and David Pryor. The piece asserted that the federal appellate judge was "nothing less than a constitutional radical" who would apply the First Amendment's "freedom of speech" clause only to "political speech."*

Moreover, Spectrum *contended, the nominee had rejected the Enlightenment concept (underlying the Declaration of Independence, the Constitution and the Bill of Rights) of natural, antecedent rights. "'Natural rights',"* the editorial observed, *"may well be a philosophical fiction, but if so, the doctrine has acquired during the past two centuries of historical experience the contours of working reality."*

Although he was being portrayed as an "original-intent" conservative, Spectrum *argued, Bork was in fact a judicial activist with an agenda that went beyond traditional ideological bounds. The paper urged Senators Bumpers and Pryor to "ask themselves ... whether they want to see the radicalism of Robert Bork enshrined for future generations in the volumes of the* United States Reports."

The Arkansas senators joined their colleagues in rejecting the Bork nomination.

George Bush won't be the party animal his predecessor was. He's a home sort of guy, a family man. Doesn't blow a lot of money decking his wife out in jewels and facelifts. Why, before attending some 14 inauguration balls, he dined at home with Barbara, the kids and grandkids and ate a simple, all-American meal of fried chicken with cream gravy, barbecued beef brisket, mashed potatoes, peas and carrots, biscuits and ice cream. It's the sort of gesture that inspires confidence in the man at the helm, refusing to fiddle while the nation's debt mounts.

That's style.

But then, Bush didn't actually do anything to tone down the inaugural festivities, either. They went on to the tune of nearly $30 million.

That's substance.

(March 1989)

Michael Jukes

Philip Martin

Losers Need Not Apply

AM radio's recent history is as an uplifting, upbeat medium. Sixties pop songs were mixed so as to maximize the effect when filtered through tinny dashboard speakers. But now, on the cusp of the 1990s, AM radio seems quaintly anachronistic, rather like 3-D movies or quadraphonic sound.

Many successful AM stations don't play music anymore. Some seem not to play much of anything other than network feeds and PSAs. One doesn't look for innovations from AM radio, just news and football games. Yet, just slightly to the right of center, at 1050 on Central Arkansas's AM dial, something different is happening. Here, 16 hours a day, KWNN pumps out three- to five-minute snippets of speech designed to "motivate and energize" it's listeners. Motivational speakers, secular preachers in Maslow's church of self-actualization, spin out little feel-good messages that combine tenets of Emersonian self-reliance with shameless P.T. Barnum hucksterism. It's hip, it's hot, it's here and — for now — it's in damn few other markets around the country. It's cutting edge. Somebody's going to get rich, or richer, off this.

The "hit ideas" of dozens of motivational speakers and self-help gurus such as Zig Ziglar, Wayne Dyer, Tom Peters, John Naisbitt, Robert Schuller, Bert (*Speaking to Win*) Decker, Denis Waitley and ex-Dallas Cowboy quarterback Roger Staubach are rotated much the same as the hit records are on other stations. Now Steve Allen gives toastmaster tips. Now Dr. Susan Forward, author of *Men Who Hate Women and the Women Who Love Them*, warns women off misogynistic relationships. Now we are given today's "Energizer:" a German proverb that states, "To aim high is not enough, you must hit the target." Now we are reminded to use the information to live better and happier. And so it goes. One imagines the effect these taped snippets have on post-innocence, post-Reagan ears is not too unlike the effect "Be My Baby" had blasting out of those low-fi speakers back in 1963 — they make a receptive would-be yuppie feel good.

So just as the Beach Boys made you want to surf, Zig Ziglar makes you want to sell. This is hit radio all right — good for a quick jolt to the base of the cerebellum. Though some of the messages might not stand up to intellectual scrutiny, the visceral kick is what's important. Occasionally the station will play testimonials from unidentified listeners — "It makes me feel like I can do anything." Indeed, infusing listeners with that sense of limitless possibilities seems to be the whole point behind all-motivation radio.

KWNN is affiliated with the fledgling Winners News Network, but owner Cliff Ford said it will eventually become "extremely local," with lots of emphasis on Central Arkansas business.

"It's designed for success-motivated executives, today's ever-changing young professional, anybody who is interested in self-improvement," station owner Ford said. His station began testing the format on August 15 and officially went on the air September 1, 1989. Since then it has been quietly broadcasting rotating motivational messages — interspersed with informational segments on health and lifestyle issues, business and financial news, a top-of-the hour good newscast and even an occasional commercial.

Simply put, the station offers advice on how to live better in America. Some of the speakers give advice on how to sell better, some on how to buy better, some on how to eat or manage time better, and some on how to smile better (exaggerate your smile and practice on videotape; when most people think they are smiling "naturally," they are hardly smiling at all). While the ideal market for the station may be 25- to 45-year-old males — salesmen who listen in their car on the way to sales calls — Ford insists the format has the potential to cut across demographic boundaries. He says a station in Florida — the first in the nation to adopt the WNN format — is immensely popular with men and women over 65. Despite low-key marketing — Ford said the big push is coming soon, with TV and print campaigns planned — the station has begun to attract attention from advertisers as well as listeners.

"We've had tremendous response from all kinds of people," Ford said, modulating his big, classic "on-air" voice. "Basically, we're finding that people — adults, really — are listening to us. Everyone from people just out of college, in their first job or looking for their first job, to leaders of the business community, people who've made it. We feel we have something to offer anybody. I've even heard that there's a rival radio station in this market that has suggested their sales people listen to us when they're in their cars ... I've never heard of that before."

Though the format seems novel, perhaps it shouldn't. The ethos of salesmanship and boosterism is an essential part of our national character. The discovery of the New World exercised a sort of natural selection among our European ancestors; while the lazy, the rich and the rooted remained at home, the dissatisfactions of others drew them over the blue horizon. Americans have thus long been comfortable with the idea that every man is captain of his own destiny. Americans not only believe in the possibility of self-improvement, we believe that if we can dream it, we can be it — if we act enthusiastic, we will become enthusiastic. Instinctively, we believe — or yearn to believe — in the power of positive thinking, even when we feel too battered down to practice it. We make heroes and icons of the Self-Made Man — even when these men turn out to be selfish rascals, we pay them a sort of grudging respect. The loud lout in the Day-Glo Dacron suit becomes a man to be reckoned with when his name is dropped in *Forbes* or *Fortune*.

Winners News Network recognizes that nothing is more American than the desire to better oneself. Though the 19th-century Industrial Revolution's cult of success placed surprisingly little emphasis on comparing oneself against "the competition," by the turn of the century, "winning" had displaced mere self-contentment as the yardstick of success. As businesses became bigger and more bureaucratic, ambitious young men had to struggle against their peers for the attention and approval of their superiors. Men of approximately equal abilities, competing for a limited number of places, faced the prospect of becoming lost within the corporate labyrinth unless they were somehow able to gain an "edge," to insinuate themselves into their boss's consciousness. In this era, self-help books bloomed on the shelves and topped best-seller lists.

One of the more durable of these books, *Letters from a Self-Made Merchant to His Son*, by *Saturday Evening Post* publisher George Lorimer, celebrated "will-power, self-confidence, energy and initiative" as values necessary to successful men. Later, Dale Carnegie and Norman Vincent Peale refined the Lorimer doctrine. Carnegie's famous course involved pragmatic cynicism, sort of a Gordon Lish approach to becoming beloved. Act like a gentle, thoughtful person, remember people's names and treat them decently and they will think kindly of you. In the end, they will want to help you enrich yourself and become more powerful.

Carnegie and Peale and the motivators who have followed them refuse to accept diligence as the sole key to making it, as surely as they reject a well-done job as its own reward. Sure, it helps if a man loves his work — if you love your work you're likely to work longer and harder. But, most importantly, these new prophets embraced the desire for more money as a useful incentive. Napoleon Hill, in his *Think and Grow Rich* — a work which is featured on KWNN as sort of a golden oldie — maintained that a man *could not* amass great wealth without first working up a "white heat of desire" for money. Success became an end in itself, victory over one's competitors was the true affirmation of one's manhood. In the 1950s, the self-sacrificing organization man in the gray flannel suit was seen as something of an ideal; in the 1980s, that ideal has been subsumed by the entrepreneur, the individualistic executive who sees his competition not only in the high buildings across town, but at the the next desk.

One needn't feel ashamed about growing rich — after all, in this land of opportunity the means to be wealthy are within the reach of all those shrewd and tough enough to implement them. Horatio Alger's Ragged Dick and Sam Walton both prove the theorem. Great wealth is not achieved by wimps or even 1970s-style New Men. Recently, Bruce Williams — arguably the most popular talk radio host in America — advised a man who had the financial "opportunity of a lifetime" to sell his house, despite his wife's objections, to raise the capital to close the deal. If his wife wouldn't accept that, Williams added, perhaps the man should divorce his wife.

Though KWNN is one of only five or six stations in the nation who have adopted the motivational format, it seems a natural outgrowth of the financial advice call-in shows which have proliferated on AM radio. Though there is some repetition, KWNN's library of more than 800 tapes is vast enough that one can listen to the station intermittently for weeks without hearing the same message. And besides, motivational messages are generally designed for repeated listening.

"People don't listen to us all day," Ford said. "They may only listen to us for 15 minutes or so at a time. But the thing is, when they listen to us, they really listen to us. It's not like a music station where they can tune out the music." Or the commercials. Ford said KWNN intends to integrate sponsor's messages into the mix in such a way as to make them as attention-holding as the motivational messages. He hints at a seamlessness between ads and infotainment material.

Despite the inherent cynicism of some of the motivators (many of whom seem to be saying nothing more profound than "nothing succeeds like the appearance of success"), there is a disarming innocence about KWNN. Relentlessly upbeat, with jingle singers chirping "For Winners Only" every couple of minutes, the station rolls on, visualizing the "world as it can be."

You Can't Have One Without the Other

In August 1989, Gus and Maria Gusek were married after they met through a personal ad Maria had placed in Spectrum *a couple of months before.*

Within a few weeks, they had decided they were right for each other.

"I knew right after the first date," Maria said. "I was miserable when he didn't call for a few days."

"We figured 'why wait?' We both knew we'd found the right person," Gus said. "There was no reason for us not to be together — and we both knew it."

Bill Jones

Shame

Salman Rushdie, the Ayatollah and the Persecution of the Mind

Of all the tyrannies on humankind,
The worst is that which persecutes the mind.
— John Dryden, "The Hind and the Panther" (1687)

It is intolerable that a man should fear for his life because he has written a book. It is intolerable that a spiritual leader should incite his followers to murder. It is intolerable that the Western traditions of free artistic expression and critical inquiry should be compromised by the threats of those who adhere to a narrow and fanatical world view.

Yet the appalling affair of *The Satanic Verses* has shown once again the extent to which, in this Age of Terror, civilized peoples of every nation are obliged to endure the outrages of a collective mentality that evidently has never outgrown its early-medieval tribal ethos. The ancient Greeks had a name for their Persian enemies that these 20th-century intellectual terrorists have earned — barbarians.

Salman Rushdie lives under armed guard in a country where the police carry no weapons. The Ayatollah Khomeini, *imam* of the minority Shi'ite Muslim sect, exhorts the faithful to send the author to Hell in the name of the one true religion, "the straight path — the path of God" (*Quran*, Sura 42, Arberry translation). No word of apology will suffice; nothing but Rushdie's death can redeem the honor of Islam.

Meanwhile, the publisher in New York temporarily closes its offices; the publisher in Paris declines to print the book; major American bookstore chains remove the offending volume from display shelves. And in the northern English city of Bradford, three Labour Members of Parliament attend and applaud a public burning of the book, while in Canada the government blocks further printing of Rushdie's work as it cravenly consults its hate-literature act.

Whatever political purpose is served by the Ayatollah placing a bounty on Rushdie's head, it is clear that many Muslims around the world genuinely feel affronted by the publication of *The Satanic Verses*. Their faith is centered in a book, the *Quran*, and they take words on paper, as we have seen in the past few weeks, quite literally and quite seriously.

The Prophet himself, according to the historical record, had little patience with dissenting voices. After his victory over the pagan Arabs in the crucial battle of Badr, Muhammad ordered the executions of two men who had unfavorably compared passages in the *Quran* with Jewish and Persian scriptures, and he approved the assassination of a woman satirist named Asma bint Marwan. Following the occupation of Mecca, he also sanctioned the executions of yet another satirist and a singer.

A cultural chasm appears to divide certain varieties of Islam and the West on the issue of the limits of creative liberty, and here, if a dangerous precedent is not to be set, we must acknowledge the differences between us and assert the primacy, in our culture, of the values we cherish.

The author of *The Satanic Verses* is a product of both cultures, and his latest book is a somewhat autobiographical account of the ordeal of dislocation. An Indian-born British subject of Muslim background and atheistic opinions,

Allen McMillan

Salman Rushdie has written an Islamic *Candide*, a satirical novel exploring the immigrant's place in an unfamiliar world. The principal characters are Saladin Chamcha, an Anglicized Indian who has made a fortune in British television commercials and radio shows as "the Man of a Thousand Voices and a Voice," and Gibreel Farishta, an Indian film actor who has achieved superstardom playing Hindu animal gods.

At the beginning of the novel, when the jumbo jet they are passengers on is blown up by a terrorist, Saladin and Gibreel fall, like angels, from the sky, heading straight toward "Proper London, capital of Vilayet," a magical-realist's Britain. Awaking after their miraculous landing on a "snowbound English beach," the two find that they have been reborn with new, and apparently opposite, characteristics. Throughout *The Satanic Verses*, Rushdie deals with the loss and recovery of identity, love and faith. Blending good and evil in his "angelicdevilish" duo, the author affirms the hope for renewal "in spite of all [one's] wrongdoing, weakness, guilt — in spite of [one's] humanity." It is a message that has been shouted down by the cries for Rushdie's blood.

Few, if any, of the writer's would-be executioners have read the book they deem so blasphemous, but, even if they troubled themselves to do so, it is questionable whether, given their murderous literalism, they would grasp the novel's postmodernist method. The believers, however, do have a point — *The Satanic Verses* is indeed blasphemous, but not in the limited, sectarian sense in which the term is understood by fundamentalists of any religion.

The novel's real blasphemy has nothing to do with whores in a dream assuming the names of Muhammad's wives, or even with the implication that divine texts may have all-too-human authors. Rather, *The Satanic Verses* is blasphemous in the same way that *Moby-Dick* is blasphemous — on a grand metaphorical scale. Like Melville's novel, Rushdie's allegory poses questions about the nature of good and evil that cannot, finally, be answered — questions that in the asking betoken an unwillingness to credit the word or Word of any putative authority.

It is this humanistic challenge that renders *The Satanic Verses*, along with many other great works of literature, so subversive of the claims of any system to completeness, perfection and ultimate truth. And it is this refusal to submit, on the apostate-Muslim Rushdie's part, this refusal to accept limitations on the play of intellect and imagination, that has set him at odds with Islam, the community of submission.

The *Quran* is a source of spiritual refreshment and aesthetic pleasure for the non-Muslim as well as the Muslim. Each of the 114 Suras which comprise the book is prefaced with the invocation, "In the Name of God, the Merciful, the Compassionate." In Sura 5 (and again in Suras 9, 33, 42, 58 and elsewhere), the reader is assured that "God is All-forgiving, All-compassionate." It is shameful that these words — which figure so prominently in every Muslim's life — have been so little-heeded lately in the Islamic world.

It is also shameful that, at the beginning of this surreal drama, so many institutions in the West, from governments to chain bookstores, showed such little regard for the principle that, above all others, distinguishes free societies — the right to speak, write, hear and read what we please, whether sacred or satanic. Unless we act upon the ideals we profess, we forfeit any moral standing to claim them as our own.

(March 1989)

Censorship, American-Style

In February 1987, Anthony Moser wrote a story — "Socialism, American-Style" — that characterized the nation's farmers as "the most dependent of our citizens, tied to an intricate network of government loans, subsidies and outright handouts."

Such intemperance could not escape notice, and Spectrum *subsequently lost the local Skaggs grocery chain as a distribution point after, a Skaggs spokesman informed us, two farmers from rural Lonoke County complained about the story.*

At the time, the grocery store was distributing 1,200 copies of the paper every two weeks. They let us back in a few years later. Then they were bought out by Harvest Foods. Who kicked us out. Then let us in. Then kicked us out again.

Philip Martin

Fear of a Black Aesthetic

My closest friend, a fearless little blond kid, kicks around the University of Chicago in a Public Enemy T-shirt and stirrup pants, inviting the ire of those humorless enough to take legible clothing seriously. Some folks really just don't get it — though Chuck D.'s genius sting and Flavor Flav's freaky jitter make her a minor fan, she's not witnessing for Professor Griff. If her T-shirt *means* anything, let's say it's an ironic comment on the current wave of afrocentrism, a playful token of solidarity with the struggle. Like Emma Goldman and Prince, baby'll be dancing through the revolution.

Public Enemy, of course, is not much loved in the land of Saul Bellow and Allan Bloom, where they're still waiting for the Zulus to produce a Tolstoy so they can read him. It is always a mistake to confuse pop culture with literature, and no one ought think Chuck D.'s labyrinthine internal rhymes carry anything close to the intellectual and moral gravity of Count Leo's laundry lists. Still, it might be interesting to note certain casual parallels between Carleton Ridenhour — Chuck D.'s real name — and, say, Ezra Pound. Like Pound, Ridenhour is a recombinant artist from a petit bourgeois background. And wearing a Pound T-shirt around the U of C could also be taken either as an endorsement of facism or a manifestation of the rock 'n' roll ethic. Some people might take offense — personally, I think one ought be generous when dealing with stuttering whitegirl hearts and mad poets.

Tolerance is what's called for here. Peace, love and understanding. All that crap. All I really want to know is how does an outsider-by-pigment approach a black popculture without becoming a dilettante, an aesthetic bootlegger or another liberal maschocist paying to be abused?

Relax, chief. Rock 'n' roll is basically a mulatto species, an electron spinning free from the collision of black and white musical cultures. It belongs to us — all of us. Sam Phillips knew what he was doing when he went after a white boy who could sound black — just like Maurice Starr knows what he's doing with those soul-suckled homies from Boston, the New Guys In The Room (whatever). Call it cultural imperialism if you want to, but the plain fact is both Jordan Knight and El DeBarge have equally legitimate claims on Sam Cooke and Buddy Holly. El just sings (a little) better. Lou Reed wasn't exactly kidding when he talked his way through "I Wanna Be Black"— and neither is Chuck D. when he dismisses Elvis as a racist on the aptly titled *Fear Of A Black Planet*.

What everyone knows and nobody hardly ever says anymore is that, in the words of W.E.B. DuBois, the essential "problem of the twentieth century is the problem of the color-line." Rock is one of the few areas where that line gets erased regularly. Since the Weavers bowdlerized Huddie Ledbetter's "Goodnight, Irene" (*"If Irene don't care for me, I'm gonna take morphine and die"*) into a Hit Parade ditty, white artists have subsumed and often denatured black music. Pat Boone's shameful race records and the British blues debacle gave way to the doomed gift of Jimi Hendrix, the brittle sheen of Motown and the fierce innovation of James Brown. And what of Prince's pan-ethnic élan, Michael Jackson's sad confusion and the quadroon chic of Sadé and Terrence Trent D'Arby? And Sigma Chis play P.E. in their Jeeps as they cruise the sorority row. Though it harbors its share of bigots, rock has always been a cultural blending pond.

We ought not require rock stars to be philosophers — or even very bright. Maybe we should demand they have a sense of humor — something apparent in Chuck D.'s cameo on the new Sonic Youth album when a slippery Kim Gordon sidles up to him to ask what he's going do for the "girls" victimized by "male, white, corporate oppression." (Word up, indeed.)

If the tepid Farrakahnism espoused by Public Enemy is a little hard to take in cold type on a lyric sheet, give 'em a beat and some strangulated guitar and, if you were born with rhythm, you can move to it. Danceability almost always redeems — and sometimes transcends — suspect politics.

(August 1990)

Anne Neville

TV Makes You Dumb

You've got one, your mama's got one, your brother's got one, your baby's got one — and it's doing nothing but bringing you down.

That's the only logical conclusion to be drawn from the latest annual Nielsen report, released in May with the usual fanfare and largely unexamined since. For the most part, the Nielsen readings on what we watch, in what numbers and for how long are reported variously, then promptly forgotten (*The New York Times*: "Televised Fare Entrances Nation — Market Prices Drop, Traffic Woes Lessen"; *USA Today*: "We're Couch Potatoes!"). Most often, the few people outside the industry who care about the ratings want to know how their own favorites rank; they feel a certain pride of ownership when one of "their" shows soars to the top. It makes them feel good, somehow, when the rest of the nation ratifies their enjoyment of Bill or Phil or Roseanne or Diane. (That last, incidentally, could be either Diane Chambers *or* Diane Sawyer. Both are blondes who have done well in the ratings; although one is fictional and the other purportedly not, they are all but indistinguishable in the viewing.)

So, for the record, is the viewing public. In 1988, the year covered in the 1989 Nielsen report, 98 percent of American households had at least one television set. Those sets were turned on for an average of nearly seven hours a day, reaching an estimated 232.8 million people. To put that in some sort of context, consider that *I Love Lucy*, television's first true socko-smash hit, made history in 1952, when it became the first television show ever to have been seen in 10 million homes. These days, by contrast, the *average* prime-time sitcom flickers its way into about that many living rooms on a regular basis.

The presentation of the Nielsen report contrasts sharply with the information conveyed by its figures. Slick and glossy, the report features few words — after all, television isn't about reading — but lots of colorful graphs and cheery illustrations of WASPs enjoying their televisions. Not a soul in any of the merry, cartoon-like drawings is anything other than white and prosperous-looking.

The Nielsen numbers point to a somewhat different reality. Average weekly viewing in the U.S. tops out among households with more than three people in residence and an annual income of less than $30,000. Contrary to what those who tout the educational merit of television would have us believe, a common-sense reading of these figures indicates that TV does absolutely nothing to improve the lot of the people who watch it most. If television is such a force for communicative good, shouldn't poor people with lots of children be the best-informed among us? Indeed, by its very nature, the tube may be drawing us all down in ways that have little to do with specific programming and everything to do with the limitations of the medium itself.

Despite the shiny presentation, television can easily be construed as The Enemy. Not merely because watching television and being poor go together like Geraldo and lesbian strippers, but because television represents a gross tyranny: that of the many by the few.

In greater numbers than ever before, we as a nation are receiving more information than any people at any time in history. Yet, by all indications, we seem to know and understand less and less all the time. Since 1945, our experience of the world has changed drastically. For the first time in evolutionary history, it has become mediated, rather than direct. "You are there" no longer applies only to the firsthand experiences of a single lifetime, but to anything, anywhere, that can be reached by somebody with a video camera. Revolutionaries in Beijing and South American rain forests are at least as real and perhaps even more accessible than the Little League ball game down the street.

Actually, however, the apparent experience of a given event through television consists of no more than sitting in front of a lighted screen, watching an artificially constructed, heavily edited melange of images flicker by. Viewers are inundated by fragments of mediated information conveyed by even the best-intentioned television programming (the "serious" TV, which theoretically pulls the gutter stuff up for an acceptable overall average), giving them little time to reflect. Information presented in quick-cut, rapid-fire bits and pieces leads to no great understanding, no concept of interconnection or overarching issues. Television offers little more than infobits, presented without a larger context that might give a sense of their importance or aid in their retention.

A great problem in all of this is that the overloading and fragmentation discourage involvement in the world and lead to passivity. TV aficionados tend to believe they "know" a thing by virtue of having seen it televised. This belief may manifest itself in any number of ways, but the danger is that it may discourage a television viewer from seeking out the real thing. Believing they have full knowledge and grasp of an issue, TV viewers often simply give it no more thought.

By its very nature, television is a medium more suited to communicating images than it is to conveying substance. Besides Nielsen's proudly presented great unwashed, only a few yearning idealists actually believe otherwise these days. How else to explain NBC's recent concurrent decisions to award *Today Show* anchor Bryant Gumbel a three-year, $7 million contract and to dismantle its Chicago news bureau?

Moreover, the concept of diversity in television is absurd. That's heresy around the Nielsen camp, of course. The Nielsen report proudly announces that "the average U.S. household can receive 27.7 channels today including those available via cable services." In other words, in this great, free country of ours, television works to cater to the taste of every American. In fact, however, the experience of watching the most idiotic sitcom differs little from that of watching the most acclaimed documentary, regardless of however much the concept of quality television depends on the myth that they are not at all the same thing.

Picture the audience at a multi-ring circus, with the folk watching the elephants believing their experience differs from that of the people absorbed by the performance of the acrobats. On any given evening, nearly 100 million American television viewers are doing exactly the same thing, believing themselves to be exercising individuality.

This is not the behavior of intelligent folk — and the people responsible for television's fare know they are catering to the stupid. For proof, one need look no further than "Family Hour," during which millions of people balance their dinners on their laps and chew mutely during programs, speaking during commercials only to request condiments.

And what are they viewing so intently? Shows revolving around people who rarely, if ever, watch television. Instead, they solve crimes, raise perfect children, have brilliant careers — generally while either going braless or trying to persuade someone else to do so. Viewers are presumed to be undisturbed by this flagrant tension between content and context — and indeed, no one seems bothered.

In Bill Cosby's model telefamily, there is certainly no "family hour" television viewing; no TV trays for the Huxtables, no sir. Yet Cosby's show has been a dinner-time megahit, because *nobody gets it*. Now, in a series of brief spots touting his show's nightly *kiddie* dinnertime syndication slot, Cosby — addressing the audience "just like regular folks" — invites young viewers to have mom dish him out a serving of vegetable when he joins them for dinner.

Date Rape

Attempting to account for the six-year life span of the syndicated program Love Connection, *Philip Martin wrote in February 1990 that "William Wordsworth, who lived some time before cable television really became popular, once noted that mankind suffers from a 'degrading thirst for outrageous stimulation.' As a corollary to that proposition, we might add that some people are willing enough to participate in their own humiliation so long as they can be assured that sufficient millions of people will have an opportunity to view their degradation."*

The concept involves video-matched contestants who describe their dates for the edification of the studio and home audiences. "There is an honesty to this show," Martin commented. "It sandblasts human nature down to its core pretensions. For these contestants, dignity seems no more valuable than some archaic tin trinket; if it can be bartered off for even the briefest celebrity, well isn't that better than just throwing it away for free?"

Television viewers don't see this sort of thing as pandering, condescending and internally contradictory. They think it's cute. They're stupid. If they were smart, they'd be *doing* what Cosby does, not sitting with their mouths full and *watching* what Cosby does.

A significant amount of formal research suggests that television actually *makes* people who watch it stupider than they might be otherwise. One study, conducted at Yale by psychology and child-study professor Jerome Singer, indicates that kids who stay glued to the tube understand less about everything, including television, than those who do not. Among other things, these children seem less able to follow the plots of the shows they watch, more likely to accept superheroes' feats as literally possible and less able to understand the concept of commercials than their light-viewing peers. They also exhibit less general knowledge, which may go a long way toward explaining why Americans have become so ignorant of current events and newsmakers in an era when most receive the bulk of their news through television and when *60 Minutes* rides high as a Nielsen top-10 hit.

Television is perhaps most dangerous because it squelches the imagination. When we think about almost anything — historical scenes, fictional characters, current events, foreign countries — it is an image from television that most often leaps to mind. Only in the past 50 years has this become the case, but it has entirely changed the way in which we see the world and the amount of intellectual energy we are willing to expend to grasp it. We no longer have to work for our images. Walt Disney or Bill Cosby or Peter Jennings or Aaron Spelling provides them for us.

And we let them.

(August 1989)

Rod Lorenzen

As Southern as Moon Pies

At midnight on a recent Saturday, a joint near the town square of Oxford, Mississippi, literally vibrates with the sounds of a steamy blues ballad. Outside on the inevitable porch, local people mix with tourists and pilgrims who have wandered out in need of fresh air. All of them want to put off going to bed for awhile, and a few, remembering their Southern hospitality in spite of the hour, talk politely with a lifelong Arkansan who hasn't been feeling too Southern lately. He has come armed with the questions a character in William Faulkner's *Absalom, Absalom* raised more than 50 years ago — "Tell about the South. What is it like there? What do they do there? Why do they live there? Why do they live at all?" — and finds that while everyone has an opinion, answers are as scarce as Yankees. Still, if there is a place to try and find out about the South and how Arkansas, perched like a reluctant bather on the edge of Dixie, fits into it, Oxford might be it. Earlier in the evening, the town was host to a party for a new book called *The Encyclopedia of Southern Culture*, an ambitious hulk of a book which took 10 years to produce and runs more than 1,600 pages.

It purports to tell everything about what Southerners have been, but readers could come away from it without much of an idea of what we are now. A lot of books and magazines have tried to explain the downtrodden, sorry past of slavery and racism and reconcile it to the modern South, hustling for new industry and — finally — integrating its schools. This contrast is an enigma which will take the visitor from Arkansas into a long, sleepless night.

Larry Brown, a captain of the Oxford Fire Department who grew up in rural Mississippi, is a good ole boy who represents the South of the storytellers to which Arkansas certainly is no stranger. On the porch, Brown talks in the soft, earthy drawl you find easily in Arkansas. In 1980, he got the notion he could pick up some extra money by writing fiction. After eight years of struggle, he has turned what otherwise might have been a cruel joke on himself into a book of short stories and a brand-new novel. Recently, he sold the country store he and his wife, Mary Annie, ran in nearby Tula. Now he just writes and puts out fires. Unlike some of his contemporaries, who worry that "Southern writer" status might limit their appeal and the audience for their books, Brown doesn't fret about being labeled. "Hell, naw," he says. "I'm proud of it." Brown is 38 years old, an ex-Marine whose father died when the writer was but 16. " I'm proud to be a Southern writer and particularly proud to be a Mississippi writer."

Those who have read his work know his writing is smooth and deft, catching the speech and rhythms of the common man, elevating them the way a good writer can. Brown writes about Southern roots — perhaps that is the story here. He seems sure of it. A young woman who works on the staff of Mississippi Governor Ray Mabus compares notes with the Arkansan on everything from the Delta their states share to Baptists, blue laws and contraceptives in schools. She is repulsed by her state legislature, which she says takes care of itself and its friends first, then spends a few days toward the tag-end of the session thinking about the rest of Mississippi. She and the visitor agree the mutual problems of their states seem insurmountable at times, yet there is confidence and hope in her voice. "We have more black legislators now than any other state," she points out "and they are speaking for white people too. We are finally getting a broader representation."

Earlier, the Arkansan stood on the veranda of Square Books where voices

Grade Inflation

Jess Henderson and Jane Wood's June 1986 cover story detailed how the Arkansas Industrial Development Commission "routinely fudged the scorecard of its triumphs." Though the AIDC claimed responsibility for attracting 10,653 new jobs to the state in the years 1980-1986, Henderson and Wood revealed the number was inflated, and the real number of new jobs was only about 52 percent of the claimed total. It was not the last time Spectrum *would point out AIDC dishonesty.*

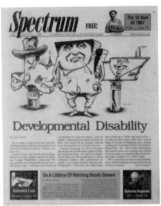

Mascot

The Arkansas caricature which debuted in issue 26 came to become a sort of mascot for Spectrum, *reappearing periodically throughout the years. Credit should be given to the Cranford Johnson Robinson agency's ad campaign for the Arkansas Industrial Development Commission, from whom the "Arkie" character was appropriated.*

from the party below competed with the folksy ramblings of a bluegrass band and answers about being Southern only seemed to diffuse themselves. So much of our history is bound up in places like Oxford or Little Rock. Much of it has gone, yet so much remains.

Over on the town square, a Confederate soldier stands on his pedestal and watches over a crowd of several hundred who will wait for hours to get their copies of the *Encyclopedia* signed by its co-editors and a flock of its contributors. At the A.G. Nielson Department Store, established in 1939, the wind breathes life into four flags, one of them the Mississippi state flag with its Confederate stars and bars showing in one corner.

Oxford is a story-book kind of place, the picture of quaint Southernness. It is a city of rare cultural wealth which houses the University of Mississippi, the Center for the Study of Southern Culture, and a colony of good writers. Square Books is one of the country's finest bookstores with its bountiful sections on literature and history where a visitor might lose himself and take time to rediscover his heritage between the pages. People dressed as famous Southern characters wander through the state and into the party below. An Ole Miss art teacher, Lisa Howorth, is dressed up like Tammy Faye Bakker, with painted-on tears spilling down her cheeks. An authentic Dolly Parton struts past. Actually, she is Jane Burdine, mayor of neighboring Taylor and head of a town council comprised of three artists and two farmers. Water-filled balloons, she confides, help provide the expansive Dolly frontage.

William Ferris, one of the co-editors of the *Encyclopedia,* is dressed up in an Elvis outfit. The Kudzu Patrol, employees of the bookstore, have wrapped themselves in genuine kudzu vines with leaves as big as Moon Pies that flap as they walk past. Barry Hannah, the nationally prominent author who lives and works in Oxford, is the only person who's dressed like a writer, but then this is everyday wear for him. He wears a dull-pink sports coat, a snapbrim hat with matching headband and shades. Maybe Faulkner himself would dress that way nowadays, but that's another one of those questions.

A garish Southern parody is being played out here. Though the joke's on us, it's okay. The white-trash appeal of Elvis and commercial country music with its woeful studies in cheatin' and drinkin'; the sad come-on of the South's religious leaders who fall from grace only to be reborn again and again; the old politicians who wear string ties and have to remind themselves not to use the word "nigger" — these are the images that bring back the questions.

The Encyclopedia of Southern Culture is perhaps the definitive work on the South and its culture — that integrated pattern of human knowledge, belief and behavior that depends upon man's capacity for learning and transmitting knowledge to succeeding generations. Even so, Arkansans could spend hours pouring through the fat volume and still not find much they didn't already know about how they might connect to the rest of the South. One supposes we are different in Arkansas, with our hill folks and the cowboys and people in the central part of the state trying to be big-city. While the book is meant to be a general reflection of the South, the casual browser might fear we'd been written off.

Orval Faubus is there, along with five thick paragraphs on the integration crisis of 1957. We find mention of the entrepreneurial genius of Sam Walton, who has gone on to great wealth but left behind a South full of abandoned Wal-Mart strip centers from whence his stores have moved to newer and bigger quarters a mile or so down the highway. Baseball pitcher Dizzy Dean shows up. The beloved Razorbacks don't, although rival coaches Frank Broyles and Darrell Royal are cited for their coaching success in the same paragraph. There is a picture of the Buckstaff Bath House in Hot Springs but no mention of any others or the city's famous bottled water. Nothing is made of Hot Springs' past as a former safety-zone for gangsters like Owney Madden or Al Capone, who used the baths to treat his venereal disease. No mention is made of Hot Springs as a former gambling paradise where casino owners and lounge owners politely dished out credit if they could find your name in their Dun & Brad listings.

In 1953, we are told, a Cotton League baseball team from Jackson refused to play a Hot Springs team because the Arkansas team fielded a black pitcher. Two years later, a Pine Bluff team in the same league signed three blacks, then let them go because of pressure from out-of-state teams. Nothing on the musicians from the Arkansas side of the Delta who first played and have preserved the Blues. Glen Campbell gets mentioned, but not Johnny Cash. In the movie section, we see Gil Gerard, but not Mary Steenburgen. The visitor wonders if anyone remembers or cares that Dick Powell was from Little Rock and guesses not. The *Arkansas Gazette* is mentioned as a Pulitzer-Prize winner as well as "the paper of choice" in Arkansas, but not as the oldest west of the Mississippi. Perhaps that is the problem here. Going west out of the South, Arkansas lies across that big river and so it tends to get left high and dry, in spite of the fact that Little Rock is listed as one of the South's notable cities. We are lauded for our hospitality to strangers and hailed as a rising star in the Sunbelt South with our cosmopolitan feel and high regard for good manners and good cooks.

Otherwise, there are few things mentioned with which Arkansas might distinguish itself or lay claim to Southern kin. On the national scene, William Fulbright and Brooks Hays are listed and Hope is cited as the watermelon capital. John Gould Fletcher, our one important contribution to the world of poetry, is mentioned as part of a group of Southern writers whose agrarian theme on work and leisure was popular 40 years ago. None of our writers are mentioned, but the book seems to concentrate on obvious, established choices such as Faulkner and Eudora Welty and Flannery O'Connor and Willie Morris.

So far as Arkansas is concerned, this massive book seems to close in on itself. Still, its purpose is noble and courageous and the Arkansan has to remind himself that he is being fussy and sensitive. There are answers here if one were to read it in its entirety or until the light from dim memories begins to glow. All that pales so quickly these days in the face of the television set where announcers prattle in flat, neutral tones as though the slightest twang, the dropping of a "g" might remind us of who and where we are.

Morris, the writer from Oxford who left the South and wrote about it in *North Toward Home,* recalls that every time he came back he felt that Southern culture was an actual force which smothered him with its language and religious fervor and double standards and how all this drained away when he boarded an airplane to go back to New York.

As the party winds down, Charles Wilson, one of the co-editors of the book, confirms that it is this sense of place which defines the South.

"When I was little," he says, "we used to drive from Texas up to see relatives in west Tennessee and we always stopped at the Razorback Drive-In on Roosevelt Road in Little Rock." The Razorback, long gone now but once known for its down-home fare, had waitresses there who said "hon" a lot and knew about hospitality.

"That was Southern," Wilson recalls. But to find this anymore you have to get out of the big city where waiters won't have to explain that they will be your servers for the evening.

"Yes," Wilson admits, "we're all getting much more like the rest of the country but religion is one of the great continuities. The South is still a region that could be defined by Baptist and Methodist churches. Polls show that religion brings people together in the South and that pattern is so deeply ingrained. It makes sense that religion would be attractive to people who have lived with a lot of hardship."

Flannery O'Connor once wrote that the South is not so much consumed by

Shopping the Wal-Mart Way

"This store is the biggest goddamn thing that ever hit this town," boasted a Wal-Mart manager, and Spectum *was on the scene in December 1985, providing an early report on what Sam Walton had wrought in rural America. Randal Seyler observed that in many communities the local Wal-Mart had become "an ad hoc center for social interaction among people from all economic strata," a substitute for the old courthouse square.*

"I think Wal-Mart represents a change in our philosophy of economics," commented Dr. Jerry King, assistant professor of sociology at Arkansas State University at Jonesboro. "Wal-Mart is a kind of smorgasbord of mass consumption ... There's nothing perceived as sinful about going to Wal-Mart. In fact, if anything, we're really conforming to the American Dream, which means getting all the stuff you can get."

The arrival of a Wal-Mart in a small town, Seyler noted, means jobs for those without higher educational credentials — an opportunity for many in straitened rural economies. But other area businesses are often blown away; in Pocahontas, Arkansas, for instance, the once-bustling Sterling, Ben Franklin and Fred's stores all went under. Now, one customer said, "Necessity is the reason people come to Wal-Mart."

Issue 54, July 1987.

religion as it is haunted by it. It seems a nice way of saying we like to party hard on Saturday night and be able to feel guilty about it on Sunday morning.

Ferris, the book's other co-editor, directs the Center for the Study of Southern Culture and is a former consultant to the Arkansas Heritage Commission. "In Arkansas," he points out, "you have three distinct cultural zones — the Ozarks, the Delta and Texas. It's a real important dimension of the *Encyclopedia* that it puts all this experience side by side. You have an extraordinary array of politicians and cultural figures who are part of Arkansas and the South and yet are very different."

"Arkansas has a lot of population change with retirement communities migrating in. Those people adapt and, in some ways, become more Southern than we do." Arkansas and the entire region, Ferris believes, will continue to assert itself in music, literature and politics and "embrace an international vision."

"Our politics," he says, "will become more multi-racial and shift from the old-guard, solid-South to a more varied constituency. The South will be the country's most interesting area politically with the young black and white leadership." The image of the Southerner as a redneck, however, will be harder to scrape off than an old bumper sticker. So, too, will the reality of economic inequality for black people.

"It's easy for those stereotypes to continue for people who don't have the resources others do," Ferris claims. "In the South, we've turned that into a source of pride, however, with blues and country music. The stereotype is only part of the bigger picture."

Down on the square, they are eating greens and cornbread and a paté made from black-eyed peas. Willie Morris, we are told, has shown up for a moment, then taken off, as though the Southernness of the party might have been too much for him to bear. Didn't someone once say that part of being Southern has to do with not saying anything about it? But that approach is sneaky and evasive, it squeezes the life out of the questions about the South and leaves them cold and mute as statues on a courthouse lawn. How will we know if we don't ask?

From the middle of Mississippi, you can drive north for hours and not see much of anything but the kudzu-ridden corridor of I-55. Then there is Memphis and a hard left turn that takes you into flat Arkansas farmland. The visitor heads west, toward home, uncertain if he has answered any of the questions about Arkansas, and how it fits into the Southern jigsaw. There is more to consider than things from the past, and he senses there are other things which have hardly begun to be written about or felt or thought. He remembers a T-shirt worn to the party by Richard Howorth, the owner of Square Books and someone who has worked for a different and better South — one in which the Arkansan might find a place. Maybe the answer was on Howorth's shirt and we have only to pick the correct one to have the correct message to take home. His shirt read:

> *We shall:*
> *a. overcome*
> *b. rise again*
> *c. endure and prevail*
> *d. all of the above.*

(August 1989)

Philip Martin

Tanya Tucker is Out Shopping or Something

Little Rock isn't mentioned once in the skimpy official biography of Tanya Tucker her people Federal Expressed to me in anticipation of an interview that didn't happen. The interview didn't happen because Tanya Tucker didn't call me like they said she would. Her road manager did call — finally — from O'Hare International Airport in Chicago, to tell me that he had just put "The Texas Tornado" on a plane to Indianapolis and that she wouldn't be calling me after all.

It's probably best that she didn't call; if she had, then we would have spent maybe 30 or 40 minutes exchanging vague pleasantries and talking about her new album and about how much she loves Little Rock and how happy she is to be back in Arkansas. And I would have probably written something along the lines of:

Tanya Tucker, who has some tangential relationship to Little Rock, is coming home to sing at the Arkansas State Fair.

"I'm really happy and proud to be back in Arkansas singing for all the good folks there," Glen Campbell's former paramour said. "I've got a lot of friends in Arkansas and I'm really anxious to see them all again. I love fairs and we're going to have a real good time in Little Rock."

And then we probably would have talked about how amazing it is that the little girl who sang "Delta Dawn" is now 31 years old (on October 10), which really isn't very old but heck, she's already had 17 years of flat-out celebrity which is a lot more than the 15 minutes you're supposed to get and she would say something like "Yeah, I've been lucky but I've worked hard and I've been through some tough times too."

I would have tried to ask her about her wild reputation and she would have laughed and said, "Well, Bill, if I'd done half the things people said I've done I'd be dead by now."

Honestly, I'm glad I didn't talk to Tanya Tucker because if I had talked to Tanya Tucker she would have probably just been another disembodied celebrity voice calling from some motel room somewhere to give me the same quotes she's given everybody else at every other newspaper in every town she's played and it would have all been stale and plastic and "nice." That's how she would have come off, because she's a pro and that's how professionals come off when they talk to newspaper people, and judging from the interviews and the press packet they're pushing a new, more demure Tanya Tucker these days.

Her fact sheet makes her looks like she's campaigning for sophomore class favorite (*"Fun ... A tradition!! Training cutting horses, scuba diving, skiing, cooking Mexican food, redecorating her home, enjoying the company of other Nashville songwriters ..."*) with this rather unflattering photo — it makes her face look puffy — of her in a flannel coat with ribbons in her hair and an expression that suggests she's shy or soft or something.

Sorry, Gnashville P.R.-type folks, but I don't want my Tanya Tucker reduced to nice, bland celebrity mush. I want my Tanya Tucker to be bawdy and arrogant and drug-stunned and sexy in a white-trash, soulful way. I want Tanya Tucker to be like her voice sounds, like sweaty, grimy, full-throttle sin in the back

Sex Therapists

In October 1989, JoBeth Briton profiled fun couple Elton and Betty White, the city's favorite dirty ditty singers. Elton, a six-foot-three, 32-year-old black man, and Betty, a 63-year-old white woman, had been married the previous June after being together for "five or six years."

While their brand of ukelele-strumming, soft-porn balladeering (mostly about body parts and the exchange of fluids) was most often regarded as a novelty, Little Rock disc jockey Jerry Coburn, who helped bring the duo to a sort of local prominence, didn't think they were a joke.

"I'm in the minority," Coburn said. "I consider them to be American urban folk artists and in that genre I see them as being as good as anybody in America ... I've heard hundreds and hundreds of artists, and nobody sounds like them."

Arsenio Hall evidently had never heard anyone like them, either. Indeed, he seemed truly amazed when 10 seconds of Elton and Betty's homemade video rolled on his late-night television show.

seat of a rusted-out Oldsmobile up on blocks in the dirt lot behind Jeeter Lester's silverwood shack. I want her hair-pulling mean and hot as Georgia in August. I want her turned around backwards on her album covers, her butt thrust out like a challenge. I want her to come across like Brenda Lee crossed with Sean Penn; I want her to smash some cameras, to be difficult and high-strung as those over-bred horses of which she seems so fond.

Look, I know the real Tanya Tucker is not some soft-focus ingenue. When she was nine years old her father Beau — an itinerant construction worker with tattoos — drove her from their home in Wilcox, Arizona, to Nashville in a brand-new Cadillac. They had a good time, but when they got back to Wilcox, Beau had to give the car back to the bank. The real Tanya Tucker is a trailer-court Madonna, *Lolita* written by Erskine Caldwell, a gone little girl who had this world-weary husk in her voice by the time she was 13. Despite the tutelage of hack producer Billy Sherrill (who along with Chet Atkins almost killed country music in the 1960s, but that's another rant) the real Tanya Tucker (so the legend goes) passed on tripe like "The Happiest Girl in The Whole U.S.A." (which later became a number one hit for Donna Fargo) and recorded, in March 1972, the difficult and poignant psycho-drama "Delta Dawn" as her debut record.

"Delta Dawn" was one of the great country songs of the 1970s, grand and sad and wounded and Tanya sang it until it hurt. It still does. Helen Reddy? Helen Reddy couldn't carry Tanya Tucker's jock. Tanya owns that song and no long, tall, pop-singing woman from Australia ever stood a chance of wrestling it away from her, even though Tanya was only 13 years old and plain as a runty brown puppy.

It wasn't a one-shot. The hits kept coming, and though they might not have been as memorable as that first one, a few came close. "What's Your Mama's Name Child," "Blood Red and Going Down," "Lizzie and the Rainman," "Would You Lay With Me (In a Field of Stone)," "The Man Who Turned My Mama On" — Tanya Tucker tore it up in 1973, 1974 and 1975, and qualified for the Country Music Hall of Fame before she could buy beer. She made appearances on almost every important network variety show — and they had a lot of those shows back in the mid-1970s — and was a perennial nominee for Country Music Association Awards. It's to her credit that she was too much of a natural artist to win many of those awards — something about a big full voice coming out of that little girl was a little frightening. Somehow, though she was surrounded by advisors and Sherrill-types, she avoided the deadly slickness that infested country music in the 1970s.

And all of a sudden — on one of those album covers from the mid-1970s — she wasn't plain anymore. In 1978, she moved to Los Angeles, and in a career move as calculated and risky as when Bob Dylan picked up an electric guitar for the first time, they stuffed little Tanya into Spandex and released an inchoate rock 'n' roll album called *TNT* (not hardly a joke, her version of "Not Fade Away" stands up with the Stones'), canceled almost a million dollars in country concert dates in an effort to change her image, and set to work on the "Ms. Bad Ass" reputation she still wears on her sleeve and on the license plate of her Mercedes convertible. By the time Tanya was 24 she was better known for her affairs with Don Johnson, Andy Gibb and — most notoriously — Glen Campbell, than she was for her music. Tanya Tucker became kind of a joke, one of those demi-stars whose private lives stoke the tabloids. *People* magazine became her official biographer: Tanya and Glen sing the National Anthem together at the Republican National Convention, Glen turns up outside Tanya's Bossier City, Louisiana hotel room, screaming obscenities and threatening violence. The police are called and the Rhinestone Cowboy is led away ...

Tanya used to tell reporters that Glen Campbell was the "horniest man" she'd ever met, and he used to call her a "raunchy young broad." She says that she called the whole thing off after Glen got "violent" but I bet Tanya got her licks in. Just can't feature her backing down from any mere man.

By 1982, Tanya Tucker was broke. Her daddy Beau flew out to L.A., paid her bills and moved her back to Nashville. Tanya flew to New York for a weekend where she took up with the doomed Andy Gibb, who had just been dumped by Victoria Principal. That weekend stretched into a couple of months, and — though she kept working — the next five or six years blurred into a boozy, reeling reverie that finally landed her in rehab in January 1988.

I doubt Tanya would have talked to me about that part of her life. According to *People*, she's got a sign on her bedroom door that says it all: "No One Gets In To See the Wizard. No Way. No How."

All that stuff's a closed chapter now, Tanya's a survivor who's been through Betty Ford's clinic — where she was (good girl) predictably stubborn and refused to open up in the touchy-feelie, group therapy sessions — and presumably she's tempered her appetites for alcohol and cocaine and swung away from the rock 'n' roll tendencies and started to rebuild her country career, which sputtered but never completely went out during that lost decade. The party line seems to be that Tanya is back with her family now, living — if we are to believe her press materials, which I don't as a matter of principle — a fairly boring existence on her ranch near Nashville.

She stills does 200 shows a year, she stills records a new album every 10 months or so, and though her voice has ripened into a slightly less raw instrument than the throaty, honey-over-gravel growl she came out with, it's still distinctive and supple. Tanya Tucker is back, y'all, and if you don't like it I get the feeling she might come to your house with a shotgun and call you out. Nothing you could do but cower under the bed and wait for her to go away.

She hasn't gone away yet. If we're real good, maybe she won't.

(October 1989)

Anne Courtemanche-Ellis

Expressions of an Ozark Culture

Someone once wrote that the Ozarks are "a shy landscape." Shy they are, and from at least one perspective, the quilt-makers of the Ozarks give the same impression. I once asked a quilter I'd never met if we could meet at the only cafe in our county seat, Jasper. This quilter, a woman who'd raised 11 children in a bona fide hand-hewn log cabin, replied that she'd never been in the Ozark Cafe, and, if I didn't care, she'd rather meet in the laundromat next door.

Drawing attention to one's self in this way is almost a sin in rural places like Newton County. A quilt-maker who lives in the area was asked once to embroider her name not on the back of her quilt, but on the front, right at the top. She responded, incredulously, "Just like painters do?"

Thus, the refined tone of four quilting exhibitions taking place in Little Rock would strike awe in the hearts of mountain quilters. The shows — at the Decorative Arts Museum, the Arkansas Territorial Restoration, the Heights Gallery and at the National Quilting Association convention — reflect a different world, where quilters express themselves without the traditional constraints of style and culture that have restricted the women of Newton County for so many years.

Not that these quilters haven't enjoyed some exposure beyond the county line. The works of several Newton County women have been displayed as far away as Madison Avenue, the Williamsburg Museum in Virginia and at an exhibition in Bogota, Colombia. But their so-called "scrap" quilts — those made from pieces of fabric left over from other projects — are almost never displayed, even though their artistry can rival that of the quilts now being shown in Little Rock galleries.

Scrap quilts are made to keep the family warm, rather than to be prized and stored away as heirlooms. The author of *A Legacy of Ozark Quilts,* Michael Luster, once described them as "short on elegance." But like the creeks that run through the Ozark Mountains, these quilts generally get more interesting after you explore them further. Just as the tiny creeks are as much a part of the scenery as the more famous rivers, so these quilts are just as interesting — in their own way — as are those that are more patently artistic.

A quilt of unknown origin made during the 1930s in Swain, which is just up the road from Nail and Deer, reveals the creativity of Newton County quilters in spite of — or, perhaps, because of — an incredibly sparse pallet of fabrics to work with. Every other square of the quilt is pieced with varying diagonal stripes, and the top is sewn together not with thread, but rather with the string that once held a feedsack closed tight. Quilting authority Geri Waechter explained that many vendors of sewing supplies never got as far as Jasper during the Depression.

The diagonal designs on the Swain quilt were not randomly determined by the size of the maker's scraps. Many of the light shapes of muslin were pieced together with muslin scraps too small to fill the light space the maker needed to achieve the overall balance of the quilt. The solid blocks were dyed, probably with rusty nails, giving the quilt a subtle yet also dramatic tone. Ilene Jones Goldman of New York, who bought the quilt recently, said it would introduce "inspired reality" to her Park Avenue condominium.

Another very "real" quilt is a unique adaptation of a traditional pattern known as "the Spool." Made in Low Gap, north of Jasper, the quilt dances with fascinating rhythms. Just when the viewer's eyes have focused on the spool in the design, other intricate abstract compositions suddenly pop out. These endless tactile combinations — tender ginghams, raw plaid silks and intricate homespun prints—could never be duplicated in another medium.

So what might the makers of these "everyday" quilts have to say to the pioneering exhibitors of the Art Quilt show? When a Newton County quilter asks what a quilted wallhanging could be used for, she's also wondering what fabric can do better than any other medium. If fabric is more fun to touch, why do these art quilters from Maine want to encase their quilts in wooden room dividers? What is it about Ruth McDowell's reminiscent pond quilt, with three-dimensional water lilies, that makes it more effective (though less gutsy) photographed than in person? And what about that extraordinary patchwork quilt by Pamela Studstill? Is she trying to put one over on us by painting in all those stripes to make it look like she did more piecing?

Newton County quilts are as distinctive from "art quilts" made by urbanites as the mountain women who make them are different from their city-dwelling counterparts. The trappings that encrust urban life and all its conventions are alien to the women of the Ozarks. On the 100-mile stretch of highway between Russellville and Harrison, it's hard to find even one traffic light or fast-food outlet. One Ozark quilter, Carol Ray, has run her sewing machine on power from a small generator for the past seven years, and in a pinch she's used ashes from her wood-burning stove to make the soap with which she pre-shrinks her fabric. Another, Mary Olson, has what she jokingly refers to as her quilting "studio" — one mini-Singer sewing machine — wedged between the kitchen stove and a deep freeze packed with the lamb and beef her family slaughtered. The top of the freezer doubles as the ironing board.

Yet the home-grown Newton County quilters do take kindly to the New Age transplants who have moved into the area, and they generously share their strong sense of place with the new arrivals. Life here is simple: when asked if she was born here, one quilter said no, she was from a different area entirely — she's from Deer, which is a full 12 miles up the road. A 94-year-old quilter, whose favorite pattern is "Road to Oklahoma," wouldn't let his wife hook their home up to the new public water supply, because he didn't want all those pipes cluttering up the house.

One quilter, whose most recent work took her seven years to complete, spends most of her time quietly farming in Walnut Valley with her mother. She doesn't get to see her sister very often, since she lives 15 miles away. But she scored a big success not long ago when her quilt was named Show Favorite at the Newton County Quilt Show. It was a "Double Wedding Ring" design carefully made from three-quarter inch, postage stamp-sized pieces of fabric. Someday, she wants to make a quilt picturing her farm. When she does, it will show an always freshly painted white farmhouse over a hundred years old, the first in Walnut Valley, uncharacteristically complete with a broad bay window in front and endlessly mysterious barns behind. She loves a challenge so much when she quilts that she'll probably solve the problem of opening up her quilt to the interior of her home: at least 14-foot-high ceilings, tall-posted iron beds and new kitchen cabinets painted as fresh as the house's clapboard exterior.

That's a fitting subject for a Newton County quilter: her art is drawn from her own remote surroundings, simple and shy and distant from urbanity. It may not be high art, but it is truthful art — an expression of a culture most of us just pass through on our way to somewhere else.

(June 1987)

Runaway Train

Spectrum *associate editor Anthony Moser took on Academy Award-winning actress (and native Arkansan) Mary Steenburgen with his September 1987 review of* End of the Line. *The film was shot primarily in North Little Rock and had its "gala world premiere" at Little Rock's Cinema 150.*

Though it was an apparent labor of love for the locally bred Steenburgen, who served as one of three producers as well as taking a small role, Moser described the film as "an incredibly, unbelievably bad movie" in which Arkies were portrayed as so hickish they made "Minnie Pearl look like Margaret Thatcher."

The Washington Post *noted Moser's hometown slam in a lengthy feature about the film which bore the headline, "Stony Reception in Little Rock."*

Philip Martin

It's Over for the Voice

He didn't die young enough to be forever preserved in our memory as a beautiful boy, but Roy Orbison was never a beautiful boy anyway. He had bad hair and weak eyes; he was fat and his skin was pale and sallow.

To watch him onstage was to feel embarrassed for him. He looked clunky and painfully sincere, and worst of all, like he didn't quite get it. Orbison looked a little like a rube Elvis impersonator checking out of the Motel 6 at 3 a.m., or maybe someone's sad dad trying to approximate Marlon Brando in *The Wild Ones*. Black leather and prescription shades failed to camouflage the heavy shyness that rooted him to the stage, locked him up and bent him slightly forward at the waist, his guitar held up under his chin. Roy weren't no dancer, no Jumpin' Jack Flash, no swirling dervish in yellow tights ... just a big lumbering boy from Texas.

But rock 'n' roll is an ultimately democratic art form, in so far as it acknowledges that even geeks have something to say. Roy Orbison wasn't much good at moving around, but the boy could flat-out sing.

Orbison's voice was an uncanny, utterly redeeming instrument, maybe the best voice ever to mine that curious vein of popular music we call rock 'n' roll. It was seamless and true and it invited comparisons to Caruso. Orbison could glide through five octaves effortlessly, easily reaching notes in his super-natural voice that other singers could approach only in falsetto.

It was sweet and it was sad; Orbison's *bel-canto* tenor lent a bitter resonance to the scary words he sang. Orbison was rock's first real neurotic. Songs like "It's Over," "Only the Lonely," "Running Scared" and "Crying" ached with unrequited desire.

Orbison's life imitated his art — his first wife died in a motorcycle accident in 1966 and two years later two of his three children died when his Nashville home burned. His career also faded in the late Sixties, but he never stopped touring, never went gently into oblivion. He hung on, a lumpy figure giving concerts that took on a pathetic kitsch. It was only in the last couple of years that Roy Orbison rediscovered his artistic compass. In 1986, his haunting "In Dreams" was an integral part of David Lynch's schizoid *Blue Velvet*, and then the next year he contributed a shivery ballad (about suicide, typically enough) to the magnificent *Less Than Zero* soundtrack. Last year he goofed with the great as a member of the Traveling Wilburys. Ironically, the *Traveling Wilburys Vol. I* album is the biggest-selling record Orbison ever enjoyed.

The posthumously released *Mystery Girl*, Orbison's first album of new material in nine years, will no doubt be snatched up by the sentimental and the curious; it is chocked with familiar melodrama and the songs all sound like old Orbison songs. They don't sound old-fashioned, exactly — not even Orbison's old records sound dated — but it is obvious that the various producers here approached The Voice with reverence.

Songs are set, jewel-like, rather than produced. That is at once the album's greatest vice and its greatest virtue; while there is a comforting sameness to the songs, they are disappointing in their modesty. There are no grand gestures here, and no great disappointments. Elvis Costello's "The Comedians" is perhaps the best cut here, but there are no surprises.

Born in Vernon, Texas, in 1936, Orbison was raised in the West Texas boom town of Wink. His father, a peripatetic laborer who strummed at Jimmie Rodgers songs, gave him his first guitar when he was six.

Within two years he was regularly performing country songs on the radio; at 10, he played a medicine show, and his high school classmates, a lot of whom still live in Wink, remember Orbison singing ballads during assemblies.

"He wasn't much to look at," one of his classmates once told a reporter. "But at least he did something with his gift."

Orbison formed his first band while in high school. The Wink Westerners featured an amplified accordion and they played dances and jamborees throughout West Texas with an eclectic repertoire that included "Moonlight in Vermont" and "In the Mood" as well as Webb Pierce songs. They were clean-cut kids, regulars on local television, the sort of band that a high school principal would recruit when he campaigned for the presidency of the Lion's Club.

Though only a year younger than Elvis, Orbison nevertheless belonged to the second generation of rock 'n' rollers — for Orbison rock 'n' roll was something of a commercial decision. Though he would later confess his tastes ran more to softer, country-influenced material, Orbison reformed, at the urging of fellow North Texas State student Pat Boone, the Westerners as the "Teen-Kings" to experiment with the then-nascent rock form.

Recorded at the band's expense in Norman Petty's Clovis, New Mexico, studio, the driving "Ooby Dooby" caught the ear of Johnny Cash, who suggested that Orbison send the tape to Sam Phillips at Sun Records in Memphis. Phillips — already Svengali to Elvis, Cash, Carl Perkins and Jerry Lee Lewis — recut "Ooby Dooby," giving Orbison his first hit in 1956. Unable to follow up, the Teen-Kings dissolved around Orbison, who soon became disillusioned with Phillips' "unprofessionalism."

"Sam brought me out a set of thick 78 records and said, 'Now this is the way I want you to sing'," Orbison remembered years later. "He played Arthur Crudup's 'That's All Right.' He said 'Sing like that ... and like this.' And he put on a song called 'Mystery Train' by Junior Parker. I couldn't believe it ... I said 'Sam, I'm a ballad singer. I want to sing ballads.' He said, 'No, you're gonna sing what I want you to sing. Elvis always wanted to sing like the Ink Spots or Bing Crosby'."

After a couple of years in Nashville as a staff writer for Acuff-Rose Publishing — during which he wrote "Claudette" for the Everly Brothers, "Down the Line" for Jerry Lee Lewis and some album filler for Buddy Holly — Orbison decided to try again as a solo singer.

Beginning with "Only the Lonely" in 1960, Orbison enjoyed a remarkable run of singles. In four years, he placed nine singles in the Top 10 while a number of others just missed. They were good records, marked by a haunting lushness. From a production standpoint, only Phil Spector's creations matched Orbison's operatic dramas. The songs incorporated everything from weepy steel guitars to swirling strings to syncopated Latin rhythms. Some were touched with reminiscences of classical music. They soared and swooned, with Orbison's voice building from a low conversational tone to the inevitable keening crescendo — a wired, nervous edge creeping into the high-end quaver.

Mercy. There was something odd and beautiful about a Roy Orbison song. There still is.

(February 1989)

Jim Nichols

The Feather in Country Music's Hat

The afternoon was almost blinding outside when Rodney Crowell walked into Juanita's before his sound check. Judging by his chalky complexion, sunlight didn't seem to be his closest friend; he circled the room before sidling up to the end of the bar farthest from the window and unfamiliar glare.

He ordered a cup of coffee. He was cold, he said.

He looked cold. Not cool, like on the cover of his latest album. Just cold, as in lack of warmth. Wearing sweat pants, a black leather jacket, a gold hoop earring and well-worn red baseball cap pulled too far down on his head, Rodney Crowell in the daylight looks very much unlike country music's hottest new star.

But a few minutes into an interview he seemed reluctant to undertake — his fifth of the day — it became clear that the man is like his music: the warmth and the humor are abundant, but sometimes they're below the surface. The heavy dose of those qualities on his wonderful latest release, *Diamonds and Dirt*, have shot Crowell to the top of his profession. Suddenly, after nearly 20 years in the the business and five albums, he's being called an overnight success.

"Aren't all overnight successes that way?" he said, his head jerking back as he laughs.

It was sarcasm without bitterness. He can afford not to be bitter: his album is a smash by any standard. Three singles from the eight-month-old *Diamonds and Dirt* have already hit No. 1 on the *Billboard* country charts, and Crowell has been nominated for three Grammy awards. By his own admission, he's making "a very good living." And he's married to Roseanne Cash, the hippest, most sultry woman in Nashville.

But an overnight success? Hardly.

"The thing of it is, I was producing Roseanne's records and they were hit records," he said with more than a trace of defensiveness. "I was producing a lot of other hit records, too. I was a tremendous success as a songwriter and producer, but in the public eye, songwriters and producers aren't the stars."

Crowell had just finished a games of basketball at the downtown YMCA with a few members of his stellar band, The Dixie Pearls. Seven hours after finishing his coffee, he would be on stage before a couple of hundred enthusiastic fans as the headline act in Trimble Studio's Musicians' Ball in the next room. It was the eighth stop on a 25-date tour for the album, in one of the tour's smaller venues, and only his second performance in the state.

"It was great, just great," he said of his reception at the first Arkansas show, which he played to rave reviews six months earlier. "I was completely delighted." He repaid the delight with interest at Juanita's in one of the most spectacular, rocking shows in these parts in a long, long time.

Such are the fruits of success. Until his self-recorded songs got their current heavy airplay, his stage act had been largely relegated to the role of opening act for bigger names, albeit in bigger cities. "The nature of my audience was that I was what you'd call a cult artist," he said. "What's great about radio success and hit records is that I can go into the secondary markets — let's face it: Little Rock's not considered a big city."

Crowell's road to fame began 38 years ago in Houston, where he was born, he says, to "a semi-religious mother and a semi-rebellious father" in a family solidly rooted in rich musical soil. His grandma played guitar. One grandfather was a church-choir director, the other a bluegrass banjoist. His daddy, a laborer and a honky-tonk guitarist himself, was a sharecropper's son from Blytheville, Arkansas, whose love of music passed to his son.

"The earliest stuff that interested me, from the time I was this high, was music," Crowell recalled, holding his hand two feet from the floor. "It was mystical, almost a magical thing."

Crowell's memories from that age are filled with the riveting sounds of Tennessee Ernie Ford and Hank Williams. Later, he was consumed by Elvis, the Beatles and Bob Dylan. But rock 'n' roll never suppressed his love for country music. "My enthusiasm for country music and the Rolling Stones was pretty much equal," he said. "I'd walk out of a record store with Hank Williams on one end of a stack of records and the Beatles and the Stones on the other."

At first it was the beat that drove him. Crowell took up drums at age 11, performing with local rock bands as a teenager. Along the way, he picked up guitar, occasionally playing the blue-collar bars with his dad. And he started to write. He had to. "The reason I started to write was I had so many songs in my head that I didn't have room for 'em. I had to write 'em down."

He admitted reluctantly that he wrote songs as a teenager, when he wasn't playing music or pitching a baseball, his other early love. (His eyes still twinkle as he says, with a typical lack of false modesty, "I was good.") Some were the songs of an 18-year-old trying to rebel while his parents ignored his rebellious posturing. But the songs of his youth "are buried, hidden so they can't come back to haunt me," he said, wincing.

His first "good song" popped out when he was 22. By then Crowell was in Nashville, and in 1972 progressive country was beginning to cut its swath in the staid, cliqueish country music community there. Jerry Reed enlisted Crowell as a songwriter, recording some of his tunes. Another friend introduced him to Emmylou Harris, who immediately took to his songs. Harris recruited him for her legendary Hot Band, where he played guitar alongside Ricky Skaggs and the man who became his closest compadre and most trusted music advisor, Tony Brown.

By the end of the 1970s, Crowell's work as a producer and his writing talent were renowned — he was largely responsible for the best recordings by his rising-star wife, as well as Bobby Bare and Guy Clark. His songs topped the charts for Waylon Jennings and the Oak Ridge Boys. Among the circle that became known as the "new traditionalists" — Ricky Skaggs, Dwight Yoakam, Randy Travis, *et al.* — Crowell was held in the highest regard by industry insiders.

But among fans and radio station music programmers, he was still largely an unknown, the guy married to Roseanne. His first three albums drew good reviews but produced only one Top 20 single, "Stars on the Water," in 1981.

Crowell and his wife kept partying anyway, lost in a daze of what he once called "truckloads" of cocaine. Worried friends started seeing shades of Roseanne's father, Johnny Cash, in the couple's lifestyle. Crowell and Cash saw it too. She went into rehab in Atlanta to break a drug habit that began when she was a teenager; he started attending meetings to deal with his cocaine problem.

"It was a different time for him," Crowell said, comparing his attempts at escaping self-destruction with those of his father-in-law. "Elvis Presley and Johnny Cash didn't have somebody to watch taking pills until they died. They had to be their own role models. We had them to look to, to say 'I'm not going to kill myself with pills.'"

By 1986, he said, he was clean. Clear-headedness brought a wider perspective on music, but it also brought uncertainty that evidenced itself on Crowell's next album. Fascinated by the music of Prince, Springsteen and Yes, Crowell channeled his exploration of the tight production of those rock stars into *Street*

Language. But that release, a product of Los Angeles and New York, was more craftsmanship than feeling — and more rock than country. The industry was scratching its head. Where was Crowell headed? To rock 'n' roll? The honchos thought so, distributing *Street Language* through pop channels. Despite its ground-breaking technical achievements, the album never took off.

Though Crowell was happy with the album, he knew something was missing. He was straying from his roots, he said. With some free time, he wrote about 20 songs in 1987, determined to recapture what he had lost. It was still there, embedded in a vein of memories from his childhood and his teens, when country music was real and his emotions were too. Things felt so good that before he even went into the studio, he told a CBS Records executive only half-jokingly that his next release would yield five Number 1 hits.

Then he sat down with Tony Brown and picked out nine of his best songs, then added Harlan Howard's "Above and Beyond." They were choices made with an eye toward radio and stage instead of the recording studio. Instead of dwelling on details — like "trying to get the cymbals to sound *just so*" — Crowell dwelt on the emotion.

The result was *Diamonds and Dirt*, one of the better country albums of recent years. Rising to the top of the charts were the singles "It's Such a Small World," his first duet with Roseanne; "I Couldn't Leave You If I Tried," a song that sounds like a classic from the first hearing; and the hard-rocking "She's Crazy For Leavin'," a comic take on the overheard whimpering of a pathetic redneck. A fourth single, the sentimental and melodic "After All This Time," was released last month.

"I never made records for the radio — I made records for people," Crowell said. "This is the first time I made a record for the radio. The focus on *[Street Language]* was on *producing* a record, whereas on *Diamonds and Dirt* it was on being a singer/songwriter. That's what I do best, and I realized you can't be a great producer when you're up on stage."

What he can be on stage is incredible, backed by a four-member band of virtuosos, three-quarters of whom look to be a dozen years younger than he. When he isn't cooing through an occasional ballad, he's playing straightahead rock. A song such as "Crazy Baby" is country only by virtue of a steel guitar and a Nashville return address. Crowell's music falls into a country genre appropriated long ago by rockers Elvis Presley, Jerry Lee Lewis, Buddy Holly and Roy Orbison, and maintained by Nick Lowe, the Stray Cats, Jason and the Scorchers, and the Rainmakers.

But the whole issue makes him sneer and roll his light gray eyes. Crowell has no use for music critics who insist on labeling and classifying every artist and song like biologists designating family, phylum and species. "If somebody sticks me in one category or the other, that's his label, not mine," he said.

The degree to which he'll allow that to be done is limited to the decision to promote his songs through CBS's country music office in Nashville instead of pop HQ in New York, and his choice of the contemporary musicians he most identifies with — Edie Brickell and New Bohemians, the BoDeans and Steve Earle are the first names off his lips when he reluctantly makes such a list. Everyone else's, it seems, includes Dwight Yoakam, but of Yoakam, Crowell says he likes "his look better than his music — he's got the look down."

For the time being, he's content to leave such doings to "industry observers." Rodney Crowell will just keep himself amused doing what he likes to do: shake up the country music establishment in the way only an earring-wearing, dress-in-black rocker with firm country roots can.

"I like catchin' shit," he says with a laugh. "I consider myself the feather in country music's hat."

(February 1989)

Philip Martin

Elvis Betrayed

Don Mattingly, the ballplayer, once admitted that for a significant portion of his life he believed Babe Ruth was a cartoon giant who hit a home run every time he batted.

Mattingly was obviously unfamiliar with the grainy, jittery newsreel footage that betrays Ruth as a bandy-legged fat man with an unfortunate mincing gait — a man of awkward construction and questionable appetites as well as rare gifts. It is hardly surprising that Ruth the Man suffers in comparison to Babe the Legend. When men are transfigured into folk heroes, something human is submerged. It is difficult to separate reality from the fantasy — the endeavor is almost always more disappointing than enlightening.

Elvis Presley is a figure of Ruthian magnitude — his pop legacy will likely outlast public appreciation of his vocal skill. There is a chance he will be remembered more for his generosity with Cadillacs than for his music. Indeed, given the near-religious fervor of Elvis fans, public fascination with tabloid gossip and innuendo, the still-emerging details of the singer's bizarre personality and the ever-growing myth-manufacturing capability of the media, Presley the pop singer has already been obscured by Elvis the King.

Still, even though allegations of sordid peccadilloes and generous myths inform the public perception more than "Teddy Bear" or "Wear My Ring Around Your Neck" ever did, there exists a record by which we may measure the man's *oeuvre* — the bulk of his music is readily available. Ruth left behind a stat sheet and some grainy footage — Elvis left a catalogue of recorded performances.

Unhappily, RCA — the record company which purchased Elvis's contract from Sam Phillips in 1955 — has not served the indisputable star of its roster well. Most of the packaging — especially of posthumously released material — has been shabby. Though RCA has released some valuable and worthy music since the singer's ignoble death, good material has too often seemed incidental, buried on compilation discs with little form or continuity. Liner notes — when they were included at all — have been spotty or inaccurate.

Instead, RCA consistently followed a callous non-strategy designed to maximize their profits at the expense of Elvis's artistic reputation and the pocketbooks of the faithful — who deserved better than the like of *Our Memories of Elvis, Elvis Sings for Children (and Grownups, too)* and the eight-record boxed set debacle released in 1980, *Elvis Aron Presley*.

In 1984, however, RCA released a six-record boxed set, *Elvis—A Golden Celebration*, which collected some of the best work from disparate periods of Elvis's career. Though hardly definitive — it would take more than 12 sides to collect essential recordings, much less merely interesting stuff — it was, considering the record label's history of atrocity (not only with Elvis— the posthumous "contemporization" of Jim Reeves's work was shameful), remarkably free of dross.

Celebration concentrated on the two artistically fertile seasons of Elvis's career — the nascent period between 1954 and 1956 and his Memphis Renaissance, which began in 1968. It contained live performances from Presley's TV performances, a side of Sun sessions outtakes and was unusually well-annotated and tastefully assembled.

But while RCA was certainly not a conscientious caretaker, any serious examination of Elvis must hold the man culpable for the denigration of the artist

Issue 114, December 1989.

— after all, Elvis was alive for most of his career. That he did not insist on exercising tighter quality control over his output — whether through ignorance or apathy — is not to his credit.

Before his 1968-69 "comeback," Presley was an exile not only from the pop mainstream but also from critical respect and social recognition.

Up until the time of the so-called Memphis Sessions, Elvis was comfortable with his role as a lightweight actor/singer, content to wallow in his money and his po' boy's idea of Hollywood decadence; working only as hard as he had to to get by, with thinly disguised contempt for his hardcore fans whom he (sadly but rightly) believed would buy anything with his name attached.

But in 1969, with his return to Memphis, on the heels of a highly rated Christmas special which reintroduced to the world a lean Elvis, resplendent in black leather (he starved himself for weeks before the taping, conscious of his softness and his public's expectations) and at least willing to try to recapture some of his lost credibility.

That television program, which has been rerun a couple of times in the past few years, presented a physical manifestation of an Elvis rededicated to his music-making roots. The music on the television program was not totally convincing — it was disappointing to hear Presley, whose voice had darkened over the years, attempt to sing his earliest material in their original, high and lonesome keys.

But his next two albums — *From Elvis in Memphis* and *From Memphis to Vegas/From Vegas to Memphis* — were revelatory. Elvis produced some of the best music of his life. Most of this material is familiar to even casual fans — "Kentucky Rain," "Suspicious Minds," "Long Black Limousine"— and to listen to these records is to put the lie to the hyperbolic opinion that Elvis accomplished nothing of musical consequence after, say, 1958.

It is pop music at its shimmering best — it hints at how good Elvis could have been had he been able to avoid the temptations of Elvishood and the sorry material with which he was so often saddled.

But even Elvis's earliest recordings reflect certain disturbing tendencies toward kitsch. Without minimizing Elvis's talent — he *was* an amazingly good singer, he *was* young and white and handsome — Sam Phillips seemed to have been the dominant personality in the studio, and he believed he could apply his formula to any kid with a passable voice and the proper attitude. His successes with Carl Perkins, Johnny Cash and Jerry Lee Lewis — to hit the biggest names — indicate Phillips's importance. He thought he could duplicate Elvis's success — and that's why he let Elvis go to RCA.

While Sun sessions outtakes reveal the young Elvis's weakness for schmaltz, and hint at the inevitability of his descent into facile schlock, it should be pointed out that the sides Phillips put out betray no such frailties.

Elvis had no role models — no Dylans or Lennons — who preceded him. The successful singers of his day were crooners like Bing Crosby and Dean Martin, part-time movie stars absolutely outside what would become the rock 'n' roll ethos. Given the circumstances, it is hardly surprising the King of Rock 'n' Roll abdicated. He abandoned his wild new kingdom for the comparatively safe and insular life of a Prince of Hollywood.

After returning from the Army, Elvis was understandably in retreat; having signed over his career to the high-rolling Colonel Tom Parker at its outset, he was neither prepared for nor particularly interested in making decisions of artistic consequence. Elvis was willing to go along with what Parker wanted; after all, that was what had made him rich and famous. Elvis was an arrested adolescent — a Peter Pan who never bothered to take responsibility for his career. The additional pressure of being a significant sociological phenomenon surely overwhelmed the shy Tupelo kid who had trouble playing his guitar and singing for the musicians who gathered for his first recording session.

This surmised feeling of inferiority and lack of faith in his own talent might explain why one of the finest singers of the century was reduced to recording some of the silliest songs ("Song of the Shrimp," "Do The Clam," "No Room to Rhumba in a Sports Car") ever committed to vinyl.

Elvis is the greatest tragedy of rock 'n' roll for his is the greatest talent ever squandered. Still, it is hard to argue that he betrayed the tradition, since there was no tradition with which to keep faith. Rock was, in its infancy, just another show-biz genre, and a genre few gave much chance of surviving.

Elvis was a rocker in style only. His heart and mind — apparent in his vulgar, glittery tastes — were low *bourgeois*. He would have no truck with Kerouac or Pollack; he held no pretensions to artistry, he was interested only in popular acceptance as manifested in hit records and fat wallets.

It is a shame that most people who proclaim their undying devotion to Elvis almost always miss the fundamental point of his career — that insulation and power are corrosive and megastardom is a peculiar circle of hell. Michael Jackson, to name the most obvious example, could benefit from Elvis's example — even an incredible talent must work to keep some connection to his or her audience.

Elvis Presley made that connection — but only sometimes.

(September 1990)

The Ant and The Cow

The beautiful and talented James Neff has contributed his precisely rendered, subtle and quirkily touching cartoons and story illustrations to Spectrum *since the very beginning. "The Ant and The Cow" is a fine example of his pop psycho-culture perspective.*

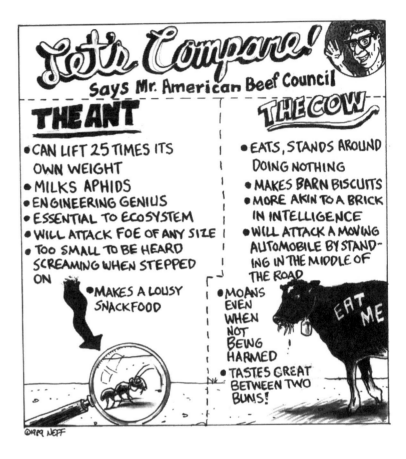

James Neff

Anthony Moser

Love American-Style

Jerry Lewis Labor Day Telethon

Nothing on television is as distinctly, singularly American as the annual 21-and-a-half hour Jerry Lewis Telethon, which is beamed coast to coast by the wacky comedian's 200-station "Love Network." If what you're looking for is tacky tastelessness, garish excess, armies of Las Vegas sleazeballs and disingenuous showbiz kitsch, Jerry's got it all.

After all, what could be more compelling than watching an already weird and unstable man, who just a few years ago underwent double-bypass heart surgery, roam around a stage for almost 24 hours with no sleep? He screams. He cries. He laughs. He moans. And above all, he begs and pleads for money.

The money is for the Muscular Dystrophy Association — Lewis's pet charity and the ostensible *raison d'être* for this 22-year-old Labor Day fixture. The victims of the sometimes deadly disease are known as "Jerry's Kids," and legions of the lame are paraded in front of the cameras in a shameless tug at the national heartstrings.

In order to unravel the mystery of the telethon's success, I decided to watch the telethon — all 1,290 minutes of it — from the vantage point of my vibrating Barcalounger. What follows is a diary of that journey.

September 4, 8 p.m.: Here it is, in all its splendor — live from Caesar's Palace, that well-known monument to altruism and charity. Since the local Love Network affiliate, KATV, Channel 7, chose not to air the first two and one-half hours of this parade of pathos, I'm forced to watch the opening 150 minutes on

Reviews

Spectrum *philosophy holds that cultural critics ought not simply reduce art to its "meaning," but instead introduce us to new ways of seeing and hearing. For more than five years, many* Spectrum *readers have turned first to the "back of the book" for our reviews of pop and classical music, theater, film, art, television and books.*

Chicago station WGN. After a rambunctious song and dance number to open the show, Jerry chides co-host Ed "Big Ed" McMahon for not being around when the festivities began back in 1966. But Ed has a pretty reasonable explanation: "I wasn't allowed to run with Jews back then, 'Big Jer'." The other co-hosts are Casey Kasem, crooner Julius LaRosa and Sammy Davis Jr., Jerry's Vegas stage partner and old Rat Pack pal. Jerry and Sammy break into song.

8:45 p.m.: Two executives of the Southland Corporation, the conglomerate that owns 7-Eleven, slink onstage. Like all the other corporate underwriters, they dole out their millions piecemeal, in an endless string of installments, so that they can get plug after plug over the course of the show. I might not have noticed this if I hadn't viewed the entire thing. This "extended tease" technique is arguably the most repugnant element of the show.

9 p.m.: Jerry switches to the New York hosts, via satellite. They are Tony Orlando and Dawn, the schmaltzy Seventies group which recently reunited after years apart. "Tony, Tony, I'm so glad you teamed up with Dawn again!" Lewis beams. "That's just marvelous! But if you expect me to get together with Dean again, you're nuts!" Then it's back to Vegas to introduce sidekick Harvey Korman, who Jerry canonizes as "the best comedic actor we've ever had in show business." Hyperbole, anyone? The cavalcade of Sixties and Seventies has-beens continues as Engelbert Humperdink sings "One World," and inserts this bit of geopolitical wisdom: "Instead of spending all this money on big bombs, we should spend it on you and your kids," he says to Jerry. Why didn't Al Haig think of this?

10:30 p.m.: KATV finally hooks into the Love Network, which they apparently love a little less than WGN does. The local hosts are early morning news reader Lorie Johnson and weather reader Ron Sherman. Johnson is drop dead, four-alarm good-looking in a long, slinky blue sequined evening gown that looks like it cost about $4.7 million. She nonetheless advises the viewers to put off buying clothes and shoes so they can "donate to Jerry's Kids."

10:58 p.m.: I knew it would happen, but I thought I'd hold out longer than this. I've already broken unto tears. A film is aired about a family with a boy of three who died from the most serious form of MD. The late child's parents then come onstage. When they begin telling their tale, I'm a goner. It's Industrial Strength Kleenex time. Two minutes later, Sammy announces that longtime telethon participant Lola Falana is now, ironically enough, an MD sufferer herself, and was unable to attend this year because of her illness. Sammy urges students at predominantly black colleges and universities to "make all the cats dig in and give," then sings "Once in a Lifetime" and "I Gotta Be Me." When he's done, Jerry screams, "He's one of kind! The last of a breed!"

11:08 p.m.: A union boss with an Italian name drags three postmen onstage to represent the National Association of Letter Carriers, who are doling out their millions in installments just like Southland. "It's a festival of love!" the Italian union boss screams.

September 5, 1:09 a.m.: The highlight of the show. Comic juggler Michael Davis performs the most amazing stunt I've ever seen, juggling an apple, an uncooked egg and a bowling ball while taking bites out of the apple every time it passes his mouth. "He's beautiful!" says Jerry.

1:30 a.m.: Lorie Johnson tells us we'll sleep a lot better if we call in a pledge. But what's this? KATV *itself* is going to sleep for the night, and they won't be back until after sun-up. The curtain comes down on the hourly 15-minute Little Rock installments, which are coming to us live from Park Plaza Mall. What a bunch of weenies! We're separating the men from the boys here, no question about it.

1:54 a.m.: The mailmen are back with "another $400,000 worth of love." This is followed by "comedian" Charlie Calas, who makes rude animal and potty noises, then lip-syncs to a scratchy record. "Brilliant! Brilliant!" Jerry beams.

2:20 a.m.: The first of a long series of taped messages from the Most Repugnant Person on Earth, talk show host Sally Jessy Raphael, the poor man's Oprah. She'll deliver four of these segments to fill up the time KATV is supposed to be filling with local cut-ins, but as noted above, Lorie and Ron are already lost in slumber somewhere. How did Sally find time in her busy schedule of interviewing transvestite sexually addicted drug abusers to do her bit for Jerry?

3:02 a.m.: Growing sleepy, despite massive infusions of caffeine and refined sugar. Rip Taylor, the Queen of Comedy, is onstage, with an act that consists of drawing pictures on his knees, playing with his silver wig and miming to records. He finally leaves the stage to make room for members of the Montana State Spurs and Fangs Club. Lewis then steps in front of the camera to announce that Harvey Korman, in addition to being the greatest comedic actor, is "one of the best men who ever lived." You know the roll call: Plato, Alexander the Great, St. Thomas Aquinas, Harvey Korman ...

3:15 a.m.: Jerry's singing again—a beacon of inspiration to victims of tone deafness everywhere. He then discusses Lou Gehrig's disease, the form of MD which felled the Pride of the Yankees. I doze off for a few minutes, but awaken just in time to hear The Ventures play the theme song from "Hawaii 5-0." Book 'em, Dano.

4:30 a.m.: Just what exactly is that stuff on Jerry's hair, anyway? Looks like 30-weight, but it might be 10-W-40 Havoline Supreme. Must be tough having to fly to the Persian Gulf every time he gets his hair done.

4:50 a.m.: Jerry's talking about Sammy again. This time, Sammy's "the singularly most talented one individual in show business history." But wait a minute — what about Harvey Korman? And come to think of it, Sammy's hair seems to have a pretty high viscosity rating too. Without an aggressive campaign of offshore drilling, this could deplete our nation's energy reserves in a matter of years.

6:00 a.m.: Dawn's early light. Not Tony Orlando's Dawn — the real dawn. Jerry's starting to look awfully tired, which sets me to wondering who's going to take over this show after all these Rat Packers check into that Great Cocktail Lounge in the Sky. Can you imagine, for instance, the "Sean Penn Labor Day Telethon": "Hey, ***hole, get off the **** stage, you spineless sack of ****! Get all these cripples away from Madonna!"

11:50 a.m.: I fell asleep for well over an hour, but I refuse to accept any penalties because it was clearly unintentional. The "magic fingers" massage action of my Barcalounger lulled me into a stupor. But I'm back.

11:55 a.m.: The president and chief executive officer of Harley-Davidson, Inc., roars onto stage for about the 400th time, with another installment of his corporate largesse. He shows a tape of a bunch of middle-aged Peter Fondas roaring down the four-lane blacktop on their Harleys in their "Ride For Jerry." Jerry, who is now referring to himself as "Super Jew," says he's just getting started "We're going to wrench your heart, touch those nerve endings and go for the jugular."

1:40 p.m.: The Charlie Daniels Band — a hardy group of Good Old Boy country rockers — is introduced via satellite from L.A. by West Coast host Norm Crosby. They sing "The Devil Went Down to Georgia," an uplifting little ditty about a man who wagers his soul to the Prince of Darkness over a fiddle-playing contest. A fine message for Jerry's Kids.

1:51 p.m.: The Italian Union Boss and Jerry are literally coupling astage. They are locked in a death-hug. Tony O and Dawn then sing "Somewhere Out There" from the cartoon movie *An American Tail*.

2:07 p.m.: An industrialist kicks in a cool million, then tells Big Jer, "I can give your kids dolls, VCRs and toys, but I can't give them what you give them,

Jerry — hope!" A few minutes later, the boss of the firefighters union comes onstage and launches into a tirade against "political hacks" who prohibit his men from "raising money in uniform." He complains about municipalities which feel it is improper for badgewielding firemen to shakedown homeowners for cash. He's followed by a Caesar's Palace official who kicks in $300,000 — which is probably what Caesar's grosses in one hour at the roulette table.

3:27 p.m.: Back at the local Little Rock cut-in, Lorie Johnson watches slackjawed as a group of rough-looking bikers from Camden — apparently inspired by Harley Davidson's devotion to MDA — strut across the stage in T-shirts, vests and chains. Their shaggy, bearded spokesman reads a lists of beer halls and honky tonks that helped them raise the money. Lorie cracks up, then yells, "All right! Bikers!" She then tells the home viewers to "Get out of that La-Z-Boy." Not on your life, Lorie.

3:32 p.m.: Spuds McKenzie, the canine "party animal" and spokesman for Bud Light Beer, is onstage with Jerry, along with two comely young ladies who are announced as "The Spudettes." Came on, all you disease victims *party down!*

4:08 p.m.: My eyes are starting to crust over. Charo is onstage singing "Luv ees in dee Air." What's this woman's problem? She married Xavier Cugat about 300 years ago, she's been in this country about 200 years, and she still can't speak English. She doesn't need a telethon; she needs a Berlitz class. As the song ends, she cuddles up against the Vegas slime sitting in the front row and coos, "Goochie, Koochie!"

4:35 p.m.: The tote board is nearing last year's total of $39 million. By the time it's all over 55 minutes from now, it will top out at $41 million. "You people," says Jerry, "are involved in a Love-In." Groovy man, cool.

5:10 p.m.: The show is winding down. Sammy sings his final number, a medley from the hit Broadway show *The Phantom of the Opera.* He's oblivious to the fact that the real Phantom, actor Michael Crawford, has already been on. "Turn your face away from the garish light of day, and listen to the music of the night." Thus spoke the Phantom, in what could be a fitting eulogy for these proceedings.

5:30 p.m.: It's over. We've met and passed our goal. Jerry promises us that "a cure is near," apparently oblivious to the news that last year, MDA research discovered that the most serious form of the disease is caused by a defective chromosome on one particular gene. Although it was good to discover the cause, it means that any "cure" will likely involve genetic engineering technology that is years — even decades — down the pike. But hey, why get picky? At least we've got $41 million of love.

(September 1988)

Stephen Buel

Put Out at First

Eight Men Out
Directed by John Sayles

The opening scenes of *Eight Men Out* portray the actions of a wealthy industrialist who is out of touch with his employees. The industry happens to be baseball, and the product, the 1919 World Series.

While Chicago White Sox owner Charles Comiskey boasts to a group of sportswriters about the prowess of his legendary team, the players are on the field, clinching the American League pennant. Director John Sayles illustrates the widening class conflict between the longwinded tycoon and his "boys" with seamless edits between Comiskey's opulent clubhouse and the spartan world of the players.

As "Commie" brags about the harmony of his team, several northern players are busy antagonizing two of their southern colleagues. As he boasts of the control of veteran pitcher Eddie Cicotte, Cicotte gets into trouble on the mound and hurls two consecutive pitches that would have been homers had they not been hit slightly foul. And as Comiskey and his court of captive sportswriters toast the White Sox and throw their cocktail glasses into the fireplace, his now triumphant players return to the locker room to discover the pennant "bonus" they'd been promised is nothing more than a few bottles of champagne. And as the White Sox soon discover, the champagne in *their* bottles is flat.

With this scene, it becomes apparent that *Eight Men Out* is less a movie about baseball than a movie about organized labor — or, actually, disorganized labor. In that sense, Sayles picks up here where he left off with *Matewan,* his 1987 film about labor strife in the coal mines of West Virginia. He has set his sights very high here, depicting in largely sympathetic tones the role of eight players in the famous "Black Sox Scandal," the tale of the team that threw the 1919 World Series. That he achieves his goal so thoroughly in a movie without a real star or even a major character is one of the many things that makes *Eight Men Out* a profoundly thought-provoking film. It is the most moving American drama I have seen in the Eighties.

The plot is hatched in a bar where the team is celebrating after the game. Sport Sullivan, a gambler from Boston, strikes up a conversation with first baseman Chick Gandil. Quite pointedly, "Chickie" starts musing about how many players it would take to throw a baseball game. Sullivan listens intently but feigns disbelief. "You say that you can find seven people on the best team that ever took the field to throw the World Series?" he asks. "I find that hard to believe." "Chickie" grins and delivers a reply that could serve as the movie's theme: "You never played for Charlie Comiskey."

For those of us not yet sure that playing for "Commie" is sufficient reason to throw the series, Sayles soon delivers extra evidence. A few scenes later, we discover that Comiskey robbed the pitcher Cicotte of his 30th victory by benching him for five straight starts, thereby cheating him out of a promised $10,000 bonus. Before he leaves the owner's office, Cicotte's eyes tell us he will now accept the $10,000 he has been offered to enlist in the fix. With him on board, the series is as good as lost.

From this point on, the film quickens in pace and intensity as, scene by scene, the stakes get higher and the team unravels. By tracking the progress of a couple-dozen characters but focusing closely on none, Sayles creates a mood of grim determinism in which no one seems capable of exercising free will. As the fix is pitched to each of the seven remaining players, each is taken aside and assured that only he stands between his colleagues and great personal wealth. An identical form of peer pressure will reappear after the series is over when the eight players face a grand jury.

Eight Men Out evokes the same free-wheeling era portrayed in *The Sting,* but Sayles points its conclusion in a very different direction. The resolution of this movie occurs not in the success or failure of the fix, but in the defeat that burns in the eyes of the vanquished. Some of the most powerful scenes in this film simply depict the sorrow or bitterness in the eyes of its characters: Cicotte's grim resignation as he realizes that he will have to throw the first game all by himself, mobster Arnold Rothstein's jealous memories of childhood and a young fan's sadness at discovering that his hero has failed him.

Although there is no one role in the film large enough to be considered for a best-actor nomination, many of the performances are exemplary. David Strathairn as the pitcher Cicotte and Michael Lerner as the gambler Rothstein speak silent volumes with their hollow, downturned eyes. John Cusack and D.B. Sweeney excel as eager young players who don't quite understand why they can't just play ball. John Mahoney is perfectly cast as the tragic ballclub's manager and author Studs Terkel is delightfully well-suited to his role as the sportswriter who blows the lid off the whole caper.

Director Sayles casts himself as sportswriter and author Ring Lardner, who, along with Terkel's character, serves as the conscience of the movie. Though his is not a large role, Sayles saves for himself many of the movie's best lines. As one of the only observers who suspects from the start that the games are fixed, he is the only person to directly challenge the players with this accusation. And early in the film he delivers a wry commentary on the extent to which Comiskey has co-opted Lardner's colleagues in the press: "Sportswriters of the world unite! You have nothing to lose but your bar privileges."

The players themselves would have done well to follow Lardner's advice. There is a definite determinist thread running throughout *Eight Men Out* and by the film's end, triumph seems to be a function of class standing. This attitude is best conveyed by Buck Weaver, the one player approached about the fix who declines to participate in it: "I always figured it was talent that made a guy big. But look at who's holding a baseball and look at who's facing a jail cell. Talent don't mean nothing."

While Sayles's own film-making talent belies this summation, he nonetheless has made his point masterfully.

(November 1988)

Bill Jones

Staring Into the Abyss

Mishima: A Vision Of The Void
By Margaret Yourcenar
Farrar, Straus & Giroux

On the morning of November 25, 1970, the celebrated Japanese author Yukio Mishima signed and dated the last page of his novel *The Decay of the Angel* and left the manuscript for his publisher's courier on a hallway table in his Western-style suburban Tokyo house. He dressed himself in the uniform he had designed for his paramilitary Shield Society, placing a 17th-century samurai sword at his side and a dagger in his attaché case.

Outside, in a new Toyota, four young uniformed members of Mishima's private army awaited their leader. When he joined them, the group set off for an appointment with General Mashita at the Japanese Eastern Army headquarters in Tokyo.

Shortly before 11:00 a.m., Mishima's party arrived at the army compound and were soon admitted to Mashita's office. During the exchange of preliminary pleasantries, while the officer was admiring Mishima's antique sword, three of the young men rushed General Mashita and gagged and bound him.

After routing aides from adjacent offices, Mishima demanded to speak to an assembly of all the soldiers in the garrison at noon. The troops were summoned, and Mishima stepped out of an office window onto a balcony to address them.

Overhead, a helicopter droned. Below, the troops jeered and cursed. Wearing a headband displaying the rising sun, Mishima appealed to his unsympathetic audience: "We see Japan reveling in prosperity and wallowing in spiritual emptiness ... We shall give it back its image and die in doing so. Is it possible that you value life, given a world where the spirit is dead? ... The army protects that very treaty which denies its right to exist ... Our fundamental Japanese values are threatened ... The Emperor no longer has his rightful place in Japan."

But Mishima's plea for a nationalistic resurgence to overturn the postwar Japanese-American settlement provoked only catcalls. Recognizing the futility of his attempt to stir the troops, the author returned to the general's office.

As Mashita, no longer gagged, begged him to stop, the writer removed his jacket, loosened his trousers, knelt, and with enormous force thrust his dagger into his abdomen, eviscerating himself. His favorite follower, Morita, attempted to behead him, in accordance with the ritual of *seppuku,* but another member of the group had to finish the job. Morita then joined his master in death.

When Yukio Mishima died, he was 45 years old, in superb physical condition and at the peak of his creative powers, having just completed his masterpiece, the quartet entitled *The Sea of Fertility*. The horror of that November morning shook complacent, prosperous, modern Japan to its foundations. According to his friend and biographer Henry Scott Stokes, writing in the October 1985 issue of *Harper's,* "Yukio Mishima's suicide ranks to this day as the single most startling news event in the postwar history of Japan."

In her newly translated book, *Mishima: A Vision of the Void*, the French writer Marguerite Yourcenar observes that, for the Japanese, "to have taken Mishima seriously would have been to deny their adaptation to defeat and to the progress of modernization, as well as to the prosperity which followed."

Yellow Peril, White Devils

John Dower's War Without Mercy: Race and Power in the Pacific War *studied the propaganda disseminated by both the Americans and the Japanese during the Second World War. The book revealed that, for the U.S., the war was cast primarily as a clash of race and culture, with economic and political considerations all but lost in the background. The Japanese, on the other hand, subscribed to a less blatant but no less vicious variety of racism founded on traditional xenophobia. Anthony Moser, writing in September 1986, found the book illuminating for its insight into "the current protectionism mania," which, the reviewer observed, may be "a manifestation of something more than just economic uncertainty."*

Politicians such as Prime Ministers Sato and Nakasone, who had secretly supported the right-wing Shield Society, were quick to denounce its leader as a madman. Other Japanese, however, regarded him as a hero. Only a couple of years ago, Paul Schrader's film biography *Mishima* generated great controversy among the Japanese upon its release.

Opinion remains divided, not only in Japan but throughout the world, regarding the motives for and the meaning of Mishima's self-destruction. Some, such as Henry Scott Stokes, see it essentially as a political act, a protest against the direction taken by Japanese society following Emperor Hirohito's postwar renunciation of his claim to divinity. Others, like Marguerite Yourcenar, view the suicide as an inevitable artistic or philosophical statement, the end toward which Mishima's fiction and politics pointed.

Yourcenar is herself a distinguished literary figure. The author of the internationally acclaimed historical novel *The Memoirs of Hadrian*, she was, in 1980, the first woman to be elected an "Immortal" of the French Academy. Her study of Mishima is an elaboration of her thesis that his "carefully premeditated death is part of his work." The book is brief, impressionistic and free from the taint of pedantry. Although it assumes at least some familiarity on the reader's part with Mishima's life and creative output, Yourcenar's extended essay makes a fine general preface to the works of this major 20th-century author.

Mishima, as man and author, was a bundle of seeming contradictions. The most virulently xenophobic of modern Japanese writers, who in *Runaway Horses* attacked "Western European ideals" as "the scum of humanism" that "degraded the exalted fervor to kill," he nonetheless wrote novels that, in style and structure, owed much to European literary traditions. Indeed, his books are in that respect much more accessible to Western readers than those, for example, of his great contemporary and mentor, Nobel Prize-winner Yasunari Kawabata.

The man who saw himself as an inheritor of the samurai spirit, who posed for photographs brandishing the sword that would be used to decapitate him, was the same man who (taking to heart Thomas Mann's dictum that a writer should look like a banker) dressed in the Western business suits that symbolized everything he hated about postwar Japan. Mishima's emperor-worshipping politics, which led him to offer the authorities the services of his Shield Society to help quell left-wing student demonstrations, did not prevent him from finding that he had "much in common" with the Communists — "a rigorous ideology and a taste for physical violence."

In her elegant work, Yourcenar hammers into unity the disparate elements of Mishima's outlook by focusing on his lifelong preoccupation with, and quest for, the Void — that Buddhist state of being described at the end of *The Decay of the Angel* as "a place that had no memories, nothing." She depicts Mishima, a man of boundless physical and intellectual energy, as one in whom the Void grew in each stage of his brief life — "the void of every life — whether it has been a success or failure, or both." In this, Mishima resembles Ernest Hemingway, to whom he was often compared as an exemplar of macho mania; both men were consumed by the Great *Nada*.

Yourcenar traces Mishima's obsession with Nothingness to his childhood, when his world was comprised of an unloving father, an absent mother and a possessive, slowly decaying grandmother who imparted to the boy "his first knowledge of the strangeness of things." This strangeness pervades many of Mishima's works, and Yourcenar is at her best in surveying the various periods of her subject's artistic development. She emphasizes the European influences in earlier novels such as *The Sound of Waves*, *The Temple of the Golden Pavilion* and *The Sailor Who Fell From Grace With the Sea*. In the four novels of *The Sea of Fertility* — named with ironic intent for the vast region visible on the barren moon — Yourcenar notes a significant stylistic change: "Instead of a Western writer's prose ... we are now confronted with a denuded style, sometimes almost flat, restrained even at lyrical moments, crisscrossed with furrows, intended, it seems, to make us stumble."

The deepest furrow for the Western reader in Yourcenar's opinion, is the theory of reincarnation that ties together characters and incidents in the four volumes — *Spring Snow*, *Runaway Horses*, *The Temple of Dawn* and *The Decay of the Angel*—that cover the history of Japan from 1910 to the 1970s. Yet the presiding spirit in the tetralogy is the Void, and even the connecting principle of reincarnation is subsumed into it. As Yourcenar summarizes the message of *The Sea of Fertility*: "From the turmoil provoked by four successive generations one after the other, from so many ventures and counterventures, from so many false successes and true disasters, what finally comes is Supreme Nothingness."

It was no coincidence that Mishima signed the last page of his last novel on the day he took his life. From the time he wrote his first novel, the autobiographical *Confessions of a Mask*, he crafted his life as if it were a work of art. "I want," he said, "to make a poem of my life." Yourcenar demonstrates the way in which life and art mixed so completely in Mishima's career, discussing at length his film *Patriotism*, in which he portrayed an army officer who commits *seppuku* on the screen. By comparing it with Mishima's own suicide, Yourcenar says, we are better able "to define the distance between the perfection of art, which shows, in the dark or clear light of eternity, the essential, and life with its own incongruities, its failures, its baffling misunderstandings due to our inability to reach, at the right moment, inside beings and to the very bottom of things."

Mishima, then, remains an enigma, and Yourcenar's book offers an intriguing clue to the ultimately unsolvable mystery. On the day he knew he would die, he left a brief note on his desk: "Human life is limited, but I would like to live forever."

For Mishima, however, the word must be realized in action and the bound spirit in bleeding flesh. His life and works, in Yourcenar's words, "superimpose on the prudent and everyday wisdom by which we live, or in which all of us vegetate, the dangerous but reviving wisdom of a freer fervor and a fatally pure absolute." They also illustrate Nietzsche's point that "when you look long into the abyss, the abyss also looks into you."

(February 1987)

Philip Martin and Anne Neville

Just Say Yes

As Woman As She Could Ever Possibly Be
Reponde deCapite
March 4, 1989

The Scene: *After the performance, an ambitious staging of the final chapter of James Joyce's* Ulysses *by an equally ambitious young theater group, two critics drive home together. A heavy rain is falling; the drops make a sizzling noise on the roof of the car. Every now and again thunder rolls and a blink of lightning makes a brief chiaroscuro of the figures. In such moments we may discern a man and a woman—but most times, only voices.*

She (too sullenly): It will have to be a rave, you know.

He: I suppose it will. After all, they deserve applause.

She: Yes. They do and we will have to give them that; we will have to be the ones to say the thing was well-played and not too frightfully muddled, that the language was rich as ever and the seven strong selves of Molly Bloom made themselves understood. It was resonant and eloquent and if not for the incessant damned buzzing of that television monitor onstage ...

He: Was that the Superego, you think?

She: Super Iago? I don't understand.

He: Neither did I, and I blame myself. The rest was great. All those Mollys.

She: Name them. Make them famous.

He: As you wish. GigiKagy ChristineWard SherwinSarjeantP aige TuffordCa seyAle xanderSha nnonW ellsKay renG ray son. They all are famous now, famous as the Big Mac.

She: At least that's something. The director was good too — he understood the thing.

He: The thing that must be understood. Tickets were reasonably priced, and the set was just so garish. Like Charles Addams meets Keith Haring. No refreshments, though.

She: It was grand. They should put it on videotape, to show the school children that Mr. Joyce is not drought, but draught.

He: I thought the third sentence — was it the third sentence? — owed much to those Calvin Klein "Obsession" ads, don't you agree? Terribly kinetic. All that reeling about and freezing and the mock spontaneity of it all. I liked that part a lot. It was funny.

She: Funny, yes, and sad and whole.

He: What does Reponde deCapite mean anyway?

She: I don't know. It looks like an Italian idiom. *Reponde de,* in French, means "answer to." But in French you have those accents ... it might also mean something about responding to a decapitation—but that's just too weird.

He: How about "a tip of the cap?"

She: That's a good guess.

He: That's all it takes.

She: Two thumbs up. And two caps.

(March 1989)

Michael McConnell

Hot Springs' Magic Kingdom

Other people's fantasies are gruesome things. They lack humanity by necessity. Their repetition and distillation hone our goofiest imaginings to a single motivating idea. Though the narrative context of this idea may vary, any details really just get in the way. A simplistic purity is required for the function of our dreams of goodness, or liberation or satisfaction. The behavior these dreams provoke, the needs they fulfill, and the obvious disparities between fantasy and reality provide artists with the stuff of great art. Descriptions of the fantasies themselves, cleansed of the difficulties that might impair their use are simply toys — platforms for simple actions. Fantasies, like toys, center on an invigorating trigger. When they fail to excite us, they are disposable.

Hot Springs — our toy town and valley of hopeful invalids — seems to bulge under the weight of its fantasy art. It lies in such abundance within the desperate whimsy of Central Arkansas's façades, that a walk down the road suggests a disorganized convention of unrealized dreams. Sculptural dragons and vapid Benini canvases alternate with chickens playing pianos and the ungodly hues of waxen presidents.

The natural beauty of Hot Springs, its history and architectural wonders could be enlivened by this kitschy charm, but tastelessness is only ironic divorced from serious intent. No one could stand in front of a dragon sculpture reading "From the depths of woe he emerges, the hidden Now unbound" without suspecting these artists see depth within their own adolescences. This particular dragon, in the window of the Debow Gallery, perfectly illustrates the lesson genre fiction and bad TV has taught generations so well. An insinuation of Big Questions amongst familiar sci-fi references could imply, if not bestow, intellectual depth on a work. That the images seldom stray from the easily manipulated devices of comic books would bore most people — but no one is ever bored by their own fantasies.

Tessarolo may be the king of toy art in Hot Springs. His show at Herr-Chambliss Fine Arts involves most creatures familiar in toy mythologies: eagles and dinosaurs pose with uncomplicated presence in their quick delineations. Scaly crawly things are doodled in doodly landscapes without much conviction and attract only as much interest as they display, though upstairs the several horses of Joy Caros invite that woozy contemplation that most soft-focus, soft-concept realism receives. We sigh at their perfect fantasy lives. *We* want to romp through the misty mist, muscling the air aside as the dewy grass swabs our clean hooves. *We* want our hair to be that thick and evenly distributed in the wind. Other than inspiring our envy, this kind of fantasy art lacks purpose so pointedly that often it must be electrically manipulated for anyone to attribute a use to it at all. Why Joy's studs aren't laquered on redwood slabs with clock hands sprouting is beyond me.

Melinda Herr-Chambliss finds a purpose in the work of Joy and Tess. Her first criteria for selecting work is an artist's résumé. A hefty résumé — chock full of foreign countries and non-English-speaking collectors. Mileage is crucial, and Tessarolo is said to have drawn hordes to his Tokyo gallery. Joy Caros has an Israeli gallery opening (despite the irony that her work celebrates freedom). So Herr-Chambliss succeeds at something others might not even try. She locates the thickest résumés, she makes sure there's plenty of work on hand, and she tests the artists' willingness to truck it all down south. Where does conceptual depth fit in?

It Is Good,
But Is It Good Art?

Melissa Mayes caught hell from readers incensed by her September 1988 review of the paintings of Donald Roller Wilson of Fayetteville, Arkansas. "Wilson's highly realistic style," she wrote, "is accomplished with astounding technical finesse. His paintings are often cluttered with an array of textural objects ranging from hairy animals with shiny pink gums to sweating pickles and dewy watermelon slices." The accumulation of images, Mayes explained, constitutes "an ongoing series of episodes not unlike a soap opera." But why, she asked, would an artist "painstakingly illustrate a story which teaches no lesson, never ends and is acted out by a group of animals wearing fluffy dresses?"

The letters came quickly. "Roller Wilson sets his standards with his tongue firmly in his cheek," said Jay King. "Ms. Mayes, on the other hand, wants her art served logically." Artist and writer Warren Criswell suggested that "Ms. Mayes lighten up a little ... forget about what art should be or should not be, and go back and have another look at the paintings." Still, Criswell concluded, "it was sort of refreshing to read a negative art review in an Arkansas publication! It was the first I've seen, I think, in the 12 years I've been here."

Up the street at the Hot Springs Art Center, Jeanne Cornerlson, God bless her, uses her mind to explore sanctity, Christianity, history and human beauty in a six-segment drawing titled *Reflections on Strength*. Her pencil defines an icon with subtlety and imagination. Imagination is not a dirty word. But fantasies and other ghosts evaporate very, very quickly when nailed to the wall.

(December 1989)

Jay Jennings

Murphy's Law

The Golden Child
Directed By Michael Ritchie

Scene: *The plush offices of Hollywood agents Mort Blitstein, Chu Wong Fu and Ari Goldberg, who trade in Hollywood dealmaking circles as Mort-Chu-Ari, Inc. A huge cigar juts from the mouth of Blitstein, who brushes ashes off his half-eaten pastrami and takes a bite. He is on the phone with Eddie Murphy, who is listening to Blitstein pitch a script tenatively called* Katmandu Cop.

    Blitstein: "Eddie. Eddie. Eddie, baby. Are you still there, Eddie? This is me, Mort Blitstein, talking, not some artsy-fartsy pansy from PBS talking about *The Autobiography of Malcolm X.* You know me, Eddie. Commercial all the way. I have no soul. You know that. I sold it last week. I wouldn't steer you wrong, sweetie. Listen to me.

    "Okay, so let's go over this one more time. You're Chandler, tough talking social worker, who ... Social worker. Uh, let's see. I think he's a guy who helps poor people — or some kind of shit like that. Don't worry, it doesn't last long. (Pause.) *Very* tough talking. (Pause.) PG-13. No, not that. No you can't say that either. Thirteen, Eddie, for God's sake, you can't say that! (Pause.) Uh, let's see. 'Damn' is okay. 'Hell.' 'Ass' is okay. You can say 'beat his ass,' 'kick his ass,' hell, use your imagination. Say 'ass' all you want, a hundred times for all I care. Let's get back to the story.

    "This social worker, see, he specializes in finding missing kids, right? So, up in Nepal ... Nepal. Go to India and hang a right, how the hell do I know where it is?! So this Nepalian kid gets kidnapped by this evil guy who's like, the devil incarnate, or a henchman of the devil or something like that. We got an Englishman, Charlie Dance, guy was in *Plenty* with Meryl Streep. Didn't see it? He was terrific. He's a first-class, first-rate actor, Eddie. Don't worry, Eddie, he won't do that. Because he doesn't have any lines, that's why!

    "So he kidnaps the kid with a couple of henchmen and takes him to Los Angeles for some reason. He puts him in a basement surrounded by evil so that the kid — the incarnation of good who comes along just once every three thousand generations — won't save the world from the evil forces as predicted in the scrolls the ancient Tibetese prophets have passed down ... Prophet, Eddie, not profit.

    "So the scrolls say that the kid must be rescued by one who is 'quick of wit, pure of heart and star of box office' — or something like that. You follow me? Don't worry, neither will the audience. Hold on, I'm getting to that. This will knock your socks off. The Tibeters send over to L.A. this beautiful woman, played by Charlotte Lewis, built like the Taj Mahal, with a couple of massive domes, if you get my meaning, and ... No, Eddie. No. PG-13, I said. Kiss, Eddie. That's all. Kiss. She's beautiful. Toward the end of the script she does gymnastics in her underwear. Absolutely crucial to the plot. The plot turns on it. Hey, I made a joke. She's doing backflips and I said the plot turns on it. Get it? OK, so I'm no comedian. I'm just an agent. How the hell do I know what's funny? She comes out to L.A. to get you cause you're the only guy who can get the kid back. You're 'The Chosen One,' according to the scrolls. No, we're going out to Nepal for a few weeks of location work. Yeah, my partner Chu has some family there and he wants to write the trip off. The original script called for the kid to be from

Seriously Now, Folks

    Possibly the most fun Spectroids have had during the first five years was in the pages of Specious, *an April Fool's parody issue that appeared in 1987 and 1988. Contributors lampooned the earnestness of* Spectrum's *lead "epics," the narcissistic obscurity of avant-garde theater, the "artobabble" of art reviewers and the bloated ego of Arkansas's secretary of state.*

    Giving in to the popular perception of the paper's New Republic-*reading writers as a cell of closet Commies,* Specious *produced Marxist analyses of* The Beverly Hillbillies *(a "savage critique of the very system they represented") and Ashley Carter's* Mandingo Master *(which depicted the "inexorable dialectical progression from individual alienation toward class liberation.")*

    But two years was too much fun, and it was business as usual on April 1, 1989.

Santa Monica, but what the hell.

"So you two guys, you and this Kee Nang chick, that's Charlotte, meet up with this motorcycle gang. Big fight scene. We'll bring them in somehow. Don't worry, it'll be logical as hell, we'll figure it out.

"Then you find out that these evil guys are trying to make the kid eat oatmeal with blood in it. Because it makes him vulnerable to evil, I guess, I don't know why, I didn't write it. It looks great on the screen. It's a visual thing. No, you don't have to eat it. Then when you're in Nepal, you have the 'Dagger of Isabel Adjani,' or something like that. And go through this treacherous test to get it. See, in Nepal there'll be plenty of chances for this 'outsider' crap the public likes so much. Like in *Beverly Hills Cop*. Sure, but this is bigger. This time you'll be way outside. Lots of cultural contrast. Funny? Hell, I don't know from funny, I'm an agent, remember?

"Michael Ritchie's directing it. No, he's cool. Remember, in *The Survivors*, he let Robin Williams run wild. Ad-libs all over the place. You're really the one in control, Eddie baby sweetie. Your picture on the posters. You're selling the tickets, Eddie. You can do whatever you want.

"Far-fetched? Don't worry, Eddie. The public loves you. You just get on the screen and flash that grin and people start to laugh. You've invulnerable. They think everything you do is funny. People just seem to laugh mindlessly at whatever you do. Search me.

"Did I tell you about the special effects? No, that's not it at all. I certainly do think you can carry the film on your own. But we got you talking to a woman who's half dragon and we got people's heads exploding. It's beautiful. This picture is going to be gold.

"Hey, that's it, *Katmandu Cop* is out. We'll call this one *The Golden Child*. After you, Eddie baby. You're going to have us all rolling in gold. Who cares if it's a lousy film?"

(December 1986)

Stephen Buel

Sympathy for The Mekons

The Mekons
Juanita's

If chart position is the only universal criterion of the commodities' worth, then by definition the record industry is structurally compelled to produce waste in vast unimaginable quantities.

— From The Mekons' "novel in progress," *Living In Sin*

The Mekons aren't buying any of that crap about rock 'n' roll changing the world. But the silent are guilty, and so The Mekons will not be silenced in spite of the apparent futility of that which they do.

In the opening lines of their epic new album, *The Mekons Rock 'n' Roll*, Jon Langford rages: "Destroy your safe and happy lives/before it is too late." Many bands espouse such mock-recklessness, but few if any are as qualified as The Mekons to state the case. For 12 years The Mekons have thrown safety to the wind as prowlers on the outskirts of rock 'n' roll. Locked out and looking in, they've intentionally avoided the mainstream — musically, lyrically and commercially. There is more than a hint of irony that they have just delivered one of their most savage and uncompromising recordings at the very time they are closest to making their first, tiny blip in the commercial hierarchy of the recording industry.

The Mekons' simultaneous longing and disdain for this blip is the ostensible theme of their brilliant new album, *The Mekons Rock 'n' Roll*. The entirety of the Twin/Tone-A&M Records release concerns itself with hopelessness and staying power, and particularly how those two concerns intersect for a band as comfortable as The Mekons are in the musical margins.

As its title implies, *The Mekons Rock 'n' Roll* wholeheartedly embraces rock as a form after a prolonged and fruitful experimentation with other styles. On *Fear and Whiskey*, *Crime and Punishment*, *The Edge of the World* and *The Mekons Honky Tonkin'*, four of the decade's finest albums, the band grafted American country-and-western and British highland-folk together with a ragged punk sensibility perfectly suited to their dire subject matter. The following album, *So Good It Hurts*, added an island influence to the mixture and produced several sterling singles but was somewhat weaker as an album. *The Mekons Rock 'n' Roll* charts new territory for the band and is likely to earn the band its broadest audience yet.

To The Mekons, rock 'n' roll is a microscope focused on "that secret place where we all want to go." But instead of giving us the answer we desire to hear, The Mekons give us the answer that is honest. When they visit East Berlin, they don't sing uplifting hymns to liberty, they bitch about how they can't buy anything. On "Only Darkness Has The Power," the sort of desperate tale of need that passes for a love song in their lexicon, Tom Greenhalgh hopes his longing for Sophie will end with the two of them living happily together — but then he adds, "I doubt that this will happen." On side two, in "I Am Crazy," Sally Timms sings a verse that may as well finish the story from the earlier song: "In the evening/I'll still stand at your gate/you'll see me/and turn away."

The Mekons, arguably the best unknown rock band in the world, dragged into Juanita's two weeks ago looking haggard and weary. They'd just completed a grueling drive from Lawrence, Kansas, where they'd played the night before,

Ending the Eighties

All right, so we stole the idea. But we had fun, in December 1989, haggling over our own list of 100 favorite albums of the 1980s. These were Spectrum's Top Ten:

1. Kate Bush, The Dreaming
2. The Clash, London Calling
3. Sonic Youth, Daydream Nation
4. David Bowie, Scary Monsters
5. Joy Division, Still
6. Public Enemy, It Takes a Nation of Millions to Hold Us Back
7. Elvis Costello, Imperial Bedroom
8. Pete Townshend, Empty Glass
9. Captain Beefheart, Doc at the Radar Station
10. Bruce Springsteen, Tunnel Of Love

Kronos Quartet (White Man Sleeps) *also made the final cut. So did Stephen Buel's culture-heroes,* The Mekons (The Mekons Honky Tonkin' *and* The Mekons Rock 'n' Roll.)

Issue 120, March 1990.

and the night before that they'd been in Minneapolis. Now, here they were in "Ar-Kansas," wondering what to do next. Told that Arkansas's peculiar distinction among the 50 states was its statistical 49th-ness, The Mekons joked that they were an appropriate band for Arkansas because they are statistically 49th among rock bands. "And second in teen-aged pregnancy," added one in jest.

Despite their press kit's observation that "over the years there have been upwards of 75 Mekons" — perhaps the band's only conceit to its own self-image — the six Mekons who came to Arkansas were very much the backbone of the ensemble that has collaborated on the band's best work.

While all are fine instrumentalists, the individual achievements of the six touring Mekons seems strangely irrelevant. If The Mekons themselves thought this mattered, they'd tell us more about themselves on their album sleeves. But they have no interest in being enshrined like a new "Dublin Messiah" — a snide apparent reference to Bono from *Rock 'n' Roll*. Indeed, The Mekons must be seen live just to figure out who is who. Visually and vocally, the band has three focuses: Timms and guitarists Greenhalgh and Langford. But there are no stars in The Mekons — no soloists, just one effortless groove. Susie Honeyman contributed her characteristically haunting fiddle playing. Lu "Mr. Knee" Edmonds on bass and Steve Goulding — ex of The Rumour — on drums provided a solid rhythm foundation. Greenhalgh and Langford swapped savage guitar licks and traded vocals, and Timms — well, her voice is simply unmatched anywhere.

Dreams that die hard, class strife and economic ruin and, of course, love gone astray — these are the concerns of The Mekons. In some senses, they are indeed an appropriate band for Arkansas. Near the end of their performance, the six Mekons proclaimed with complete sincerity that Arkansas had provided the warmest reception of their tour. Their marvelous show notwithstanding, that was the nicest present they could have given the crowd. Because it's not so much The Mekons' grim vision that draws one to the band. It's rather that they keep trying anyway.

(December 1989)

Bill Jones

Unheard Melody

The Mambo Kings Play Songs of Love
By Oscar Hijuelos
Farrar, Straus & Giroux

There are novels, and then there are novels. You know what I mean. Some are pleasant temporary diversions or current cultural obligations, but a few — *The Unbearable Lightness of Being* and *Love in the Time of Cholera* are recent examples that come to mind — become permanent features of your moral landscape. *The Mambo Kings Play Songs of Love*, the second novel by New York author Oscar Hijuelos, possesses that rare sort of transforming grace. It has the power to redefine some of the basic terms in the vocabulary of your imagination.

Hijuelos has created a multi-layered narrative in his story of the Castillo brothers, two musicians from Cuba who live in New York in 1949 at the peak of the mambo, rhumba and conga dance crazes. They soon form the Mambo Kings, "an orchestra that packed clubs, dance halls, and theaters around the East Coast." One of the greatest pleasures of the novel is to be found in the detailed footnotes dealing with New York's Latino music scene of the early 1950s, the heyday of the late Perez Prado, "when every Cuban knew every Cuban." The factual and fictional are so well blended — a complete Mambo Kings discography is even included, featuring such song titles as "The Subway Mambo" and "Mambo Inferno!" — that you may be overwhelmed by a desire to prowl through used-record shops searching for nonexistent albums.

Cesar, the older brother and vocalist for the Mambo Kings, is consumed by a voracious sexual appetite that leads him to bed nearly every woman he meets (although he returns most regularly to Vanna Vane, Miss Mambo for June 1955). His compulsive sexual conquests, however, appear to be merely so many self-prescribed nostrums enabling him to recover the fragile childhood security of his mother's unconditional love.

On the other hand, Nestor, the younger brother and the band's trumpet soloist, is obsessed by the image of one woman, Maria, who deserted him some years before in Cuba. He wears an "expression of eternal homesickness and longing for love" throughout his short life, writing and rewriting the bolero that will become the Mambo Kings' greatest hit, "Beautiful Maria of My Soul." Neither marriage to the intelligent and self-sacrificing Delores, whose initial purpose is "to release this young musician from his pain," nor parenthood — nor, for that matter, modest commercial success — ever serves to heal Nestor's wounded spirit or to reconcile him to a life without the object of his devotion, his "lost key to happiness."

Unquestionably, the high point of the Mambo Kings' career occurs in 1955, when they are discovered by their fellow countryman Desi Arnaz. He invites them to appear on the *I Love Lucy* show, where they perform for posterity the heartbreaking "Beautiful Maria of My Soul." The television episode, repeated through the years on the small screen and throughout the pages of the novel, provides a structural device for Hijuelos to move his chronicle backward and forward in time. In so doing, he links the narrator, Eugenio, Nestor's son, with his surviving uncle Cesar, through whose consciousness most of the events are relived.

Perhaps, though, "replayed" would be the more accurate word. *The*

Is Fiction Dead?

Spectrum associate editor Jess Henderson found "something terribly wrong with contemporary fiction" in October 1986. From the novels of James Fenimore Cooper onward, he said, American writers had been "enamored of strong central characters of almost mythic proportions."

But modern realism brought with it the anti-heroes, who are succeeded today, Henderson argued, by "middle-class wimps — floundering in realities too big for them." He cited as examples the protagonists of The Moviegoer *by Walker Percy and* The Sportswriter *by Richard Ford — men whose response to life is escape.*

What is missing in postmodern literature, Henderson urged, is "the sense of identity that springs from self-confidence. What is wrong is not our situation; what is wrong is ourselves. We live in an age where it is harder to be 'great' on a grand scale; therefore, we have eschewed greatness and left no room for the small triumphs that ... assert ... humanity in the midst of intolerable conditions."

Mambo Kings Play Songs of Love is both the title of the novel and the name of the group's best-selling record. The two longest sections of the book are designated "Side A" and "Side B," and in them Cesar listens to the album in a seedy New York hotel room, summoning memories on the night of his death in 1980. The author treats events in the past as if they were tracks on a scratchy LP, moving his metaphorical tone arm to repeat various selections again and again.

The theme of *The Mambo Kings* — with its meticulous reconstruction of a lost era and its conjuring of ghosts on plastic discs and black-and-white film — is the price of memory. Only Delores, the novel's most admirable character, seems exempt from the claims of the past. Nestor, haunted by the sentimentalization of a time spent with a woman who neither understood nor loved him, is rendered incapable of responding to genuine sympathy and affection. Even so, memory, however distorted and falsified by self-pity, prompts Nestor to write — and to live — one true song.

Attempting to preserve his brother's memory, Cesar in some sense assumes the identity of Nestor, adopting, as much as his gregarious nature will permit, the introverted characteristics of the younger Castillo. The recaptured past becomes his constant companion during the last two decades of his life, as he holds the inhospitable present at an ever-increasing distance.

Finally, Eugenio, angry and alienated, comes to terms with his perpetual sense of loss — his childhood, his father, his heritage — through the resurrection of two young men singing a *"song about love so far away it hurts; a song about lost pleasures, a song about youth, a song about love so elusive a man can never know where he stands; a song about wanting a woman so much death does not frighten you, a song about wanting that woman even when she has spurned you."*

As I said, there are novels, and then there are novels. Some you simply can't put down. Others you don't want to finish because you can't bear to leave the characters or their world behind: *The Mambo Kings Play Songs of Love* is one of those. But this joyously sad, wistfully comic novel is, after all, about memory, and the reader is unlikely to forget Cesar and Nestor and the unheard melody of "Beautiful Maria of My Soul."

(September 1989)

In 1990, The Mambo Kings Play Songs of Love *was awarded the Pulitzer Prize for Fiction.*

Dixie Knight

Philip Martin

Dumb Da Dumb Dumb

COPS
Fox Network

Promotion material for *COPS,* Fox Broadcasting Company's latest voyeuristic foray into tabloid television, makes much of the show's video verite format: "No scripts, no actors, no phony endings — just cops."

Just plain old, ordinary cops. The show's producers, John Langley and Malcolm Barbour, the same bad boys who brought us the Geraldoized *Doping of a Nation,* assigned camera crews to follow and videotape several members of the Broward County, Florida Sheriff's department as they scurry hither and yon, protecting and serving the populace. Langley and Barbour say they wanted to present a realistic picture of what policemen really do: to show average lawmen caught, as Allen Funt might say, in the act of being themselves.

But unlike the unwitting subjects of *Candid Camera,* the deputies of Broward County know all too well where the camera is and what it is doing. And wherever lights and camera are introduced into a situation, the situation is altered — it intrudes, the camera becomes a player; the cops, no doubt instructed to act naturally, heat up and cool down like little De Niros. The scumbags — uh, innocent-until-proven-guilty suspects — point fingers and shout at the cameramen to leave them alone with their humiliation. (Sometimes the guilty faces are scrimmed out by electronic Vaseline on the lens; more often they are very identifiable.) Often the cops themselves turn to the camera to offer the home viewers a conspiratorial smile or a wry aside.

"This guy's a real winner; he's a new one in town," Deputy Glenn Topping tells us, as his partner lifts the wig off the bald pate of a cross-dressing hobo accused of harassing customers outside a convenience store.

"Who you trying to impersonate? Your sister?" the nameless deputy asks. The case is resolved by the officers driving the transient to the county line and sending him on his way. "Now he's same other jurisdiction's problem," Topping informs the camera.

Such incidents are the bread and chocolate of *COPS*; every few minutes the officers wrestle a suspect to the ground, roughly cuff 'em and stuff 'em into the back of a patrol unit. What makes it different from the other cop shows on television, the producers insist, is this is Real Life. If someone gets blown away on this show — thankfully, no one has yet — they don't get up when the screen dissolves to commercial.

While there is some passing anthropological interest in *COPS* — no dramatic series, not even the formidable *Hill Street Blues*, has ever really captured the oddly formal policeman's *patois* — that would hardly seem to justify a series of half-hour shows. All the real reasons to watch *COPS* seem prurient ones — it offers the passive an opportunity to watch something truly dangerous from the safety of their living rooms.

There is nothing make-believe about the violence here. Look Ma, that's real blood leaking from the corner of that scumbag's mouth! Though the deputies seem like decent sorts, they are not well-served by the necessary selectivity of the director's eye. Verite is not reality, and just like the dramatic police series it presumes to supersede, *COPS* operates on the titillating rhythms of tensions and conflict.

But unlike dramatic series, which pay actors well to play the bad guys and the victims, *COPS* exploits the sordidness of real life and the misfortunes of real people — victims as well as "perps." Cameras grind away on little girls crying as their father — a suspected cocaine dealer — is wrestled away by arresting deputies. Through it all the cops seem humane, the cameras merciless.

It is hard to watch, and there is nothing instructive about it. It is hard to understand why so many police organizations have endorsed the show. *COPS* trivializes their very difficult profession — it reduces policemen to clowns and stuntmen trotted out for the Coliseum's entertainment. *COPS* is a stupid and reckless show: it panders to the mentality that watches auto racing hoping for the big crash and rents videotaped montages of horrible accidents.

(April 1989)

Johnny Shines   *Stephen Buel*

Stephen Buel

Birth of a Blues Festival

King Biscuit Blues Festival
Helena, Arkansas

Rice Miller is believed to have assumed the stage name he is now remembered by for his first 1941 appearance on Helena radio station KFFA. As Sonny Boy Williamson, a name evidently appropriated from a blues harmonica player then active in Chicago, he joined guitarist Robert Junior Lockwood in a series of lunchtime radio broadcasts that served as perhaps the single greatest influence on the coming generation of Delta blues musicians.

The broadcasts were called *King Biscuit Time* after their sponsor, King Biscuit Flour. For 15 minutes each day, Williamson, Lockwood and a revolving host of other musicians, who come to be known as King Biscuit Boys, broadcast live blues over a wide area of the Arkansas and Mississippi Delta.

King Biscuit Time became the catalyst for a new influx of blues musicians to Helena, which was already alive with streetcorner musicians and thriving black and white nightclub scenes. Elmore James, Little Walter, Johnny Shines, James Cotton, Jimmy Rogers and others were attracted to Helena by the promise of steady work or the hope that they might pick up some musical tips from Williamson or Lockwood.

Forty-five years later, Helena's essential contribution to the development of modern music is often overlooked, even in Arkansas. Recent years in particular have seen lessened awareness about the music the city exported to the world, despite the torchbearing of dozens of still-active musicians and of authors like Robert Palmer, whose 1981 book *Deep Blues* is a compelling and compre-

Whose Blues?

"A whole different segment of the population is listening to the blues that didn't before," said Jim O'Neal, editor of Living Blues magazine and a director of the Blues Foundation, in an interview with Louis Guida. *The new audience is predominantly white and, according to O'Neal, is creating a new pantheon of blues heroes in something closer to their own image. "The surge in the popularity of blues,"* Guida noted in his July 1987 article, *"is beginning to raise questions and spark discussion about the impact of white audiences and performers and the role of black musicians."*

Janice Laffoon, president of the Arkansas Blues Connection, attributed growing white support for blues to two factors: "First, blues was denied radio air time except on white college stations, and that created a white, college-educated audience. Second, blacks histori-cally have suffered from an image problem when it comes to blues ... Especially during the civil rights movement, many blacks wanted to escape from the blues. Whites ... just heard some mean guitar licks."

In the view of Henrietta Hock, a black music professor from Little Rock, "The ethnicity of the blues must be dealt with. The recognition of black blues artists is not only necessary but vital to the music scene ... because it was black people who created the blues."

hensive history of Delta Blues tradition and Helena's vital role in it.

In recent years, however, the blues have been receiving greater recognition in their native land. Nowhere has this feeling been stronger than it was at the first King Biscuit Blues Festival, held October 18 on Cherry Street in downtown Helena. The festival was a joyous celebration of Helena's musical heritage, and, as a friend observed, its setting could not have been more perfect. The blue stage in downtown Helena was next to a railroad track and in front of a levee holding back the flood-swollen Mississippi River.

There are, of course, better-established blues festivals that feature better-known musicians. But the important thing about the King Biscuit Blues Festival was that it was in Helena, which can rightfully claim to have been the birthplace of modern Delta blues. Helena was excited to have the blues again. Many blues concerts have the backing of Miller Beer and *Living Blues Magazine*, but few if any enjoy the wide measure of support that this one did. The front of the stage was festooned with placards proclaiming the allegiance of local businesses like the Home Insurance Company, H&M Lumber and Cunningham Kwik Stops.

Given that the festival's economic objective was to attract people back to "Main Street Helena," it was gloriously successful. Because the crowd stretched for blocks down Cherry Street, it is all but impossible to estimate its exact size, but it was in the thousands. It boasted numerous celebrities, from musician Levon Helm of The Band to politicians of all stripes, and dozens of journalists, including an AETN documentary crew and Palmer of *The New York Times*.

Most of the festival's strengths were provided by musicians with musical roots in Helena going back 30 or more years. Following a taped musical tribute to Sonny Boy Williamson, the first performer was Pine Bluff guitar player CeDell Davis, who trained himself to play slide guitar with a butter knife after a childhood bout with polio. Despite appearances that night by James Cotton and Bobby "Blue" Bland at a separate paid concert at the Lily Peter Auditorium, the day's highlight was the free midafternoon session that featured the remaining giants of the KFFA days, Lockwood and Shines on guitar, Sam Myers on drums and Joe Willie "Pinetop" Perkins on piano.

Shines's Helena roots go back to 1934 when he came to town to meet guitar player Robert Johnson, and then teamed up with him to play a variety of local house parties, juke joints and special events. Perkins, who played piano in Muddy Waters's band many years later, performed with Nighthawk and Williamson in Helena from 1943 on.

With Shines playing a six-string electric guitar and Lockwood on an electric 12-string tuned characteristically out-of-key, these giants of Helena's youth played a spirited series of blues standards, trading off lead singing duties between themselves and Perkins. *Deep Blues* credits Lockwood as being the Delta's first modern lead guitarist, and even at 71 his guitar still rings with a blend of traditional acoustic blues and jazzier electric elements. Although their advanced age slowed the pace a bit, and Shines punctuated his Howlin' Wolf-inspired vocals with a nasty hacking cough, their 10-to-12-song set was nonetheless vibrant and spontaneous.

The festival's weakness was the order in which the bands played. The collaboration of Lockwood, Shines, Perkins and Meyers did not close out the festival, but was followed by a series of earnest but by-comparison uninspiring blues-rock bands. This gave the whole event a somewhat anti-climactic feeling. And the abundance of bands unfortunately meant that no major performer got more than about a half-hour. But these are minor complaints for a brand-new festival which was musically superior to the eight-year-old Delta Blues Festival across the river in Greenville, Mississippi. The standard set by the first King Biscuit Blues Festival all but guarantees the event's success in years to come.

(October 1986)

Warren Criswell

Passionate Geometry

Sammy Peters
Heights Gallery

Uniqueness in the art of the 20th Century is often confused with quality. To make its mark in the upper circles, an artist's work must not only be good, it must be different. Sometimes, if it's different enough, even the "good" can be dispensed with. There's no use quarelling with this syndrome; it is the inevitable result of the high value we place on individuality. The question is: how do we define uniqueness?

The truly unique has nothing to do with an artist's choice of medium, technique or subject matter. That is, it is not necessarily attained by cleverly hitting upon an unoccupied niche in the art world. It can come from an artist working within an outmoded tradition, as in the case of Melville, Mahler or Eakins, as well as from such ground-breakers as Joyce, Schoenberg and Picasso. One feels that the works of these writers, composers and painters would have been just as great regardless of the idiom in which they were done. This is what I suspect about Sammy Peters, whose works will be on display at Little Rock's Heights Gallery through August 9.

Peters works in the modernist tradition of abstract expressionism, the style which brought American art to world prominence in the 1940s and 1950s and which has been all but smothered under the avalanche of "isms" since the Sixties. Like Adolph Gottlieb and Robert Motherwell before him, he works with a limited number of geometric forms. These have evolved out of his earlier figurative work just as Willem de Kooning's and Jackson Pollock's did from theirs. Despite these parallels, words like "derivative" or "outmoded" are not likely to occur to the viewer of a Peters painting. All such considerations are swept aside by the vitality and drama of these works.

Every abstractionist has to deal with the problem of how to — or whether to — make the world of his or her art as interesting as the real world. Peters' strategy is to start with a few rudimentary shapes and colors, set up a dynamic, unstable relationship between them, and let them interact. His paintings seem to have evolved as the universe itself has, beginning with a few elemental forces in opposition, expanding, proliferating and exploding.

What might be called the "environments" in which these dramas play themselves out are made up of rectangular color fields, sometimes flat and featureless, as in *White Roofs*, sometimes churning like a drop of pond water or the surface of the sun, as in *Vague Miasma*.

Often the most prominent of the *dramatis personae* is the right triangle, or wedge. Its base is characteristically unstable, so that it tends to eject its contents like a volcano or a wound. A double curve, resembling mountains or breasts, is frequently found near the top of a painting. In the middle region of nearly every work is a kind of horizontal barrier of short vertical strokes, which resemble coyote fences the artist said he saw in New Mexico. Equally omnipresent is a group of small bean-shaped forms resembling footprints or microbes. Sometimes, as in *Richly Blatant*, these have become trapped in loops of juicy white paint like invading germs attacked by leukocytes.

Near the end of 1985, a mutation of the wedge, an isosceles triangle, began appearing in Peters's work. In *Merger and Acquisition*, it recalls a rooftop; in *Necessary Circumstance*, the female pubis; and in *Richly Blatant*, it tries to

Gift from the Ages

Art reviewer Kathleen Harper, surveying an exhibit of sculptures by Arkansas artist Anita Huffington in August 1990, noted that the fluidity of the Greek-inspired female nudes and horses' heads "echoes the qualities inherent in or suggested by the materials themselves as they were worked." Huffington's earlier pieces were sculpted out of Virginia stone, alabaster and marble; her more recent works have been in bronze, sandstone and limestone.

The artist, Harper wrote, "carved around the stippled and nubby areas of one stone and they became the cheeks on the long, lean muzzle of Wild Horse.*" In one bronze piece, a dime-sized "imprint of a perfect scallop shell" was created by a chip accidentally flying out. Huffington named the small torso* Fossil Figure — *"I felt," she remarked, "it was a gift from the ages."*

imitate the indigenous right triangles by taking on their red coloring and volatile disposition.

Peters works mainly in oil and oil pastel on canvas or paper, usually on a large scale. There is always interplay between the dry marks and fluid strokes. The artist describes his work as "messy," and so it is, with drips, splatters and troweled textures so entangled that sometimes the painting looks out of control. This is, of course, deliberate. It is not the artist who has lost control, but the world he is depicting. It is a world in a continuous flux of upheaval and collapse, growth and decay. In *Jaded Merger*, the wedge seems to have just been reborn out of the gloom in a gush of fire or blood, whereas in *Subsequent Metaphor*, its ejected contents have cooled and petrified.

Such works are not so much finished as simply stopped, as action is stopped by a camera. A painting is a static thing that can, at best, show only a record of movement, like a seismograph, not movement itself. It is the painter's task, as it is the photographer's, to stop the action at precisely the right moment. The mood and character of a Peters work depends on this decision.

No matter what their mood, all these paintings give the impression of having been caught in the act. And it's not just paint that has been caught. In spite of their sometimes imposing physical presence, they are nevertheless *pictures*— images of something beyond themselves. They are fundamentally metaphors of the human condition. Geometry may be their language, but it is a passionate geometry.

Anton Bruckner has been accused of writing the same symphony nine times, and Sammy Peters has said the same thing about himself — that he paints the same painting over and over again. Although that criticism of Bruckner is exaggerated, it may have more validity in his case than in Peters's. You certainly don't get a feeling of repetition in a roomful of Peters's paintings. Each work demands to be experienced on its own terms. True, the "characters" keep coming back in different guises, contexts and degrees of prominence, like those in Faulkner's novels or in Donald Roller Wilson's paintings, but this only stimulates our interest in them. If there is any weakness in this approach it is only that one Peters painting by itself is perhaps less interesting than it would be in the company of some of its ancestors and descendants.

Except for a recent self-portrait, the last figurative work Peters did was in 1983. In those earlier canvases, one can find the beginning of the footprint-microbes, the proto-wedge and other embryonic forms of his present pantheon. Why were these works unsatisfying to him? I think his shift in direction might be comparable to that of a scientist who is compelled to turn from observed effects to root causes. His figures are as "messy," animated and volatile as his abstract forms, but they are the visible result of the animating forces, not the forces themselves. It is as if in his present work he is trying to penetrate the very origins of form and color, and to do this it became necessary to create the world anew. This is the necessity out of which the uniqueness of Sammy Peters's work emerges.

(July 1986)

Philip Martin

A Season in Hell

Crimes and Misdemeanors
Written and directed by Woody Allen

Woody Allen has always had trouble making the transition from wise ass to wise man. In his *Stardust Memories*, two fans approach cult-film director Sandy Bates (played by Allen) to say, "We love your work ... especially the early funny ones." In context, it is an amusing line, and not an insignificant one. Allen has never been comfortable resting on his considerable achievements as a comedian and comic writer. And sometimes his "serious" films — most notably the poorly written *Interiors* — have been flawed by overreaching ambition.

Happily, *Crimes and Misdemeanors* avoids the self-indulgent, self-conscious cerebralness that has plagued some of Allen's other work. That is not to say that this is a simple film; on the contrary, it is teeming with a dark intelligence. It resembles the underrated novels of Morris Philipson, both in structure and texture — the book-lined apartments and houses of Allen's characters seem less claustrophobic and more generous than before — and though a chilling nihilism lies at the film's core like a chocolate-dipped rock, Manhattan seems beautiful and sun-burnished, flooded with a warm gold light. At times the city seems more like Philipson's genteel New Haven than the demanding, clinical town it has portrayed in past Allen films.

It is fitting that this film — which is about, as much as anything else, *seeing* — is Allen's most splendidly visual film to date. The camera is allowed to linger ... to allow the viewer to select significant details, to glimpse the life (or deadness) behind the character's eyes. The story is straightforward enough. Judah Rosenthal (Martin Landau), a successful and philanthropic opthalmologist, has a problem mistress, Delores (Anjelica Huston), who is threatening to tell his wife (Claire Bloom) about their two-year affair. She believes promises were made and reneged upon, and she wants to confront the woman with the knowledge that her husband is a cheat. Later, she ups the stakes — threatening to go to the authorities with allegations of Judah's financial improprieties. After much wringing of hands, the fiercely agnostic Judah enlists the aid of his underworldly brother, Jack (played with convincing malevolence by Jerry Orbach), to deal with the problem.

In the middle of a dinner party, Jack telephones Judah to inform him that it's all over. Judah slips into shock, excuses himself and drives to Delores's apartment to stare into her "inert" eyes — and remove any incriminating evidence (love letters, a framed photograph of the illicit couple).

A subplot to the story involves Allen (as Cliff Stern, a nebbishy maker of obscure — and mediocre — documentaries) and his infatuation with Halley Reed (a breezy Mia Farrow), an associate producer for a public television series. Plagued by problems financing his "real work," Cliff meets Halley after his wife (played with appropriate bloodlessness by Joanna Gleason) arranges for him to take a job making a documentary about his brother-in-law Lester, a successful and self-aggrandizing television sit-com producer (Alan Alda, doing Hawkeye Pierce in a cashmere turtleneck). Cliff, of course, despises Lester — he is a vulgarian whose work makes money. And he's also after Halley.

Cliff's other brother-in-law, Ben (Sam Waterston), a rabbi facing imminent, inevitable blindness with beatific patience, is the link between the two parallel stories. As Judah's patient and confessor, he entreats Judah to tell his wife about his indiscretions, to ask her forgiveness. Though Judah and Ben respect and like each other, there is a fundamental philosophical schism between the two — the rabbi believes in a structured universe that allows for hope and mercy; Judah sees only swirling chaos in the void.

Though the film is chocked with obvious symbolism and familiar Allenisms — all the talk of eyes, the glorious old films, the crashing verbal ripostes, Judaism, love and death and sex and God — nothing seems trite. (Well, perhaps the character modeled after Primo Levi didn't have to be *named* Levy — but this slight clumsiness can be excused in light of the character's eloquent, simply declarative suicide note: "I have gone out the window.")

It is a large and uniformly excellent cast — though Allen's persona has become so iconic it's hard to gauge his performance. He's just there, wry and whiny — Spike Lee's schleppy godfather. Landau is imperious, especially in his dialogue with Allen during the film's crucial penultimate scene. Huston, as the neurotic airline attendant who becomes Judah's mistress, is desperately frumpy, and brave beneath a frightening hairstyle. Waterston's brief performance is affecting. The limited Alda, having (one hopes) finally decided that he cannot *be* Woody Allen, has decided to join him, and is put to good use.

Crimes and Misdemeanors is an unsettling film, flawed only in so far as it will be misunderstood by many, if not most, of those who see it. One shouldn't leave the theater thinking Woody Allen doesn't believe in Hell.

(November 1989)

Michael Keckhaver

New Ground

Tiny Lights
Juanita's

Music critics are rather a slack lot. They tend to follow the path of least resistance. They like bands that sound like other bands. Rather than write: "Predictably instilled with a vacuity reminiscent of interstellar space lashed to a thudding, synthetic corporate-beatdrone," it's much easier to simply say: "It sounds like Janet Jackson." Performances that defy categorization, on the other hand, force the critic to come up with new categories, coin new descriptive phrases. For these rare performances, simple comparisons just won't suffice.

So it is with Hoboken, New Jersey's Tiny Lights, who made their Arkansas debut at Juanita's Cantina Ballroom March 19. After their second year in a row of giving a smashing, critically acclaimed showcase at Austin's South by Southwest Music Conference, the Lights loaded up and headed for Little Rock to play for a disappointingly small crowd. The folks who did attend were treated to an eclectic musical performance the likes of which have not been seen in Central Arkansas since Eugene Chadbourne raked the walls of several local venues some months back. The drummer played saxophone and tablas. The bassist played trumpet. The singer played violin. The cello player played bass. The guitarist was the only band member who stuck with his instrument all evening, compensating by switching styles a couple dozen times per song.

Free-form jamming, extremely tight arrangements and some delightfully original medleys were the cream that rose to the top of a witty, sometimes bizarre repertoire. The group mixes traditional rock methodology with traces of Celtic ruminations, ethereal jazz and Colemanesque explorations to reach a thoroughly unpretentious, delightfully original flavor. Easily half the songs performed at Juanita's began as free-form improvisations that eventually wound up (or down) to one of the band's originals or a drastically revamped cover.

Hendrix was interspersed with Public Enemy in a massive funk-fest that eventually broke into a Sly and the Family Stone medley. P-Funk's "Tear the Roof off the Sucker" was surrounded with an Eastern-tinged cello solo. A rap/scat intro by singer Donna Croughn segued into a wah-wah violin solo, which, in turn, mutated into a tricky jazz-cum-psychedelia that would have done Syd Barrett proud.

Guitarist John Hamilton swung wildly from straightahead-boogie to upstart funk vamps to three-notes-a-minute psychedelic washes and proved an able singer as well. Equally comfortable with white noise feedback or clean and corny flat-picking, Hamilton pumped in the rock fuel to the band's folk/rock vehicle.

Unpredictability was the key element in the band's set. Andy Demos would slap his drums in wildly varying tempos for a bit and then jump out in front of his kit, pick up a soprano saxophone and honk elegantly for a few bars before resuming his duties as rhythm underpin. His virtuosity on sax lent just the right touch to the songs he saw fit to augment. Bassist Dave Dreiwitz traded his four strings for three valves on occasion and bleated out some high-pitched trumpeting, squealing one second, oozing blues the next. Croughn even proved an able jazz drummer on a couple of songs. With all this exchanging of instruments one never got the feeling the band was showing off. Each change-up was evidently crucial to the task at hand and the panorama never once lapsed into mere novelty.

The ability of these musicians to communicate non-verbally, in effect creating their own language with their instuments, was a wonder to view and the few people who showed up sat enraptured from beginning to end. Versatile to the point of disbelief, Tiny Lights effortlessly shattered the concept of "nothing new under the sun" and proved that there is still much unexplored territory in the realm of rock.

Opening for Tiny Lights was Washington D.C.'s Strange Boutique. Although the dictionary defines "strange" as "previously unfamiliar," Strange Boutique's dreamy, atmospheric sound should be very familiar to any fan of the late, lamented Pauline Murray & the Invisible Girls. Heavily phased guitar, sometimes acoustic, sometimes electric, sparse drumming and up-front bass formed the superstructure of a short set of semi-dirge tunes. Fronted by an able female singer, the Boutique evoked the sombre timbre of bands like Joy Division and, especially, A Certain Ratio. Somewhat recycled and wholly homogenized in technique, the band still provided 30 minutes or so of pleasant pop musings that, if not overly exciting, were inventive and relaxing. With more time to stretch out and a larger, more enthusiastic audience to play off, Strange Boutique might offer the entire meal rather than solely a light entree.

(March 1990)

Bill Jones

A Summons to Responsibility

Missing Measures
By Timothy Steele
University of Arkansas Press

Think about any art form in the 20th century — music, the novel, architecture, dance, painting — and the idea of radical experimentation inevitably comes to mind. Modernism elevated novelty of execution, regardless of the medium, to unprecedented heights, granting it the status of ideology or revealed religion. The problem, as the century ends, is that what Robert Hughes called "the shock of the new" eventually wears off, the inheritors of the original movement forget what animated their revolutionary ancestors and the whole enterprise loses its impetus, becoming stale and derivative — the very faults that novelty sought to banish.

This is the situation of the dominant mode of poetry written in the English language today. A century after *vers libre* triumphed in France, many British and American poets (and their readers and critics) remain convinced that free verse is the only authentic poetic method. In *Missing Measures: Modern Poetry and the Revolt Against Meter*, Timothy Steele argues that those contemporary poets who have forsaken traditional form have failed to "liberate" verse and have sacrificed the rhetorical advantages of metrical composition without understanding what they have lost. Steele, a poet who along with Richard Kenney and Tom Disch is numbered among the "New Formalists" now leading a prosodic revival, examines the factors that have led to the decline of meter in 20th century poetry and presents an eloquent case for the enduring strengths of ordered expression.

The book is addressed to all who believe, with the author, that "poetry can speak with special vividness and comprehensiveness" to the central issues of human experience. It is precisely that "vividness and comprehensiveness" that Steele believes is abandoned in the "revolt against meter," which champions instead a "musical indefiniteness of form and matter." Clarity yields to an increasingly private, self-referential language in much modern free verse, where difficulty is regarded as a guarantee of depth and solipsism a token of sincerity. Yet, as Steele demonstrates, adherence to regular meter never stifled the individual voices of Shakespeare, Milton, Pope, Wordsworth, Yeats, Frost or, more recently, Larkin, Wilbur and Gunn.

The great proponents of *vers libre* in English were Ford Madox Ford, Ezra Pound, William Carlos Williams and T.S. Eliot, who defined free verse as the absence of pattern, rhyme and meter. Steele devotes considerable attention to their theorizing and propagandizing — as well as to earlier pronouncements by Edgar Allan Poe and Walt Whitman. The author provides an illuminating analysis of the modern reaction to the overripe style of many Victorian poets and the metronomic scanning of lines practiced in late-19th-century schools. Steele contends that Eliot and Pound confused *meter*, a "specific form of poetic rhythm," with *scansion*, a sing-song reading of lines designed to determine metrical identity. The result was a devaluation of form at the hands of two of the most influential poets of the century, based in part on their misapprehension of

Poetry's Perils

Examining the cultural role of contemporary poetry in March 1988, Bill Jones noted that The Los Angeles Times Book Review *had in the past year discontinued publishing reviews of new books of poetry. "There seems to be some cause for concern," he commented, "when a major book review abandons an entire literary form."*

In interviews with several practitioners of the art, however, Jones found evidence of renewed vitality. Many younger poets, reacting to the "private mythologies and private languages" of modernism, have adopted a simpler, more accessible style, while the Neo-Formalists have returned to traditional structure. Another group is resurrecting narrative verse.

Although major publishers — many of which have been absorbed by corporate conglomerates with no previous experience in publishing — are less willing to risk the typically slow but steady sales of poetry volumes, regional and university presses are taking up the slack. Further, Jones reported, the proliferation of "little magazines" and the success of revived poetry readings in clubs and coffee-houses — such as those in Little Rock's DMZ, a venue that often attracted crowds of about 100 poetry lovers — indicated renewed vitality in the oldest of literary modes.

But, sad to say, Little Rock's "Readings" were discontinued in May 1989.

the nature of meter.

Steele's explorations lead him into related fields of inquiry, all of which have relevance to the subject of his well-documented study. He reaches back to antiquity and forward to the present to trace the evolving relationship between prose and poetry, from "Prose Seeking Order on the Model of Poetry" (Aristotle, Cicero) to "Poetry Seeking Freedom on the Model of Prose" (Hopkins, Williams). The author discusses the historical development of the rather arbitrary distinction between "poetry" and "verse" (a putatively inferior variety of poetry), showing how Eliot, in a discussion of Kipling, linked "verse" to mere metrical competence and "poetry" to "a musical pattern of emotional overtones." The suggestive is exalted above the definite in both form and content.

One of the most intriguing chapters in *Missing Measures* concerns the misapplication of scientific principles to the free-verse movement. Steele observes that in an essay on the "Image," Pound seems to advocate, paradoxically, a "poetic method whose 'scientific' character is designed to provide a mystical experience." If, with Pound's fascism in mind, this sort of mumbo-jumbo doesn't strike the reader as somehow ominous, the author suggests a connection between the "triumph of experimental poetry and art in the first half of this century" and the "triumph of reactionary pseudo-scientific political ideologies in the same period." Steele effectively invokes modernism's flirtation with — or in some cases seduction by — totalitarianism to undermine the "scientific" and libertarian claims of free verse.

At times Steele presses so hard for his own cause that he comes close to denying any legitimacy at all for free verse. The "radical subjectivism in poetry" that produces free verse, he contends, also produces a "dictatorial" poet who "versifies by fiat." On the other hand, meter "asks obedience of and offers rewards to all poets equally." Steele asserts that the absence of formal standards applicable to free verse requires that "the poet's self-expression be accepted on its own terms, however arbitrary and obscure they may be." But surely this is overstating the case. In the past century readers and critics have adapted to the innovations and idiosyncracies of novelists from James Joyce to Kathy Acker and have managed to find appropriate responses to such free verse classics as Eliot's *Waste Land* and Pound's *Cantos*.

If there is a flaw in Steele's otherwise scrupulous scholarship, it is his unrelenting Apollonian tidiness that concedes as little merit as possible to the disheveled, unwashed enemy. In his concluding assessment of the free-verse movement, he finds nothing but failure in its attempts to expand the range of subject matter, employ a more natural diction and create a new metric. Still, the argument for the "new formalism" (a label Steele dislikes) is, despite its occasional stridency, generally convincing and always compelling.

Missing Measures is, by any standards, an important book — it is easily one of the most significant critical works to appear in recent years. In it, Steele has issued a summons to literary responsibility for general readers, students, teachers and, above all, poets. Anyone interested in the fate of poetry and the health of our culture should read the volume, confront the issues it raises and bear in mind the author's counsel: "The only novelty sure to last in poetry is the novelty of talent."

(July 1990)

Philip Martin

Celtic Soul

Richard Thompson
Arkajun House

Something about Richard Thompson inspires reverence. My closest friend says, "Hey stupid, it's his bulging talent," but I'm not completely sure that talent — or even minor-key genius — can account for the thousand-ton hush that fell on the Arkajun House crowd when this scrawny little Brit began to whisper his left hand up and down the neck of his weary Martin.

There is always cause for concern when a performer is treated like a holy man by his fans. Right-thinking people get nervous when the roar subsides; there is no target more tempting than the rock poet too sensitive to live. Anyone — including Elvis Costello — who steps on stage naked but for an acoustic guitar is suspect.

Richard Thompson, nearly 40, with a critically acclaimed catalogue that reaches back to 1969 and his work with Stonehenge-obsessed folkies Fairport Convention, is not nearly so obscure as a lot of rockcrit types would have you think. Though his albums have never sold remarkably well, it's likely even non-fans might recognize a few of his songs. Jo-El Sonnier recently had a country hit off the poppy "Tear-Stained Letter," and *Rolling Stone* cited two albums he cut with his then-wife Linda in its "Best 100 Albums of the Last 20 Years" list in 1987. In some quarters, Thompson is regarded as something of a secular saint, undervalued and mystic, with a kind of sated patience twinkling behind his beatific blue eyes.

Thompson's albums have always been worthy bits of craftsmanship, surprisingly accessible and admirably restrained — never as desperately down-beat as, for instance, Jackson Browne at his most confessional. And besides, Thompson can rock too — wildman-zombie guitar parts, like Jimi Hendrix with good sense, or Robert Fripp with the starch excised.

Still, given the hype, one approaches Thompson cautiously. But Thompson overcomes the singer/songwriter milieu by virtue of a committed intelligence coupled with an immense virtuosity. Simply said, he is one of the best guitar players ever to mine the thick vein of rock 'n' roll, occasionally chipping away at the edges of the genre but more often simply twisting its conventions in a modal swirl of hammer-ons and pull-offs. An obvious English folk influence is redeemed by restraint and a true rock 'n' roll heart. Thompson is no Ry Cooder-style archivist; his playing is delivered from nostalgia by wit and taste.

Oh, and his technique is spooky. He could drive nails through the fretboard with his shuddering pinkie. What B.B. King wrenches out of an electrified Lucille, Thompson seems capable of wringing from his flattop — such is the controlled power of Celtic Soul. Alternately spraying the crowd with stinging arpeggios, clanky shuffle chords and buttery, melt-in-your-heart microbursts, Thompson wove in some fine, understated songwriting. His voice is serviceable and expressive, melodies are lovely, if borrowed (if that's a crime, Dylan's on death row and all pop culture is on appeal) and his lyrics are understated, honestly raw and infused with a gentle fatalism. Thompson typically unpacks his psyche into unsentimental songs about bomb-hearted lovers and odd broken outcasts. His best lyrics are queer and quirky, often laced with a wry misogyny or undercut by a self-deprecating twist. Like Pete Townshend, Thompson is listenable even when he's corny and preachy — a brittle honesty rescues even his most specious ideas.

Speaking of Townshend, I had never noticed — least not until deep into the second set when Thompson got to "Jerusalem on the Jukebox," a song off his latest album — the vocal resemblance Poor Richard bears to Pete. Of course, it sort of helped that "Jerusalem " quotes Townshendesque chord patterns (complete with ringing upstrokes). Just in case anyone missed the point, Thompson covered "Substitute" a few songs later.

To sum it up, Richard Thompson is an exquisite talent who is capable of surpassing the expectations imposed by his press clips. Not even jaded ears are immune to the power of his raw guitar and throat. He's no shaman, but he's no swindle either.

(May 1989)

Michael Jukes

Anne Neville

Sad, Sadder, Sadist

Sexual Personae
By Camille Paglia
Yale University Press

In Madeline L'Engle's subversive adolescent classic, *A Wrinkle in Time*, one character slyly introduces himself as "the Happiest Sadist." Call Camille Paglia the Happiest Sadean.

Her new — and first — book, *Sexual Personae*, an ambitious tome whose stated purpose is to trace themes of decadence and sexual unrest in art and literature from the ancients through Emily Dickinson, owes much to the infamous Marquis. Early on, she postulates a Sadean universe, then dovetails nearly 3,000 years of diverse artistic and literary tradition to fit neatly within its bounds. It's an ambitious approach — and certain to get her talked about in all the proper circles — but more than anything else, *Sexual Personae* harkens back to that old musical question: What do you do with a drunken sailor? So

Looking at Porn

In June 1987, Spectrum *looked at pornography. Bill Jones reviewed two books that surveyed the history and social impact of the slippery subject.* The Secret Museum *by Walter Kendrick emphasized literary works and treated the category of pornography as an invention of the 19th century middle class. The author chronicled the continuing attempt to locate "the chimera of artistic value."*

The Question of Pornography *by Edward Donnerstein, Daniel Linz and Steven Penrod, on the other hand, summarized the results of research on the effects of media portrayals of sex and violence. The study suggested that violence rather than sexual explicitness causes negative changes in male attitudes toward women. Jones found the two books together "a welcome corrective to the inanities of the [1986] Meese Commission Report."*

inebriated is Paglia with her own insights that she sees evidence for them everywhere. Her provocative and sometimes quite stunning observations are buried in such an avalanche of theoretical self-justification that one really does want to throw her in a lifeboat 'til she's sober.

In setting up a Sadean framework for her critical theory, Paglia has posed for herself difficulties she never convincingly surmounts. One of a growing number of academics who counts the Marquis among the significant philosophers of the Western World, she considers him the brilliant Enlightenment counterpoint to Rousseau. Within this school of thought, Sade's modest assortment of philosophical treatises and prodigious output of erotico-philosophic novels are considered an important defense of a world view postulating humankind's essential selfishness and cruelty. In direct opposition to the Roussean concept that humanity in its natural state is good and civilization a corrupting force, Sadean discourse postulates a malign Nature, whose children are characterized first and foremost by their amoral egoism. Thus, civilization functions as a positive force, restraining humanity's evil impulses, keeping natural vice confined to the seething underbelly of private aberrations and allowing the continued functioning of the species.

Paglia, who considers Sade's opus "a comprehensive satiric critique of Rousseau," sees civilization as locked in a death struggle with nature, which she views as an inescapable hierarchy of the strong and the weak. Man, terrified of women's primal strength and the fetid, procreative chthonian nature to which it is inseparably linked, has established a culture that allows him to be stronger than she. In the West, it is the life of the mind, not that of the womb, which is most highly valued. Sky trumps earth. Apollo's aristocratic aboveness holds sway over the Dionysian fecund liquidity of the "invisible sea of organic life," manifest in the uniquely female processes of menstruation, childbirth and lactation. Art, literature, and civilized culture are all in the Apollonian mode, representing as they do a transcendence of the organic. Dionysius rules over the amoral, the procreative, the ecstatic; "frosty Apollo" transcends through "sculptural coherence and clarity." Born of fear, Apollonian higher culture and, in particular, the cult of high beauty is man's escape from and weapon against primeval, humid female Nature. Thank goodness for that terror, intones Paglia; were it not for man's need to project himself beyond the swamp we would all still be living in "grass huts," so earthbound is woman in her accepting, cyclic, natural sympathy.

Though it is certainly intriguing, Paglia's Sadean construct is sadly based on a too-simplistic reading of the prolific Sade. His work simply cannot be accepted as a high-flown intellectual rebuttal to Rousseau and allowed to pass as coherent philosophy. Let slide Sade's own sexual tastes and practices — which, although they certainly never approached the gross atrocities clinically detailed in such horrific wonders as *Justine/Juliet* and *120 Days of Sodom,* do suggest that idiosyncratic kinks played at least as much a part in his story lines as the shimmering intellectual highmindedness with which Paglia implies he probed the depth of depravity to prove an intellectual point. Concentrate instead on the question of the philosophy itself. Never does Paglia defend her placement of Sade among the great Western philosophers and her high ranking of him is as questionable as his philosophy itself.

Briefly, Sade's thought is problematic because it is internally inconsistent throughout his work, he documents the "perverse" behavior of primitives, ancients and his own contemporaries to shore up his vision of the naturalness, and as such the goodness, of his cruel universe. Ultimately, however, his libertines strive ceaselessly to execute their cruel, passionless, motiveless acts in order to establish and celebrate their separateness from nature's tyranny. They wish to affect the natural order, not to act within it, and in their will to disrupt lies the Sadean paradox, which Paglia never acknowledges — let alone addresses —

in her haste to get on with the ferocious pagan dance.

For Paglia, Sade's work is emblematic of her view that cruel nature lies just beneath the surface of civility; she sees the Dionysian/Apollonian schism as a theme underlying all of nature and art. Like the new reader of Freud, who suddenly finds great significance in the fact that almost everything in the world is indeed longer than it is wide, she gazes about wide-eyed, and everywhere see sex-as-violence and male loathing for fetid femaleness. More disturbingly, she see the Western tradition of art and literature as both product of and inseparable from this fear and loathing. Themes of cruelty, sadomasochism and sexual revulsion are for her not simply present in great works but seem to be the very elements that make them great.

Most of the authors and artists she cites are male, and she accepts unquestioningly their right dominance in the world of arts and letters, parroting that old standby *ipso facto*-dismissal of women's talents as obviously inferior because genius will out, regardless of societal constraints — and, my dear, women simply haven't achieved the greatness men have. It's all so trite and cyclic, one simply wants to slap her. As her sole example of greatness in a female writer, she cites Emily Dickinson, whom she christens "Amherst's Madame de Sade" and examines with an eye to celebrating her sadomasochistic imagery.

Dickinson is legitimized for Paglia because she participates in the tradition of Dante, Spenser, Blake and Baudelaire which, as it is presented in *Sexual Personae*, is characterized first and foremost by spiritualization of cruelty and atrocity in the best Nietzschian tradition. It is only what Paglia sees as her "detachment from her gender" that allows Dickinson to be great, the expulsion of "chthonian femaleness from her world." Citing William Blake's idea that "imagination must separate itself from female nature," Paglia praises Dickinson's "poetic self-masculinization," calling the poet "a male genius and a visionary sadist" in justification of her life and works.

Sexual Personae is so maddening primarily because Paglia's intelligence and critical talents are so evident throughout. Her analysis is fascinating and a significant contribution to critical dialogue, but her need to make everything fit into a construct leads her far too often into speciousness. Ultimately, she comes across as a happy slave, an apologist for ensconced male-bias academic prejudice. Like Sade's Juliet, who rivals her male tutors in cruelty and barbarism, yet ultimately cannot break free of the ugly edifice of their *regles du jeu*, Paglia is trapped within a critical paradigm whose bounds she cannot escape because she has accepted them unquestioningly. For all her fine insights, it never occurs to her to spurn the fraternity, to leave the castle and view it as the artificial structure that it is.

(May 1990)

Michael Jukes

Even before the February 1990 debut of Flying Snake, the poetic cartoons of writer/artist/musician Michael Jukes infused the back pages of Spectrum with a healthy impatience with convention. Flying Snake — a "merchandisable metaphor" — is an alert, sassy, and utterly unflappable creation who embraces the world of the mundane with touching relish.

David Bailin

Spectrum[1]

A posthumously published collection [is] discovered after his death.[2] [Here] essays, poetry, history, philosophy, social commentary, science, "serious" fiction and miscellaneous efforts,[3] skating rinks, day care centers,[4] radio stations, walking courses and community centers, fast food joints, mobile home parks, Baptist churches, the $1 movie theater and two liquor stores[5] [become] a literal representation of the interior of a solid, respectable family's house.[6] To trace themes of decadence and sequel unrest in art and literature from the ancients — confined to the seething underbelly of private aberrations — concentrate instead on the question of the philosophy itself.[7] Offer some hope, but not enough to warrant the proclamation of a new golden age.[8] Dispel the feeling that there is a glass ceiling.[9] [Consider rather] a little less literal, with more graceful variety and nuance in phrasing[10] — immediately more intimate and contained — a wax tableau of a reclining woman, played continuously by a musical clock,[11] comes to terms with history by filling the air with incessant chatter.[12] Across the room at a half-dozen tables, salespeople sit with customers.[13] Similarities emerge:[14] check everything out, don't take everything at face value.[15] — figures far apart from the whole picture.[16] "It's hard to get a perspective ..."[17] Half-dozen factories expanding, a major thoroughfare widened, police and fire station enlarged, golf course designed, stakes marking a shopping center, a hospital, restaurants, several small businesses,[18] discarded bone, viscera, feathers and fat that accumulate[19] lead to realms of metaphysical mystery.[20] A customer dines alone and reads at his table — a mild fellow with whom she has made eye contact.[21] A shred of romance informs us.[22] A poor, ravaged tropic made all the more desperate by "the grotesque tinkering of theorists"[23] ... lost, arcadian virtues.[24] This was not a simple slip of the tongue.[25] Served to divert attention from the realization[26] of this autumnal tale of two alternative American dreams[27] — with supporting cast,[28] bloodied but unbowed indeed.[29] Hunched over papers and pointing at figures[30] a sort of shadow remains alive.[31] But "keep the champagne corked"[32] appeared with 18th century spelling and typography.[33] From this perspective, the past is present.[34]

Birthday Bash

In June 1990, to commemorate its fifth anniversary (and to provide the editors a chance to slip away to a convention in Denver) Spectrum *invited some of its critics and friends to write essays on what the newspaper was doing wrong. Here's what we printed on the front page:*

"I'm still waiting for Spectrum *to find its identity, and I hope it does not identify with the folks who will pay $1.95 a minute for someone to talk nasty with them on the phone and with those so bereft of personal charm that they must advertise in a newspaper for companions."*
— *John Robert Starr*,
Arkansas Democrat *Managing Editor*

"[Spectrum] has adopted a traditional print-media bias that blames nearly all the ills of the news world on TV."
— *Jeanne Rollberg*
UALR Journalism Professor

"Your hip thirtysomething-style trendiness is wearing thin."
— *Anthony Moser*
Former Spectrum *Associate Editor*

"We know that Juanita's is doing a great job of bringing in all kinds of amplified music. However the obvious geographic closeness of Juanita's to Spectrum *makes you guys look lazy, or inbred, or both."*
— *Lee Tomboulian*
Pianist, writer, and contributor

*(*Spectrum's *offices were, at the time, located above Juanita's, a restaurant and nightclub which really* did *bring some of the best live music to Little Rock.)*

[1]Since arriving in Little Rock some four and a half years ago, I have enjoyed the intelligence and integrity of the writing and reporting of *Spectrum*. When I was asked to write a review of *Spectrum* for your celebration issue, I was pleased to accept. I asked for and received several issues, current and past, to look over. I thought I might deal with the paper as a conceptual art piece. But the more I read critically (not as a reader but as an artist looking for material and systems), the more I thought I'd like to do something with its text — essentially extracting the context from the content. I had been working with found text back in the early 1980s on a work I called *Washington's Profile* and thought this process might be fun. Apologies must go out to all the authors whose work I used — I took great liberties in extracting lines. There was one line I found that will be immediately identifiable by any one associated with the Editor/Publisher. It was my reaction to hearing about *Spectrum* back in April of 1986. The line is extracted from Michael Keckhaver's article called Texas Flood, issue number 125, May 23-June 5, 1990, p. 19: Hey, "... cool."

[2]Ten Years At UA Press, Dorothy Neville, No. 124, May 9-22, 1990, p. 15.
[3]Ten Years At UA Press, Dorothy Neville, No. 124, May 9-22, 1990, p. 1.
[4]McClellan Opens to the Public, Clay Hathorn, No. 124, May 9-22, 1990, p. 3.
[5]Neighborhood, Clay Hathorn, No. 124, May 9-22, 1990, p. 3.
[6]Heil Himmler, Bill Jones, No.125, May 23-June 5, 1990, p. 35.
[7]Sad, Sadder, Sadist, Anne Neville, No. 124, May 9-22, 1990, p. 15.
[8]Historical Fiction and Period Style, Bill Jones, No. 124, May 9-22, 1990, p. 15.
[9]Courtly Debate, Anne Clancy, No. 124, May 9-22, 1990, p. 4.

[10]Insightful Recital, Jess Anthony, No.125, May 23-June 5, 1990, p. 35.
[11]Insightful Recital, Jess Anthony, No.125, May 23-June 5, 1990, p. 35.
[12]Heil Himmler, Bill Jones, No.125, May 23-June 5, 1990, p. 35.
[13]Then We Ask Them To Buy, Clay Hathorn, No.122, April 11-24, 1990, p. 5.
[14]Children Of Flower Children, Clay Hathorn, No.122, April 11-24, 1990, p. 6.
[15]Children Of Flower Children, Clay Hathorn, No.122, April 11-24, 1990, p. 7.
[16]Big Poultry's Dirty Water Problem, Dorothy Neville, No.122, April 11-24, 1990, p. 11.
[17]Big Poultry's Dirty Water Problem, Dorothy Neville, No.122, April 11-24, 1990, p. 13.
[18]Then We Ask Them To Buy, Clay Hathorn, No.122, April 11-24, 1990, p. 4.
[19]Big Poultry's Dirty Water Problem, Dorothy Neville, No.122, April 11-24, 1990, p.11.
[20]Friendship and Faith, Bill Jones, No.122, April 11-24, 1990, p. 27.
[21]Rot For Rot's Sake, Philip Martin, No. 124, May 9-22, 1990, p. 20.
[22]Losing Vietnam, Steve Barnes, No. 124, May 9-22, 1990, p. 21.
[23]Losing Vietnam, Steve Barnes, No.124, May 9-22, 1990, p. 21.
[24]Just What Is This Show's Function?, Anthony Moser, No. 29, July 23-Aug. 5, 1986, p. 15.
[25]Just What Is This Show's Function?, Anthony Moser, No. 29, July 23-Aug 5. 1986, p. 15.
[26]Here Comes The Judge, Jess Henderson, No. 29, July 23-Aug. 5, 1986, p. 3.
[27]Alternative American Dreams, Bill Jones, No.125, May 23-June 5, 1990, p. 36.
[28]Alternative American Dreams, Bill Jones, No.125, May 23-June 5, 1990, p. 36.
[29]Fame And Death, Philip Martin, No.125, May 23-June 5, 1990, p. 38.
[30]Then We Ask Them To Buy, Clay Hathorn, No.122, April 11-24, 1990, p. 5.
[31]Children Of Flower Children, Clay Hathorn, No.122, April 11-24, 1990, p. 8.
[32]Outlook For the Nineties, Clay Hathorn, No. 117, Jan. 31-Feb. 13, 1990, p. 10.
[33]Historical Fiction and Period Style, Bill Jones, No. 124, May 9-22, 1990, p. 16.
[34]Historical Fiction and Period Style, Bill Jones, No. 124, May 9-22, 1990, p. 16.

Bill Jones, Stephen Buel and Philip Martin   *Dixie Knight Photography*

How We Did It

In the fall of 1990, when they had recovered from Spectrum's *fifth-anniversary celebration, the three editors began reading through all 134 issues of* Spectrum *published before the paper went weekly. They compiled long lists of their favorite pieces. Then they compiled shorter lists. At the end of the next round, they came up with 25 selections each and discovered they had two books. After long hours of trimming and trading, they produced* A Spectrum Reader. *And here it is.*

BILL JONES is contributing editor of *Spectrum*. His work has appeared in other alternative weeklies, as well as in *Southern Magazine*, *Arkansas Times*, and the *Arkansas Gazette*. A Little Rock attorney and actor on the local stage, he is a graduate of Rhodes College with an M.A. from Vanderbilt University and a J.D. from the University of Arkansas at Little Rock School of Law.

PHILIP MARTIN, executive editor of *Spectrum*, once played semi-pro baseball in Rio de Janeiro and guitar on *The Merv Griffin Show*. A former daily newspaper columnist, he is also the editor and publisher of *zulutolstoy*, an erractically published journal of "kulchur."

STEPHEN BUEL, editor & publisher of *Spectrum*, founded the newspaper in 1985, after working as a reporter for the *Arkansas Democrat*. He attended the University of South Florida and received an M.J. in Journalism from the University of California at Berkeley. His work has appeared in *The Berkeley Gazette*, *The Washington Post*, and the *San Francisco Bay-Guardian*, but not too recently.